AF572151

BRUN [illegible]

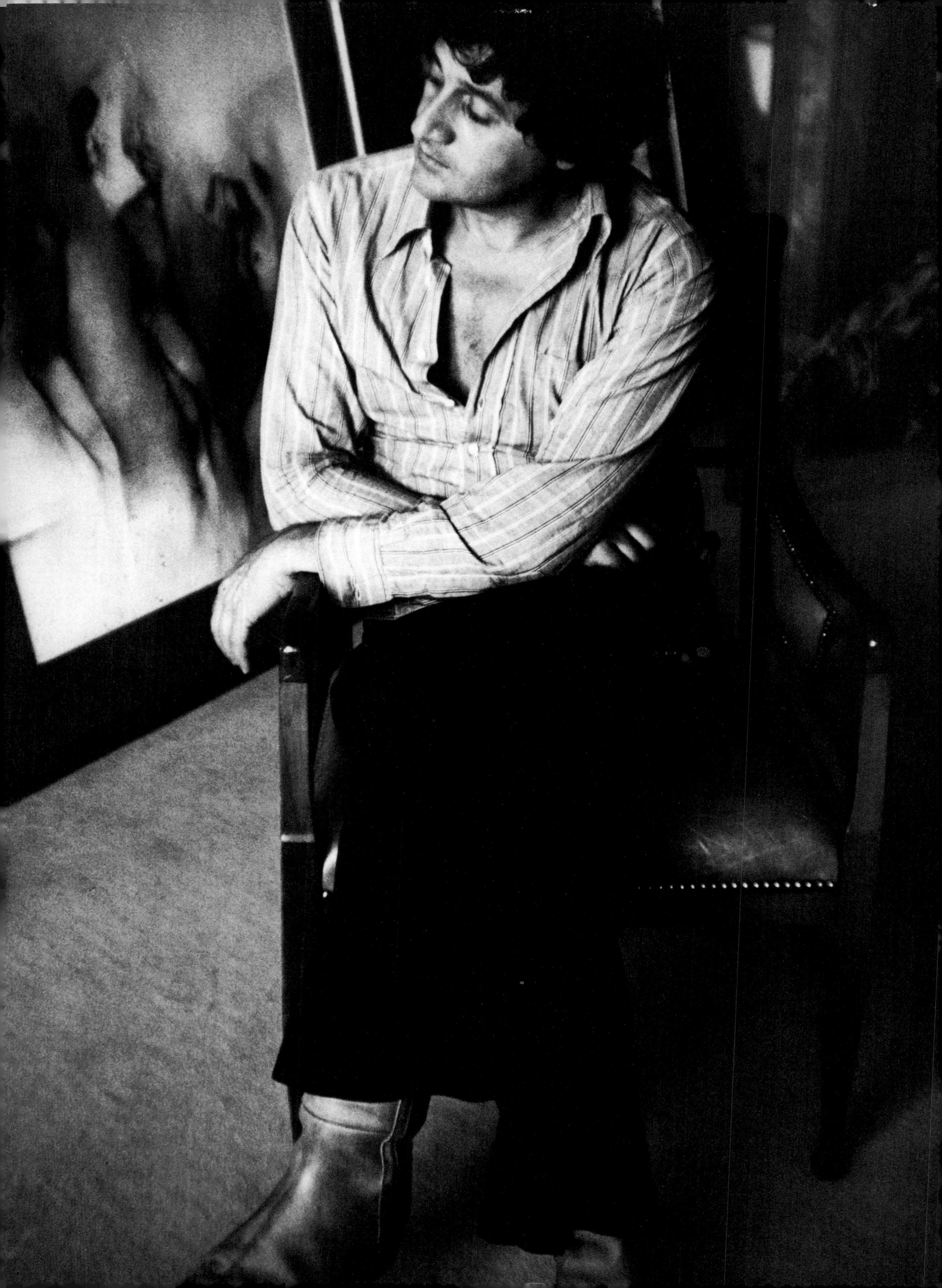

BRUNO BRUNI

Edited by
Hanns Theodor Flemming

Texts by
Hans-Harald Müller
Dieter Hoffmann
and
Max Bense

John Szoke Graphics

Offenbach am Main, Berliner Straße 218
West Germany

144 East 57th Street, New York, N. Y. 10022
Printed in West Germany
ISBN 0-936598-00-X

Hanns Theodor Flemming

Bruno Bruni

"A thing of beauty is a joy for ever"
(John Keats, Endymion)

The Return of Beauty. All the works of Bruno Bruni are characterized by a distinctive charm. They unfold in a half-world of dream and reality, perception and fantasy, intuition and perfection – images full of erotic dreams and artificial paradises. Here, fragility is vitally linked with sensualism, tenderness and élan. A new interpretation of beauty – as a surreal appearance – occurs in the art of Bruno Bruni.

Bruni's work is filled with a confession to beauty. Of course, nowadays the concept of 'beauty' implies a very intuitive interpretation. "What beauty is I cannot say," Albrecht Dürer has exclaimed. Discussing the boundries between art and non-art in his definitive book, *Aesthetics,* art historian Benedetto Croce declares: "They are purely empirical in nature and cannot be defined."

Nevertheless, we can distinguish a continuous development of the concept of beauty in occidental painting and sculpture from Greek antiquity up to the work of Picasso and Dali. Despite new variations, the ideal of beauty in art has remained true to the mediterranean roots of its aesthetic origin. This origin is particularly evident in Bruni's imagery and style which derive from traditional and new concepts in modern art.

Intuitive Perception. Benedetto Croce is right to distinguish between an 'intuitive' and a 'logical' perception of the world. The former derives from fantasy, and the latter is dominated by reason. Art belongs to the first category and is, thus, a kind of intuitive perception that manifests itself in visual expression. There is no difference between form and content in art, because content can only be expressed as form.

The intuitive perception from which Bruni's pictures originate does not distinguish between reality and imagination, fantasy and actuality. "The painter is a painter, because he sees what others can only feel or look at, but cannot inter-

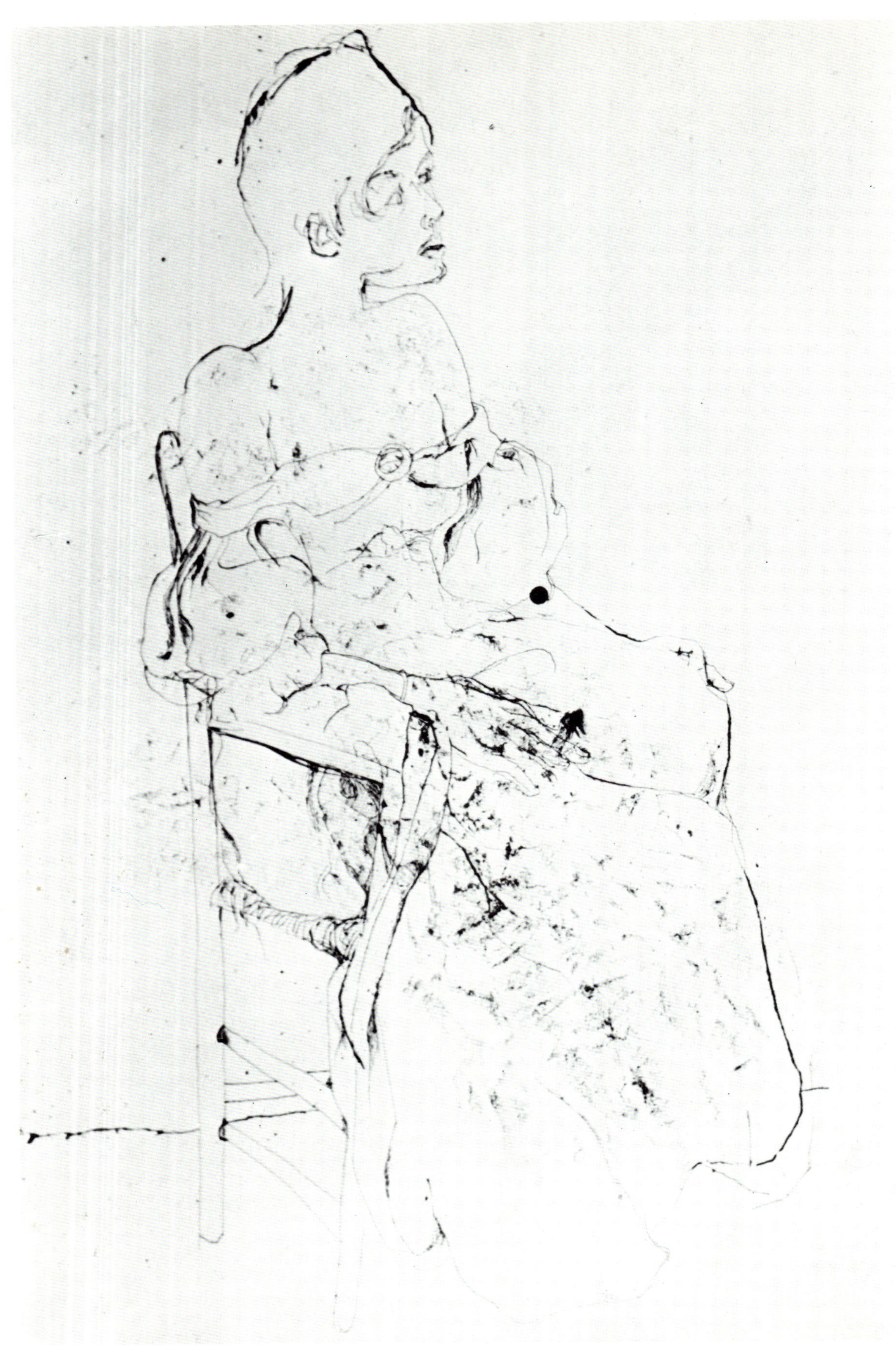

"Ute" 1961
pen-and-ink drawing, ca. 35x25 cm

pret," says Croce. Only the intuitive perception realized by the painter is relevant in a work of art – not ideological declarations of intent. Only the final work is important; its aesthetic quality and its meaning represents the totality of its artistic value.

Stylistic Features. From the very beginning of Bruni's career, elements of Surrealism and Italianità were tightly combined in a very distinctive manner. A preference for Quattrocento painting, Mannerism, fin de siècle, and 'Floreale' styles (a poetic Italian interpretation of Art Nouveau) characterizes Bruni's works in painting, graphic design and sculpture. Throughout, he remained fascinated by beauty and sensuality. The pleasure of the graceful female body is ever-present in Bruni's compositions. However, the subject of beauty is always enhanced by its surreal presentation and set apart by qualities of superb drawing and gracefully balanced compositions which derive from Italian prototypes.

Bruni's paintings overflow with Mannerist, overstrained perspectives; elongated androgynous bodies of girls with narrow hips and long legs who lift their dresses over their heads with inimitable grace; gentle hands and fingers that reach into space in a strange and ornamental way; autumn leaves, hats, coats, draped garments. Swan necks, loving couples and, above all, girls with flowing hair that evolve into flowers dominate Bruni's compositions. Subtly mixed colors from a varied palette of irridescent pink, bright green, pale purple and fiery orange accent the picture plane. The backgrounds are often colored in pale mauve, dusty blue, ocher, and velvet grey and are sometimes structured by fine lines. The female nude and the rose are presented in a symbolic relationship – figure and space melt rhythmically on the picture plane. Indeed, in Bruni's work, Art Nouveau moods and Pop Art accents are integrated, blending grace with quiet melancholy, sensualism with elegant draughtsmanship.

Career and Development. But before Bruno Bruni found his genuine style, he passed through various phases. Bruni was born on November 23, 1935 in Gradara, near Pesaro on the Adriatic Sea. Bruni studied art at the Istituto d'Arte in Pesaro from 1953 to 1959 and then moved to London in 1960. The following year he settled in Hamburg to continue his studies at the State Academy for the Visual Arts. The artist George Gresko (1920–1962) proved an important influence on Bruni's early artistic development, as did Paul Wunderlich (born 1927) with whom he collaborated in the field of lithography and became close friends.

Relationship to Gresko and Wunderlich. As an artist, George Gresko was an outsider. The style of his gouaches, drawings and, above all, etchings were on the borderline between Surrealism and Abstract Expressionism. Just before his death in 1962, Gresko was evolving a more realistic drawing style in the spirit of Klimt. As Bruni himself confesses, Gresko's strange, nonconformist personality, combining a predilection to the macabre with a biting humor fascinated his students and provided them with a powerful visual stimulus.

In his early period when he worked as a graphic designer, Bruni was still heavily influenced by Gresko and Horst Janssen. Bruni's early drawings and etchings also show the influences of Dix and Grosz and the critical social realism of the twenties. Bruni's mastery of lithography was due to the influence of Wunderlich who offered him much technical and stylistic advice. Indeed, from 1963 to 1978, Bruni made more than two hundred lithographs, many of them printed in several colors.

Turning point: "Donna-fiore". An important stylistic change in Bruni's art first appears in "Donna-fiore," painted in 1965 when Bruni left the Hamburg Art School and became independent. From then on he created a series of highly original compositions of female nudes and floral bouquets. Each shows a beautiful nude lifting her arms to pull a garment over her head; the garment then evolves into flowers or buds. Bruni's extraordinary ability to capture and modify this gesture with grace and elegance is confirmed in a later gouache, "La Sera" (1976), which shows a standing nude in front of a bed. This metamorphosis is seen again in two bronze figures, "Knospe" and "La venere annoiata" (1976), where it is effectively translated into three-dimensional sculpture.

Homage to Mannerism. The principal motif of 'flower girl' (or 'girl bud') is often presented in a window-like frame that serves to integrate space and plane, body and line. (An example might be the paintings "Interno" or "Vis-à-vis," 1965.) Some of these paintings still show the impact of Wunderlich's style, for example "Oratori," (1965) or "Cardinale" (1966). In other paintings, Bruni, like Wunderlich, chooses the highly Mannerist subject of Gabrielle d'Estrées and her sister ("Ommaggio al manierismo," 1965). The first high-point in Bruni's work was the famous lithograph, "Strangers in the Night" (1966), in which the symbolic connection between female nude and rose, posed in front of a closed door, creates a magical mood. Later, in the many versions of "Bud" and other drawings, Bruni varied this theme over and over, elaborating it with clouds, flowers, lips, hearts, mirrors, and butterflies. Next, Bruni integrated and interpreted the surreal-formal motif of a 'picture-within-a-picture', using views through windows, stretch frames and easels as in "La Modella" and "Alla ricerca del tempo perduto," 1967. The motif of the 'lying nude' that Bruni later developed into a three-dimensional scheme, first appears in early drawings and lithographs, such as "Nudino" and "Sogno."

Venus by Botticelli. In Bruni's variations of "Venus by Botticelli" (1971) we find a continuation of images and formal motifs introduced in his earlier work. The flowing lines and charm of Florentine Quattrocento painting apparently fascinated Bruni, stimulating him to create his own images of surrealist aesthetics. In his work, Bruni places Botticelli's Venus in empty, modern rooms; separates her face, hair and body so that they become individual components; and gives her a gentle nudity -- the refined, somewhat deformed sensuality of his own melodious nudes.

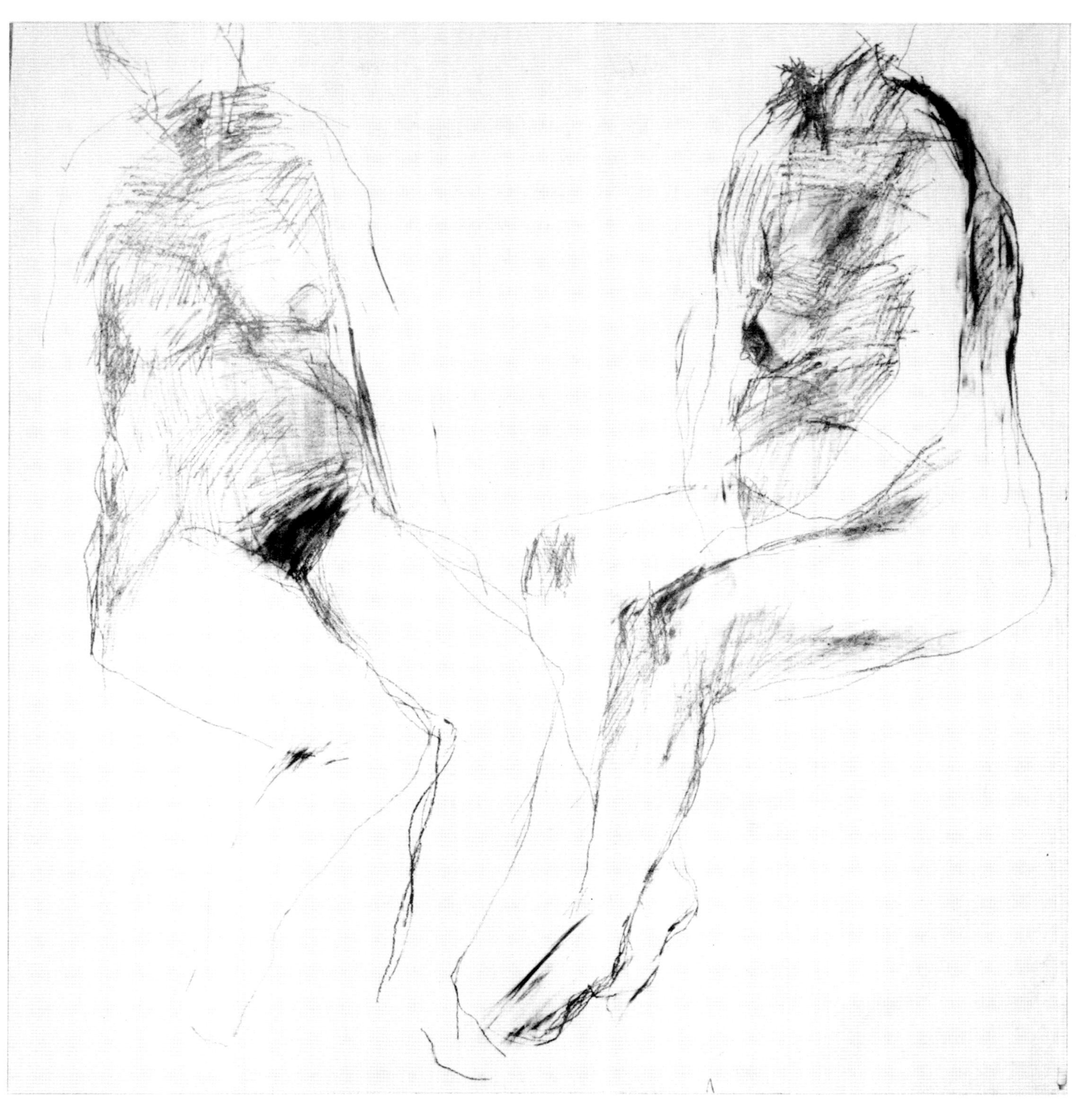

"Models" 1963
pencil drawing, ca. 90x80 cm

Ever since his first public exhibitions, Bruno Bruni has been criticized for the elegant aesthetic of his graphic design and drawing, as well as for the palpable influence of Paul Wunderlich's work on his color lithographs. What Bruni's critics did not realize was that because of his Italian background, Bruno was actually deeply rooted in the sensual and physical world of classical antiquity; Bruni's basic talent differed dramatically from the more intellectual aesthetic of his mentor. Because of the unique Italian-Germanic mixture of his background, Bruni developed a distinctively individual mode of expression that is, at its root, quite different from Wunderlich's. Rather, the connecting link between Bruni and Wunderlich is their preference for artificial paradises where the rules of form and harmony remain valid despite their liberal interpretation.

Il Cappotto. Two years before his variations of "Venus by Botticelli," Bruno Bruni had begun to explore an entirely new theme with his serigraph collection, "Il Cappotto." In Bruni's interpretations of "The Coat" by Gogol, the theme of the surreal-alienated article of clothing appears for the first time. Bruni isolates the coat, turning it into an ambiguous symbol that not only incarnates the plot of the story but expresses the emotions of heartache and melancholy. "The body vanishes, only the covering remains," explained Bruni.

Rosa Luxemburg. In Bruni's six lithographs of the Rosa-Luxemburg collection some of the tragic events are symbolized by articles of clothing, such as hats or caps. In fact, despite their political and critical emphasis, the paintings of Rosa Luxemburg show a great sensitivity to picturesque detail and graphic quality. The collection is conceived in a nostalgic manner, like an album of old-yellowed photographs. The first image shows the revolutionary as a twelve-year-old girl from a bourgeois family. The following stages in Luxemburg's tragic history – the manifestation, the citadel, the prison, revolution, and death – are symbolically implied by a variety of semantic attributes. Particularly effective are symbols of the 9th of November – flaring red flags – and the populace – a sea of faceless hats. Luxemburg's 'last greeting's is symbolized by a broken red carnation at the edge of the lithograph that shows an anonymous gathering in front of a statue of the political martyr. The last image of the sequence, "Ermordet, 15. Januar 1919," presents the same red carnation bleeding on the Landwehrkanal in Berlin in a dismal winter setting. Bare trees frame the bridge over the canal in a classical arch format. Bruni's personal feelings about the historic event are expressed in the interview on page 25. However, it is clear that even when Bruni tries to make a political statement, he remains an exquisite painter, designer and lithographer.

Amor Roma – Roma Amor. The suite, "Amor Roma-Roma Amor" (1973-74), unites the various components of Bruni's work into an exciting synthesis. The motif of the graceful girl, undressing and at the same time changing into a flower, is now intermingled with rich symbols of ancient and modern Rome... Nude and Mitra, Venus Kallipygos and the cupola of St. Peter's Church, the Pope and the Capitolean Wolf, Bernini's Saint Theresa in ecstasy – these images

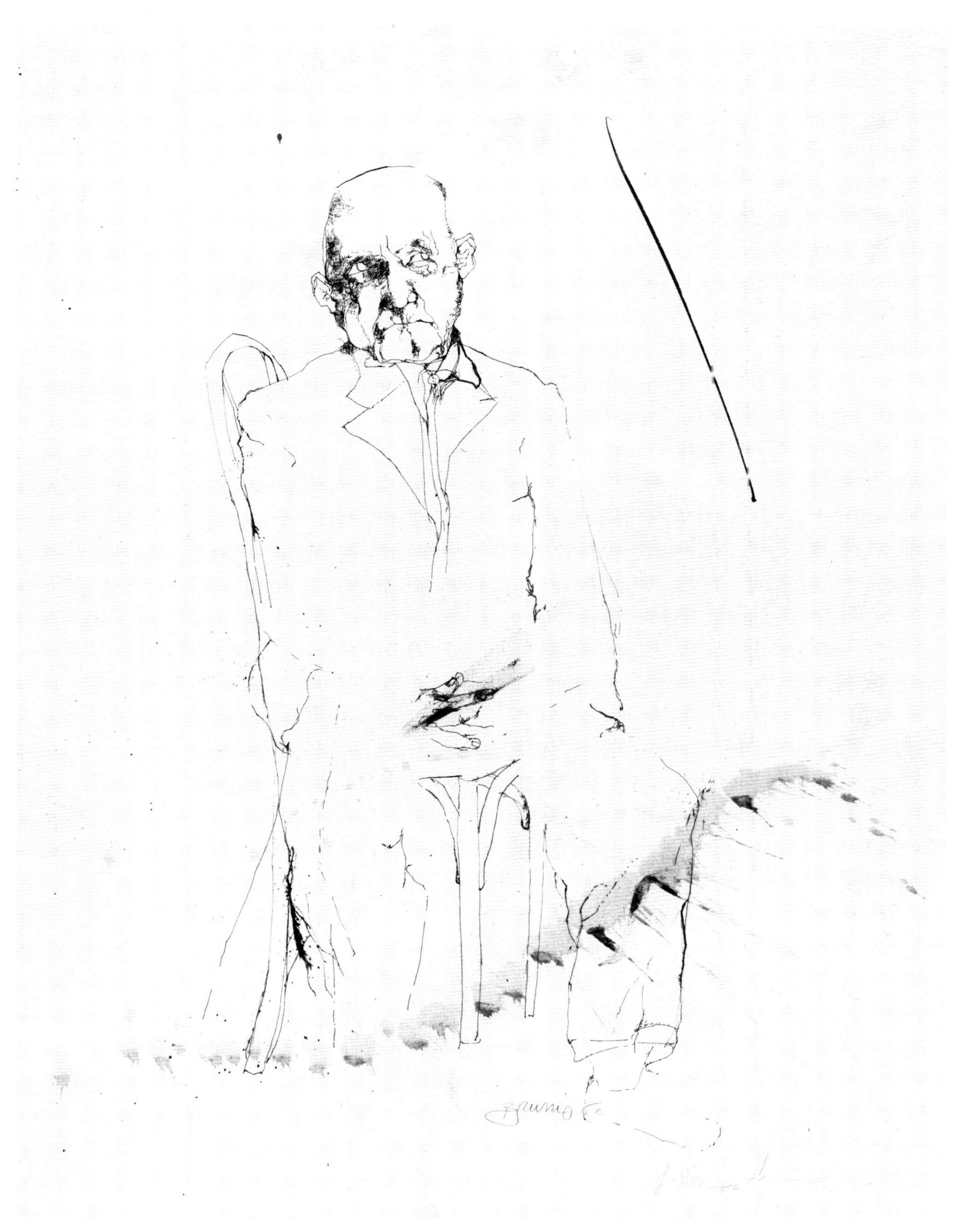

"Grandpa" 1962
pen-and-ink drawing, 49,5x38 cm

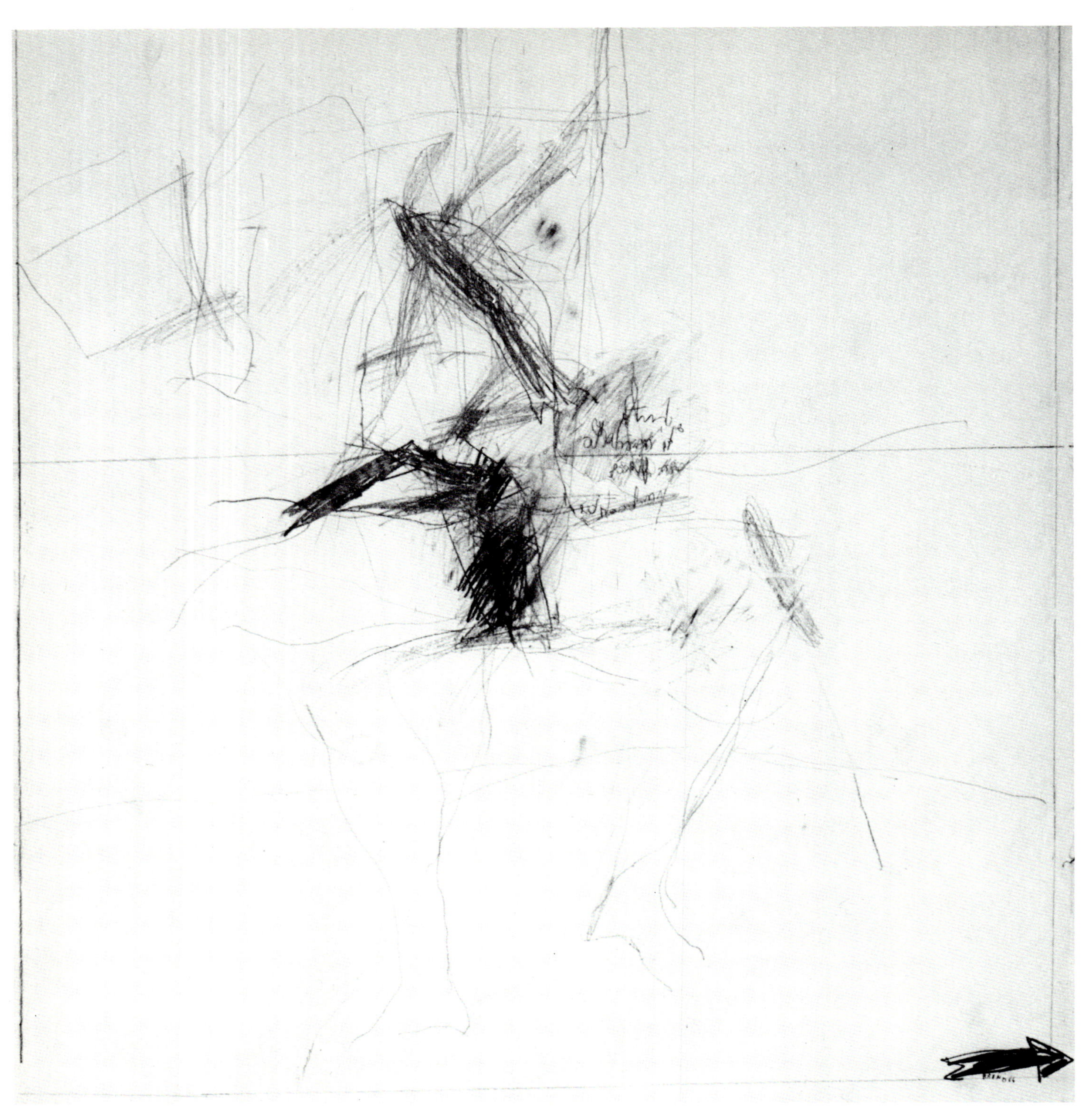

"Without Title" 1963
pencil drawing, 90x80 cm

make a picturesque graphic contrast of grace and decay, vitality and fragility, charm and tension. This ambiguous cycle functions as a homage to Rome, a city Bruni loves and where he maintains a studio.

Striptease. The suites, "Striptease" (1974) and "Les Belles et les Bêtes" (1975), are similar in style and motif. Here, the erotic element is even stronger than in his earlier work; the motif of undressing predominates. Drawing with pencil and lithographic chalk in an almost plastic style, Bruni creates an enchanting sensuality, tempting and at the same time fragile. Simultaneously, the sensualism of the images translates as pure, cool aesthetic form, arousing 'pleasure without interest', in the classical definition of beauty.

Leda and the Swan. Bruni interprets the ancient theme of Leda and the swan in an erotic and poetic way that is similar to Baudelaire's poem, "Le Cygne" from *Les Fleurs du Mal.* Here, (Leda con Cigno II, 1975) the long, snake-like neck of the swan bends and moves with elegance in the soft drapery covering the naked body of Leda. Bending backwards, Leda is gently outlined by an oval tondo and is enfolded in the wings of the approaching swan. In another painting, "Ein Auge auf den Schwan," the swan's bent neck creates a threefold arabesque, echoing the graceful body of the girl who pulls the garment over her head. In Bruni's most recent bronze statues the outlines of the swan's neck are molded into the figure of Leda, creating a single surreal entity.

Tenderness. Bruni's presentation of a loving and embracing couple in "Tenderness" (1976) is totally unique. Two raincoats, viewed from the back – the union of the slim, naked body of the girl with the man wearing a raincoat and high hat – become a metaphor for a short but intense relationship, full of tenderness and symbolizing, at the same time, the tension between frustration and satisfaction. By juxtaposing images of girl and man, female body and rain coat, nude and article of clothing, Bruni creates a unity, a tension and a harmony. "Such images have a magic effect," says Henri Alexis Baatsch in his introduction to the cataloque of Bruno Bruni's exhibition in the Gallery Brockstedt in Hamburg in 1976–77, "the objects, naked or clothed, appear to vanish after a while, but with careful observation, they reappear in the magical light that surrounds them."

Landscape elements. Even though the figure dominates Bruni's work, landscapes, or rather elements of landscapes, such as clouds, autumn leaves, deep horizons, have always figured prominently in his compositions. In "Tra de Nuvole" 1967, a graceful female nude is partially obscurred by the realistic rendering of a cloud that casts a shadow onto the window, through which other clouds may be seen. Several of the paintings from the Botticelli cycle include mountains and cypress trees of the Tuscany landscape ("Frammenti toscani," 1972). Other landscapes, such as the panorama "Fireland" (1972), originate in the artist's imagination. On occasion, Bruni unites fantasy and experience to create surreal combinations of nature, such as waves, clouds, rainbows and flying

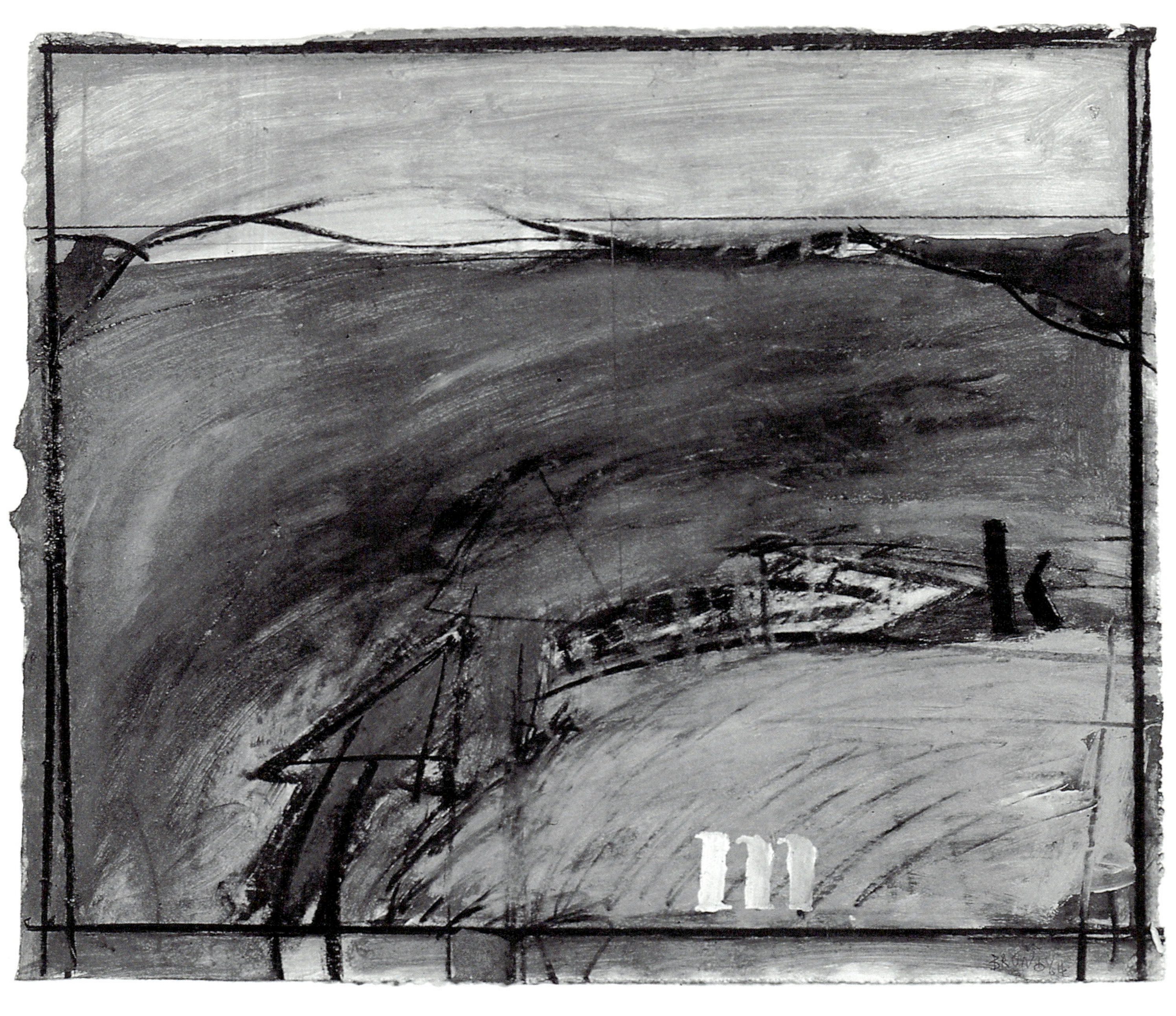

"Landscape" 1963, *gouache, 25x35 cm*

birds. Fantasy and reality are merged in "L'Alarcobaleno" – a fusion of the word 'wing' (ala) and 'rainbow (arcobaleno) – the title for both the 11-color serigraph of 1969–70 and the 5-color lithograph of 1970. In another surreal presentation of a landscape, a group of men's hats, shaped like a bouquet is confronted with stylized, bubbling waves. The title, "Discussione assurda a proposito di un onda" (1973), means an argument about a wave.

The Importance of Drawing. The drawings of any artist may be treacherous for they provide direct insight into the working method of the artist – a look behind the scenes of his studio. They reflect the process and develoment of his visual ideas, enabling the viewer to look over the artist's shoulder and participate in the process of creative intuition. Drawing is the basis of Bruno Bruni's entire work. He is a first-class draughtsman who loves to collect the drawings of other artists, be they related spiritually or not. His collection includes important drawings by Klimt, Rops, Bellmer, Magritte, Delvaux, Dix, Grosz, Schad, Beckmann, Arroyo, Gresko, Janssen, Wunderlich, Hockney, Dine, as well as bronze figures by Lipschitz and newer works of Dali and Wunderlich.

Bruni first develops his visual ideas through drawing. His lithographs are based on these drawings which have become almost as complex and elaborate as his paintings.

Large Gouaches. Bruni's large gouaches of 1975–76, exhibited for the first time at the Brockstedt Gallery in Hamburg (1976–77), tread a fine line between drawing and painting. In these gouaches, Bruni proves himself to be a draughtsman/painter as well as a painter/draughtsman, capable of all variations and subtleties. Earlier topics reoccur in these gouaches: the graceful slim nude pulling her garment over her head. Motifs such as curtains, sheets, blankets, dresses, coats and hats which first appeared in the series "Il Cappotto" and "Rosa Luxemburg," are now shown in surreal isolation. Moreover, there are configurations of masked figures and loving couples that gain symbolic meaning by their additional attributes -- images like "Autumn" and "Evening," "Melancolia" and "Infernale." The same soft accent and flowing lines of these recent drawings and gouaches prove Bruni's technical and aesthetic mastery.

Bronze figures. Bruni's fascination with the fluid, modulated outlines of his graceful nudes as seen in his drawings, lithographs, and gouaches, has recently found another medium of expression – three-dimensional sulpture. In Bruni's first surreal sulpture, "Lying down" (1975) the narrow female torso ending at the breasts, with extremely long legs, is transformed into a three-dimensional bronze. In another sculpture, the theme of drapery is adapted in a highly original way: a second 'lying girl' is partially covered by a blanket that is actually a separate piece of metal and may be lifted. The figures do not have a base and must be positioned at the edge of a table or stool so that their extremely long, elf-like legs may hang down freely. A year later, in 1976, Bruni created two standing bronze figures, "Knospe" and "Venus annoiata." Here, another of Bruni's principal motifs is transformed into a sensuous sculpture: the standing nude, lifting her garment -- now silver and shining -- with inimitable grace like a flower. Grace and surreal sensualism are intimately linked.

Bruni's latest bronze sculpture developed from preceding configurations of Leda and the Swan. Uniting both creatures into a single entity, Bruni eliminates the polarity of the sexes and creates a supernatural erotic entity.

Although Bruni was not originally a sculptor, his bronze figures are unique and have already been cited as important examples of contemporary sculpture. They reflect major characteristics of Bruni's aesthetic. In them, grace, sensulaity and surrealism combine to create visual interpretations of beauty.

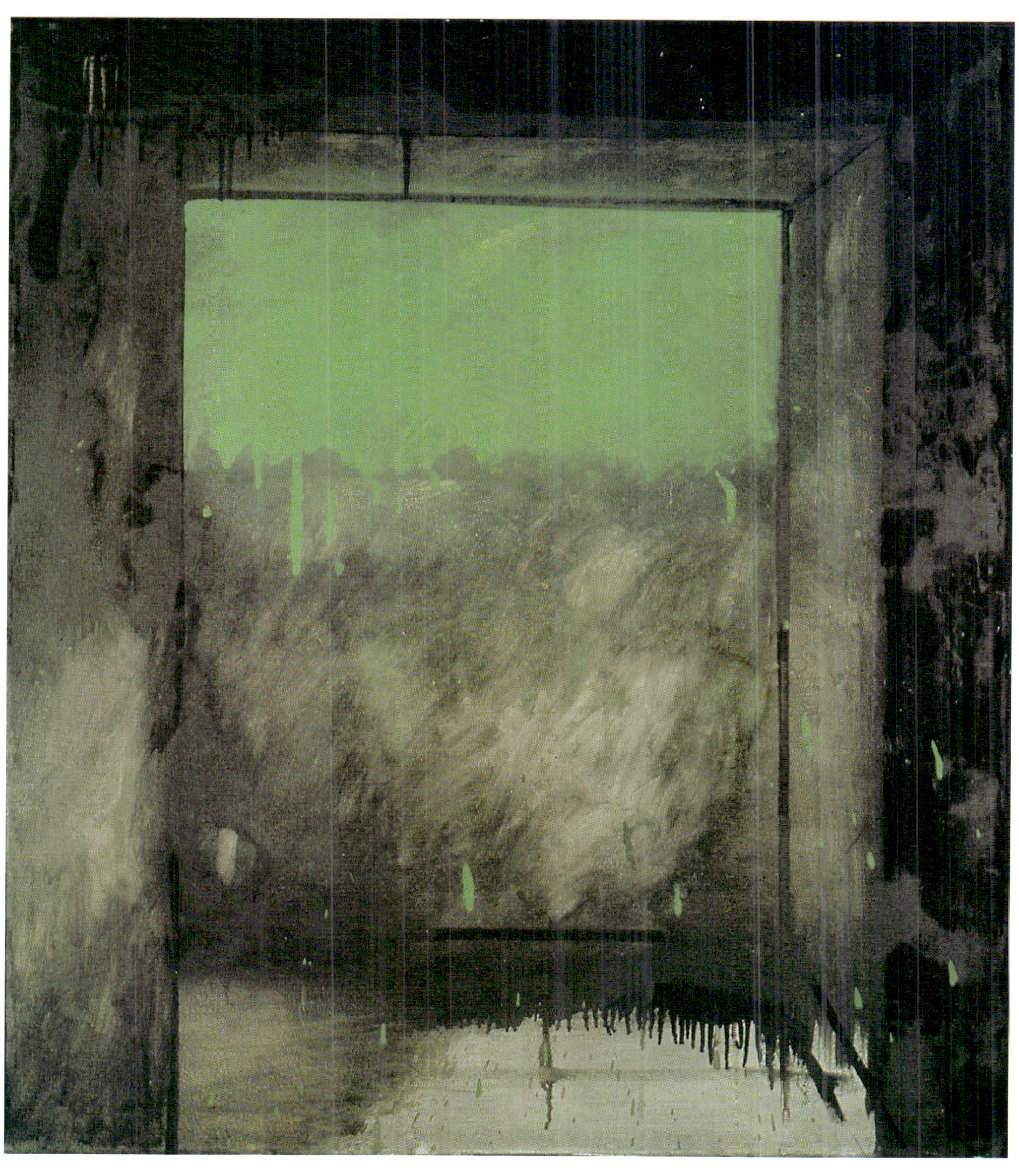

"Paesaggio" 1963
oil on canvass, 100x80 cm

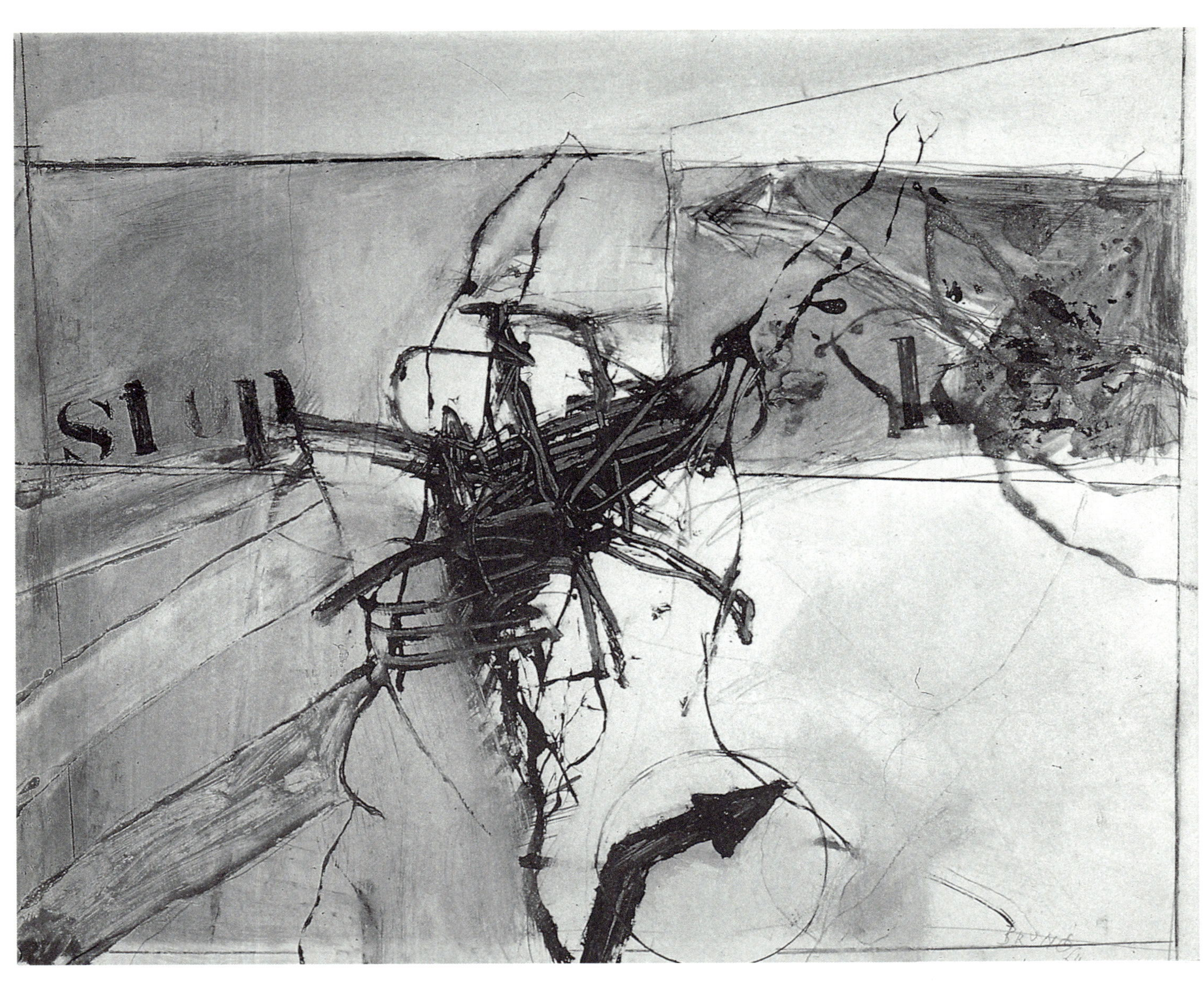

"stop" 1963, *gouache, 25x35 cm*

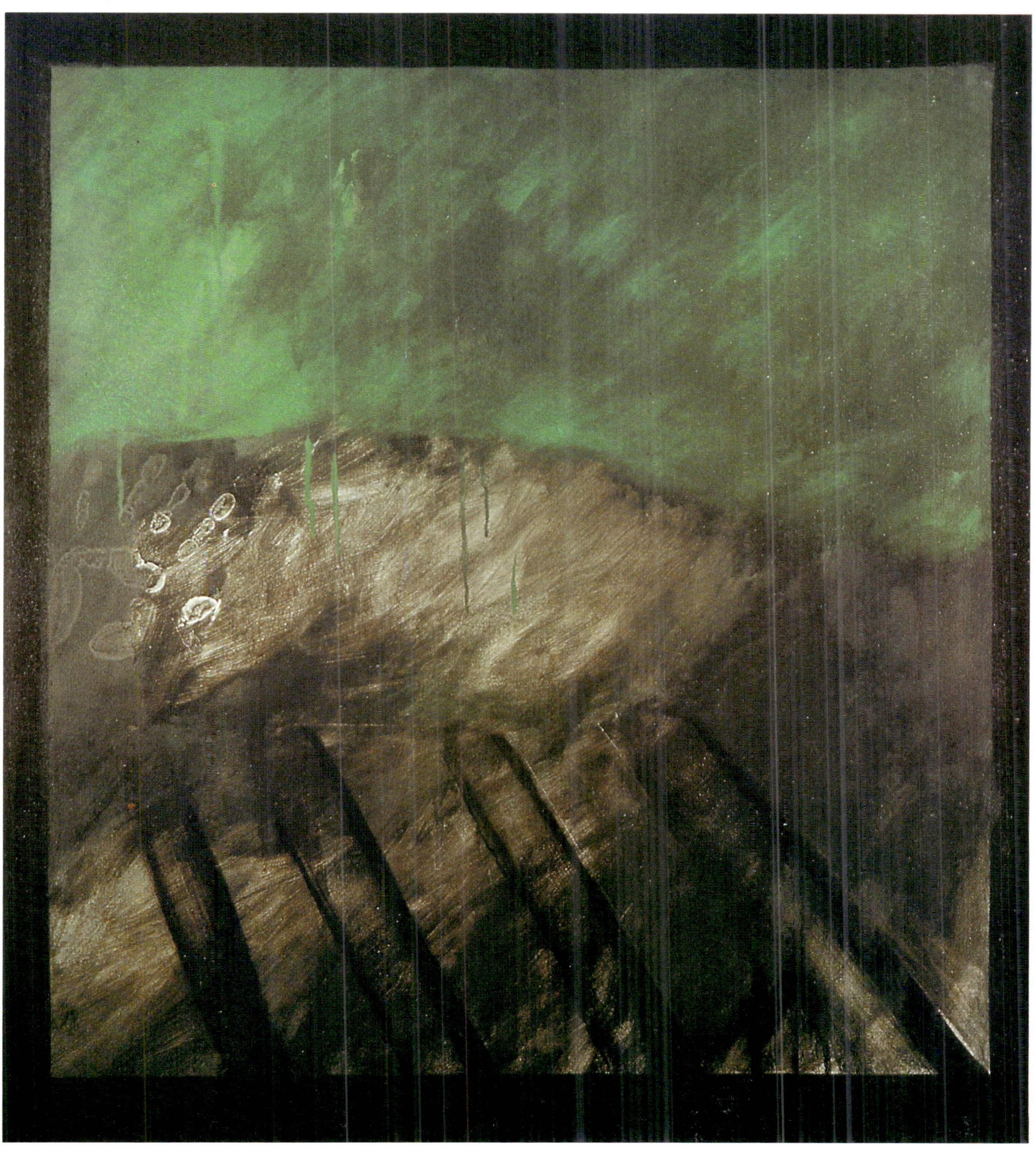

"Paesaggio" 1963, *gouache, 35x30 cm*

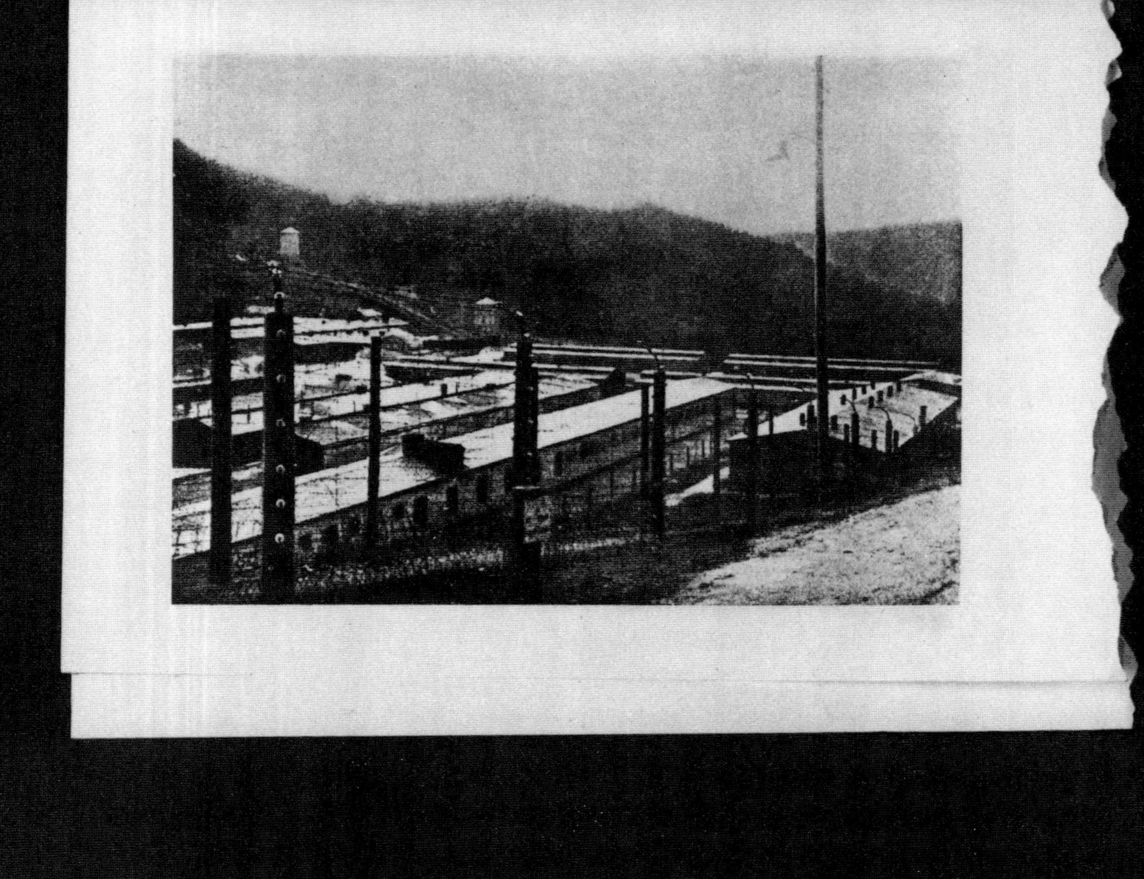

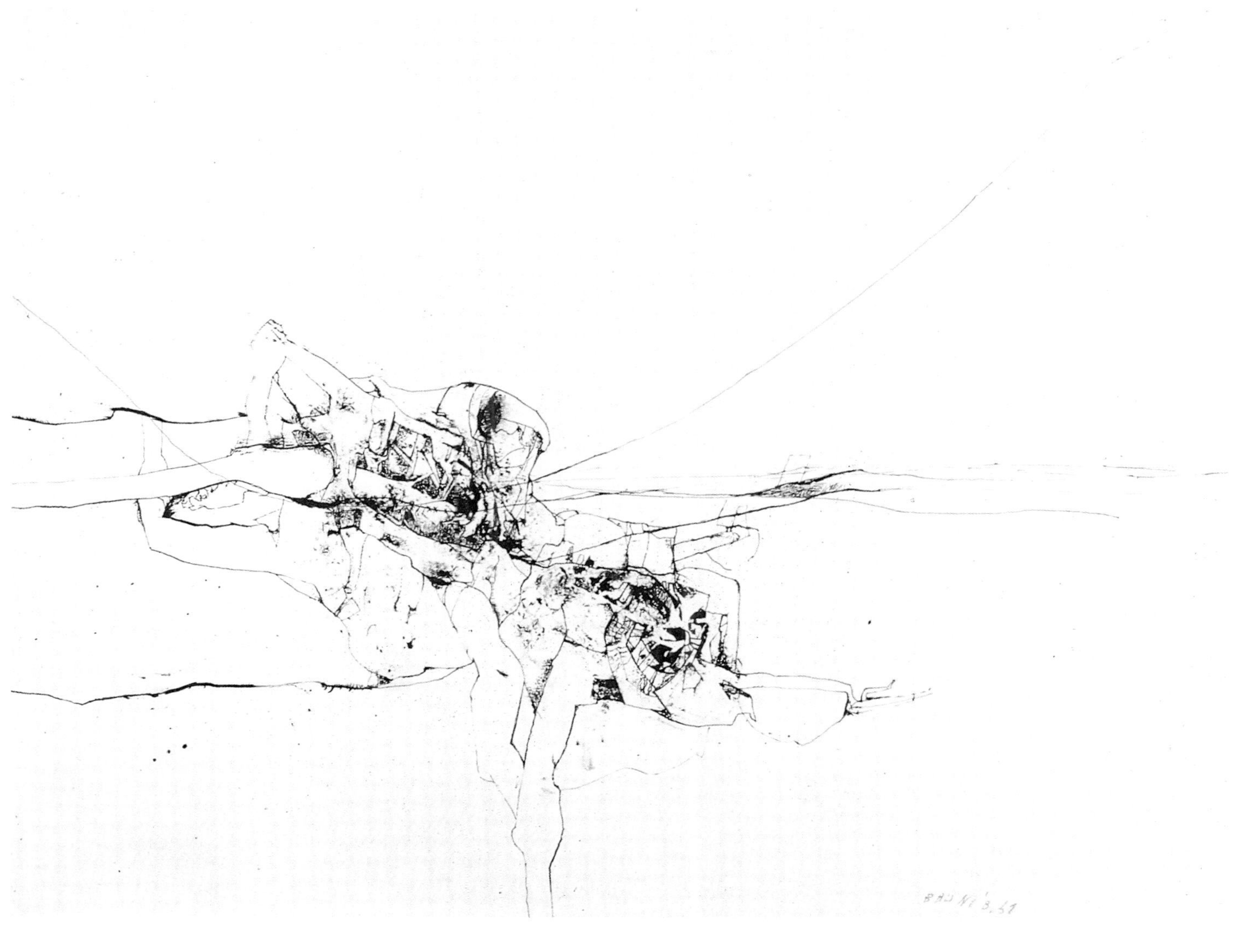

"Der gelbe Stern" 1961
pen-and-ink drawing, 23x34 cm, out of a series of five drawings
◁ Concentration Camp Photo as inspiration

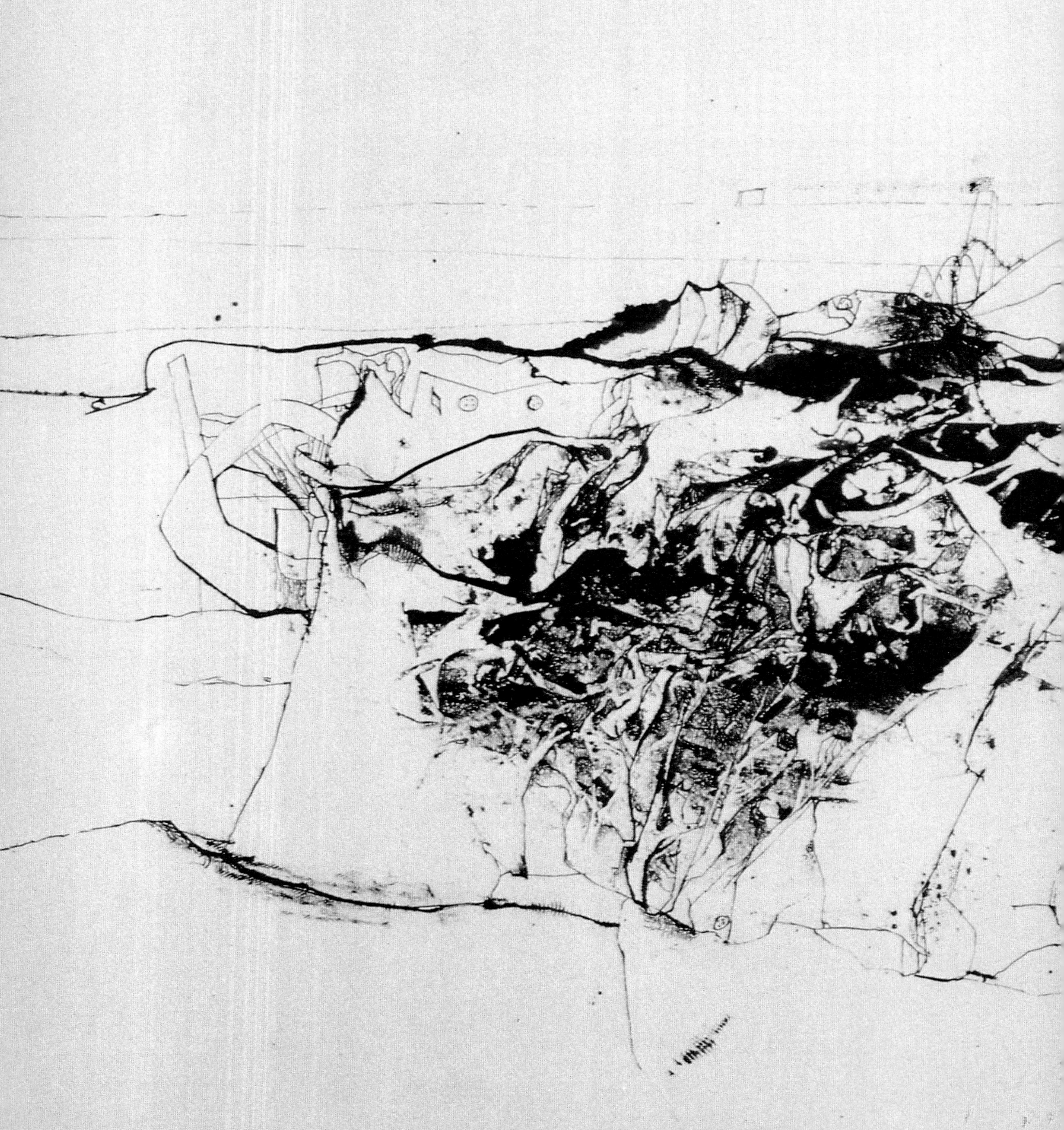

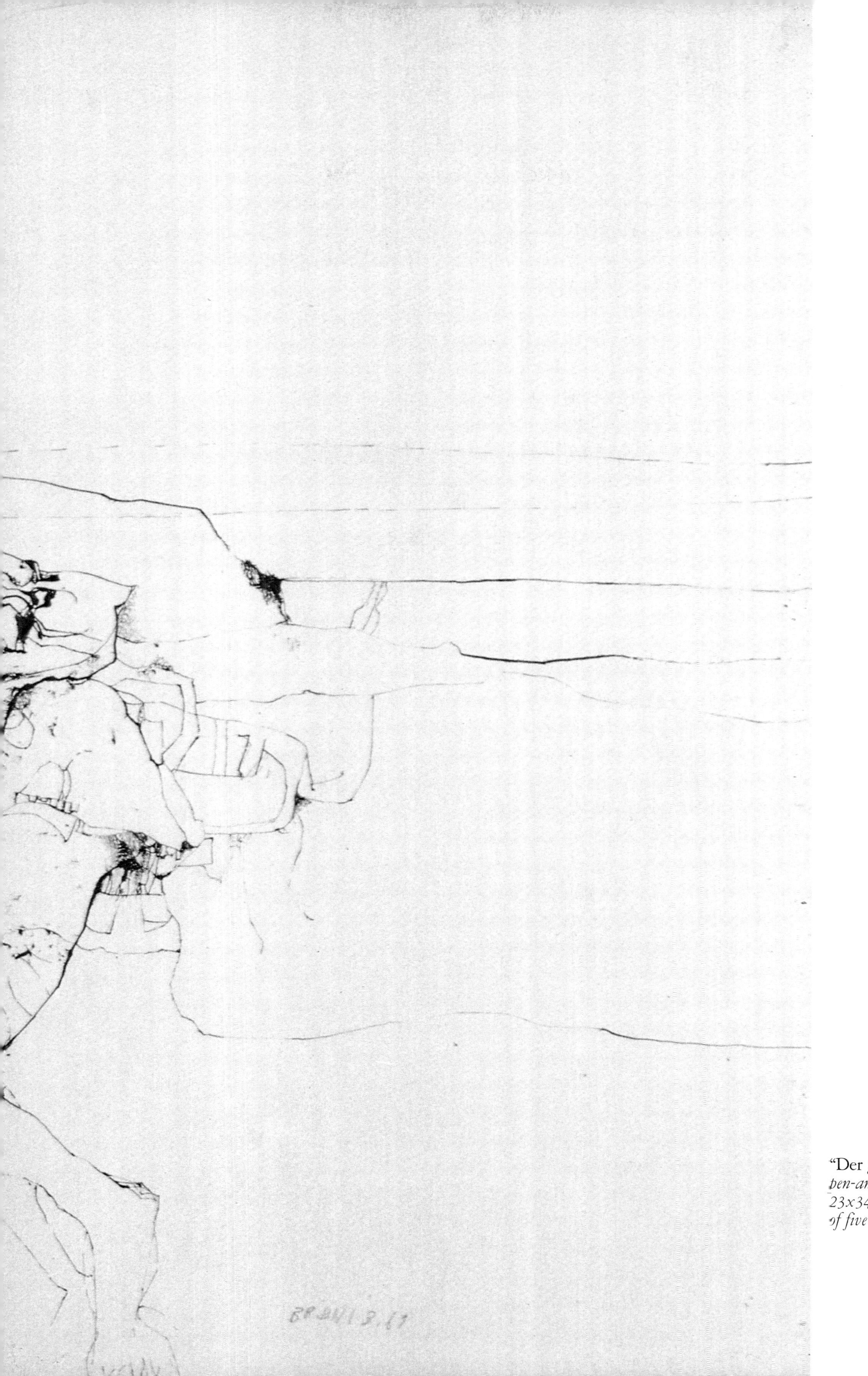

"Der gelbe Stern" 1961
pen-and-ink drawing, 23x34 cm, out of a series of five drawings

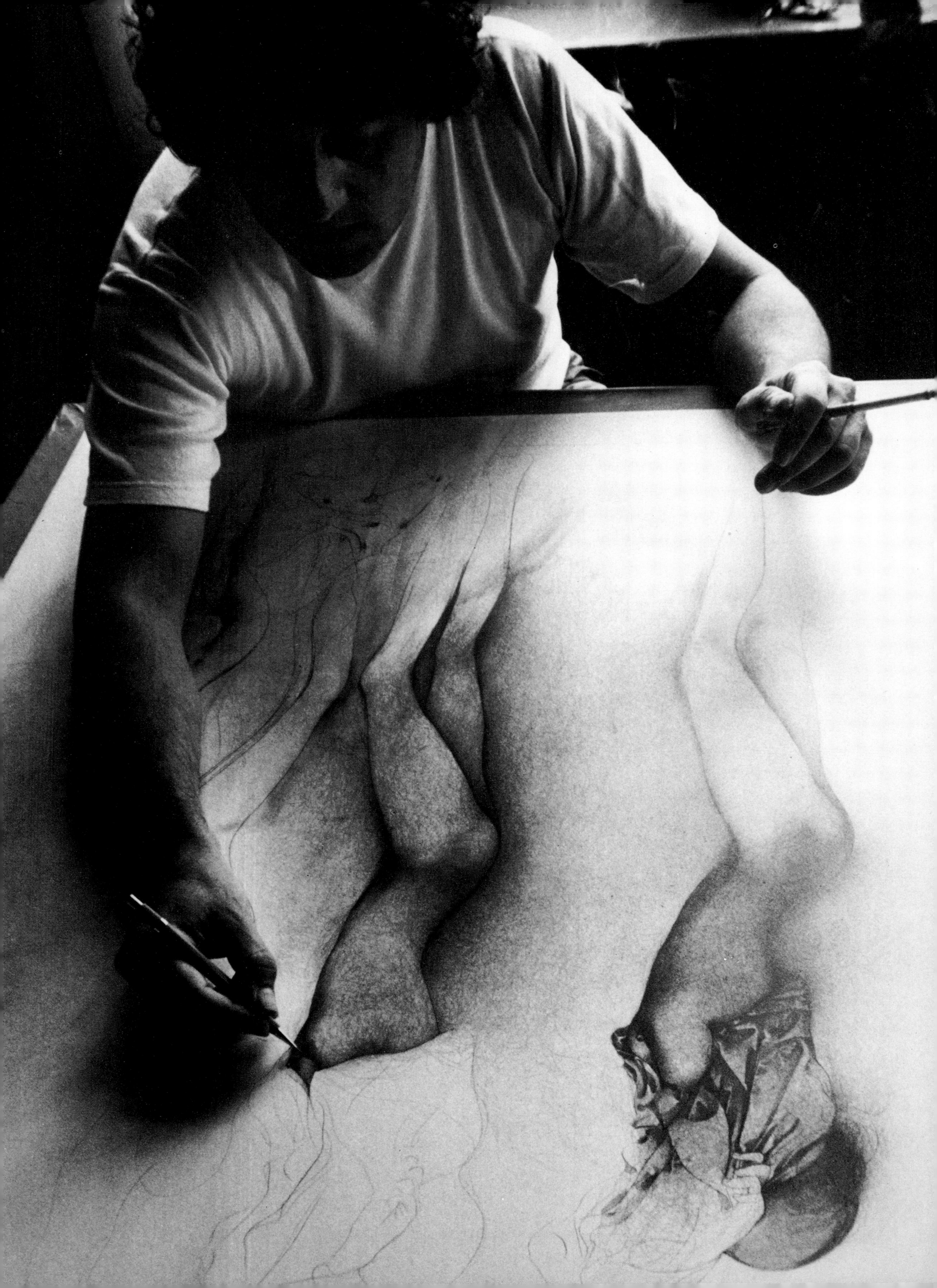

Self-Expression or Message?

A Conversation with Bruno Bruni, December 1977

Flemming: Do you prefer a historical or a poetic interpretation of your work?

Bruno Bruni: I don't want to be presented as either a historical figure or as a monument. Since you've known me for a long time and have observed the development of my work from the very beginning, you can probably judge the different periods of my work better than anyone.

Flemming: In the last *Documenta* exhibition in Kassel, work like yours and Wunderlich's, and even the entire neo-surrealist and fantastic realist schools were entirely excluded. Perhaps, your work was too beautiful, too sensual, too aesthetic. What is your opinion as to the problem of beauty and sensualism in art?

Bruno Bruni: As to your first remark: The value of these big events, such as *Documenta,* the Biennal, etc. is, in my opinion, very questionable, because art is not really the primary concern ... As to your second question: Beauty and sensualism are very important to me, but neither one is, in itself, enough. I admit that many people have criticized the inclination to beauty and sensualism in my art. Yet, whenever I have dealt with themes like "Der gelbe Stern," "Rosa Luxemburg," or "Algeria," the important issues were ignored and I was even attacked, as if beauty could not be connected with a statement...

Flemming: You are an Italian, and in your country you were confronted with reminders of antiquity at a very young age. What is your attitude to Greek and Roman antiquity, and how did they influence your former academic education and your current work?

Bruno Bruni: One cannot deny one's origin, even if one wanted to... In my country, art is not connected with a particular social class as it is in Germany; in my country the old masters are truly "popular" ... Indeed, my work could not exist without the influence of the old masters.

Flemming: Two names are quite important in connection with your artistic development and your studies in Germany: Georg Gresko and Paul Wunderlich. Tell me about your relationship to Gresko.

Bruno Bruni: I was lucky to meet such a person by chance. One cannot forget that I came from a small village and that the Academy of Arts was an inaccessible dream for me. Gresko made it possible for me to study at the art school in Hamburg, and he helped me in every respect. Without Gresko, I might even say, I would not be the artist I am today ... I also learned a great deal from Wunderlich, particularly in terms of technique, even though he was my teacher for only a short time after the early death of Gresko ...

Flemming: Despite the surreal alienation in your work, your relationship to sensual things appears to be quite basic. Do you create a great deal from your imagination?

Bruno Bruni: Yes, unless you mean "basic" as primitive; but as direct and spontaneous, I agree. However, I think that many people misunderstand the word "basic."

Flemming: Basic and sensual do not exclude the elements of reflection and thought. But I have another question concerning the role of the female nude in your art. Your manner of presenting the nude is the antithesis of the kind of profane sensualism you often find in magazines and popular pornography. Many of your paintings and sculptures, such as "Venus annoiata," exude a sensual enchantment. But you are, if I may say so, a realistic man, firmly standing on the ground. Do you see a striking contrast between art and life, or do you really experience life in the same gentle and sensitive way as is expressed in your art?

Bruno Bruni: Of course, I see a direct connection between art and life ... The great success of my *"Tenderness"* series shows that these images exist not only in my own fantasy but that they correspond to the emotions of many other people ...

Flemming: Here we come to a topic that is discussed often these days: the social relevance of art. In fact, everywhere people talk about overcoming the boundaries between art and audience. However, in those big events, such as *Documenta,* new boundaries are built up precisely because the organizers and many of the artists behave contrary to their politics, like an élite ...
You are right in emphasizing the success of your "Venus annoiata" as public approval. In general, how do you see the relationship between art and audience? Whom do you feel you are addressing with your creative message?

Bruno Bruni: Actually, I work for myself first, but the acceptance of the audience is very important to me. However, I want to emphasize that while I am drawing or painting I really do not think of a particular message ...

Flemming: How would you classify your work? Are you more of a realist, or rather a surrealist in the realm of fantasy?

Bruno Bruni: I am neither a realist nor a surrealist; rather, I belong to the school of "fantastic realism" . . .

Flemming: How do you find the specific themes of your work? I do not mean the female body, for that, of course, is a popular subject. Why did you choose, for example, themes like "Venus of Botticelli," or "Rosa Luxemburg," or "The Coat" by Gogol – to name three totally different topics? What made you paint these things?

Bruno Bruni: The beauty of Botticelli's women has always fascinated me, ever since I was a little boy. So I dedicated the series "Venus" to Botticelli in order to express my admiration for his paintings. I come from a family of communists and in Italy, Rosa Luxemburg has always remained a historical figure. I think people like Rosa Luxemburg have always been misunderstood in Germany. Therefore, I tried to express my admiration for this woman, and at the same time prevent her from falling into oblivion.

Flemming: To what extent are your Rosa Luxemburg paintings based on historical documents, and how much did you idealize your heroine?

Bruno Bruni: My paintings are based on documents; I did not idealize her. With people like Luxemburg, idealization is not necessary. Instead, I interpreted her life in a chronological sequence up until her death.

Flemming: Do you believe that because these pictures are extremely beautiful and aesthetic, they are capable of changing the sensibility of the broad public, or is it more likely that they are only appreciated by a small esoteric circle of people!

Bruno Bruni: I think that the people who did not like Rosa Luxemburg before will not like my pictures either. In fact, this series is the only one in my work of which I still have several unsold prints . . .

Flemming: I would think that people who do not sympathize with Rosa Luxemburg as a historical figure, would still find your paintings of her to be extremely beautiful . . .

Bruno Bruni: That would be fantastic – but the only pictures out of the suite that sold well were the ones that do not express the issue very clearly.

Flemming: One question about your sequence, "Roma Amor" – an especially beautiful anagram that can be read in both directions. In this suite you combine the aesthetic and the erotic element with the historical. What did you intend?

Bruno Bruni: This series was planned for a gallery in Rome as a critical hommage to the eternal city. The original idea was that every year until the end of my life I would make a painting about one aspect of Rome that I am very fond of. I could have accomplished a fantastic suite, but unfortunately I broke up with the gallery much too soon.

Flemming: This imaginary sequence would certainly have been something new in the history of art, surpassing even Vollard who often waited decades for his graphic suites by Rouault, Picasso and Chagall... But back to reality. How do you see the relationship of drawing to sculpture in your work? Only recently, with your gentle girl figures, have you begun to work in sculpture.

Bruno Bruni: I am not a sculptor in the traditional sense. The sculptures are all based on my drawings. They are - so to speak - a continuation of my paintings, my paintings realized in a different dimension.

Flemming: It is without doubt a problem to write a book about a contemporary artist. In 1955 I wrote my first book about the sculptor Ewald Mataré (1887–1965), and with good reason, he did not read it before it was printed. Mataré lived ten more years. You are much younger. But finally I would like to ask you: What are your plans? How do you see the development of your artistic career? Or do you leave that up to mood, love and coincidence?

Bruno Bruni: There is no coincidence. As Machiavelli said: "You have to search for Lady Luck to find her, as she doesn't come by herself."

Flemming: Do you find the essential impulse for your art in self-expression or in the message of your fellow men?

Bruno Bruni: First in self-expression, and if my fellow men perceive it as a message, so much the better.

"Kleines Veilchen" 1961, *pencil and gouache, 56x50 cm* ▷

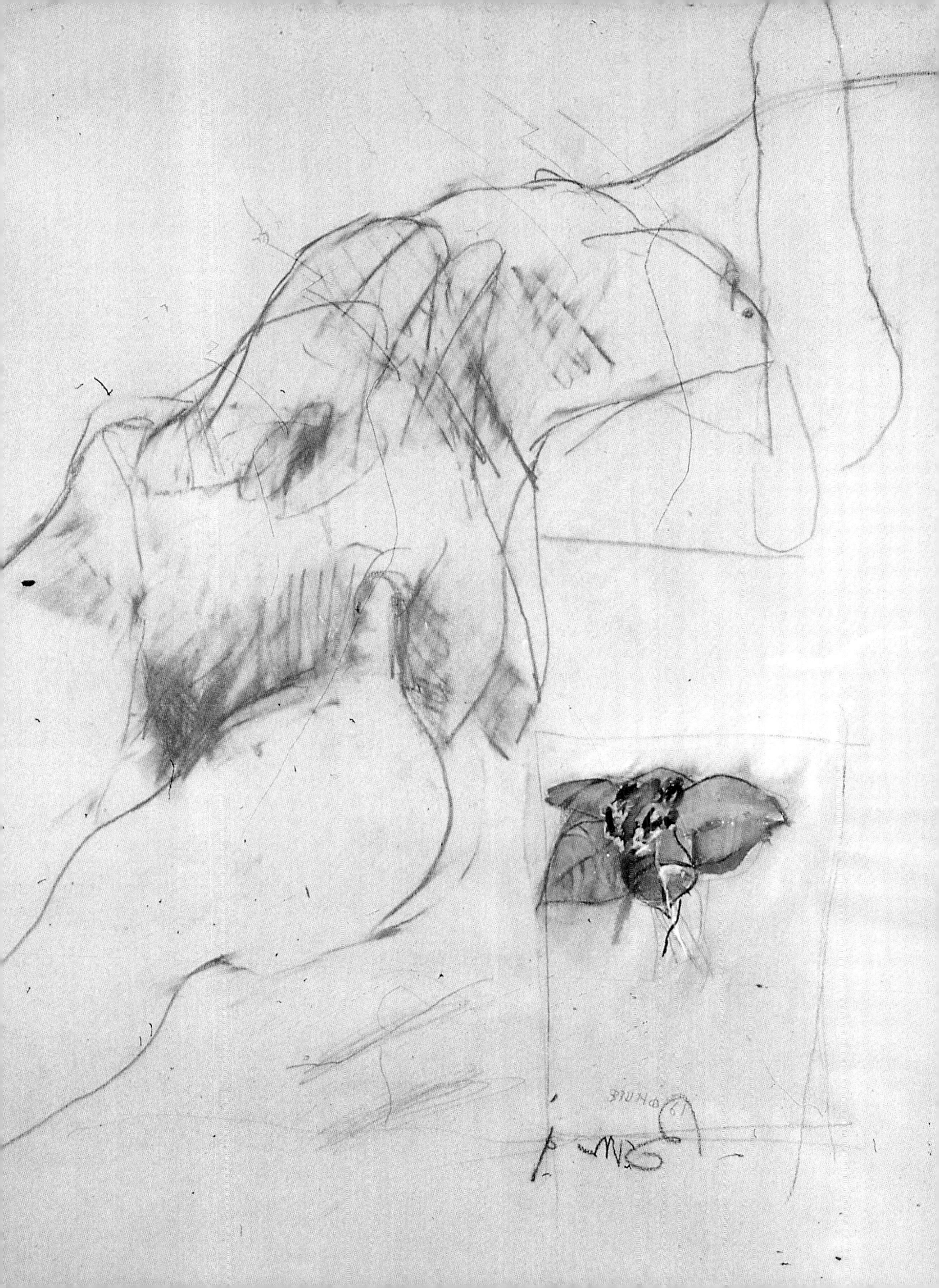

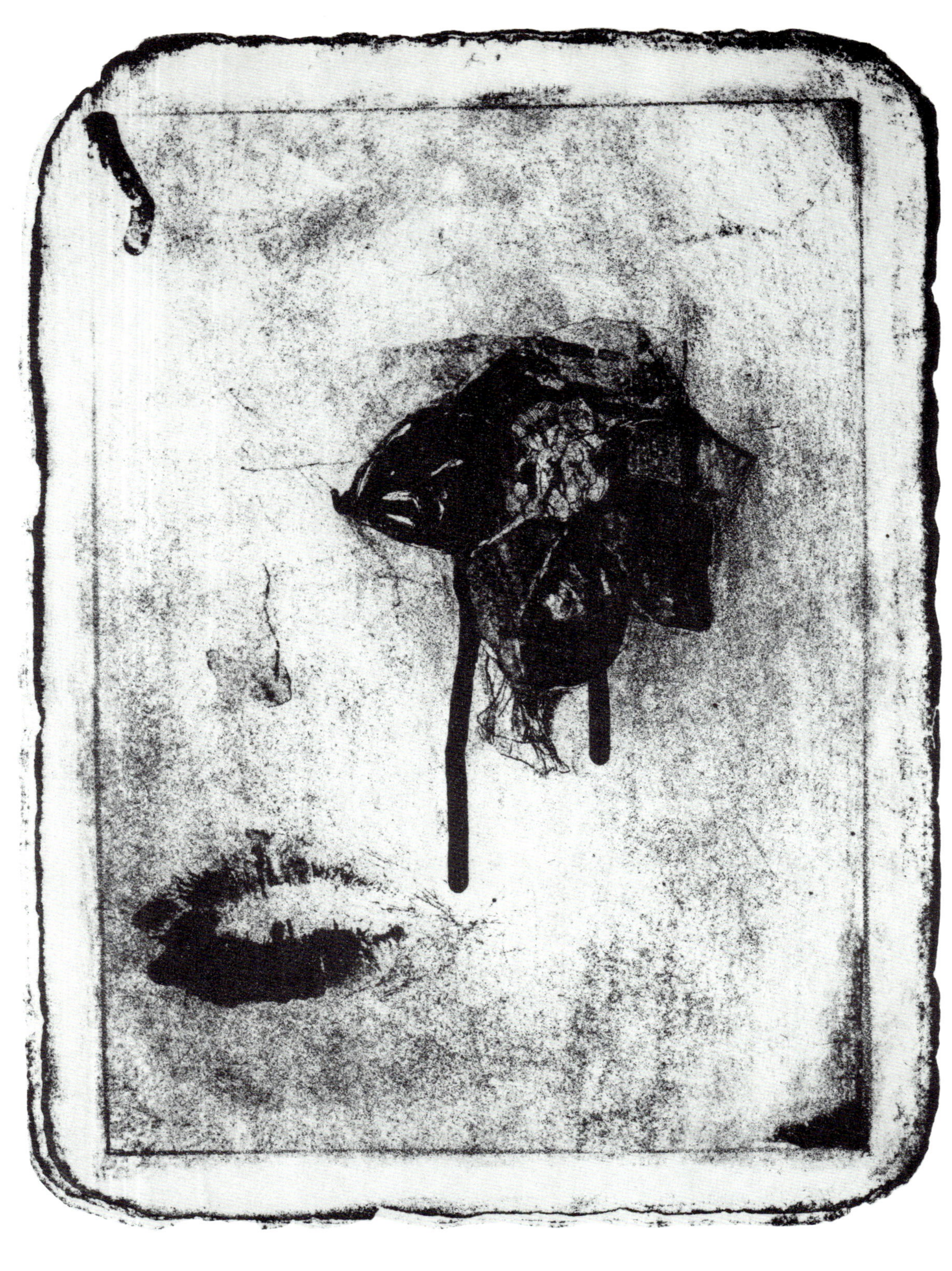

"A Dürer" 1964
lithograph in one colour, 21.7x16.2 cm

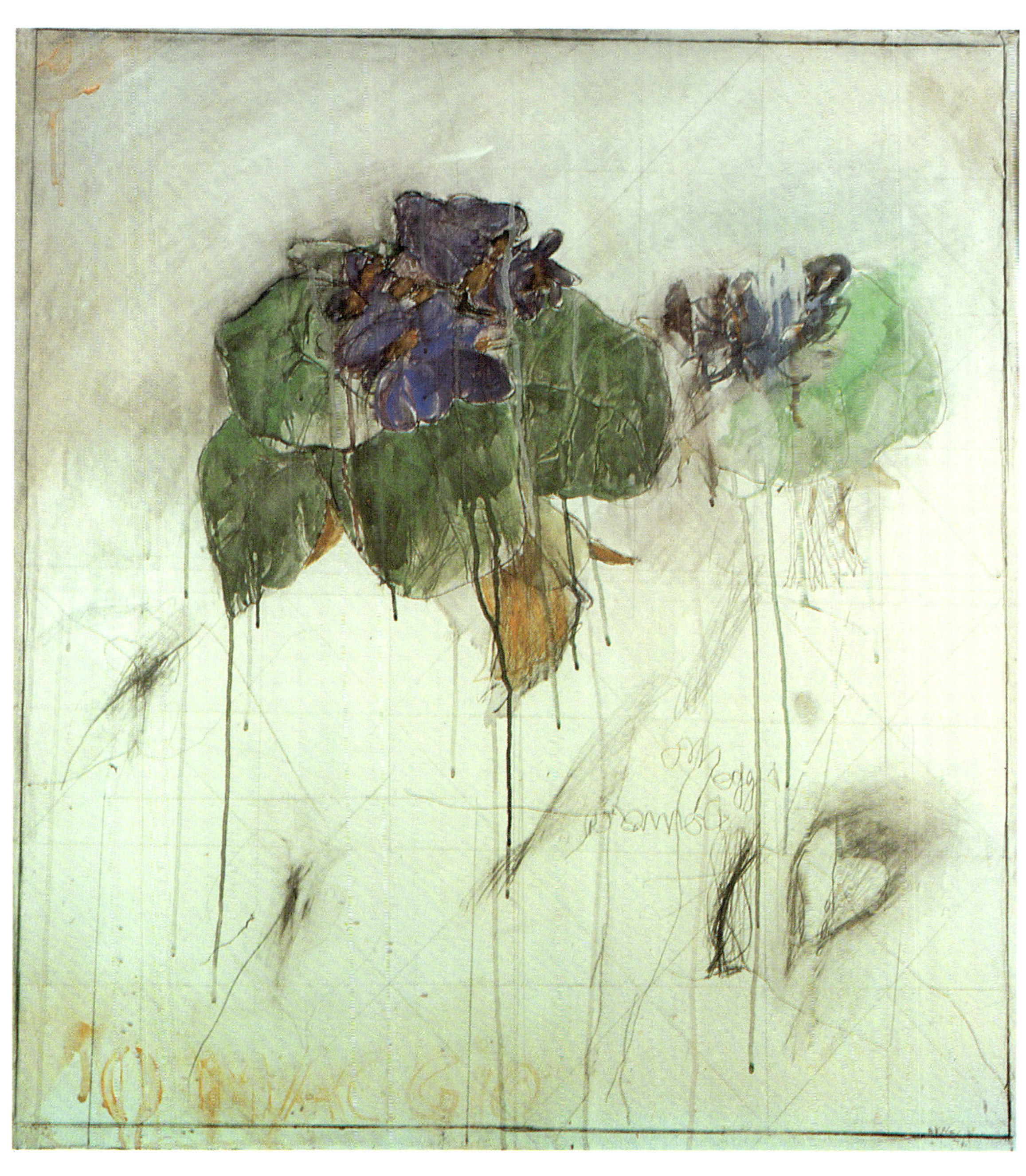

"Without Title" 1964, *water-colour, 100x90 cm*

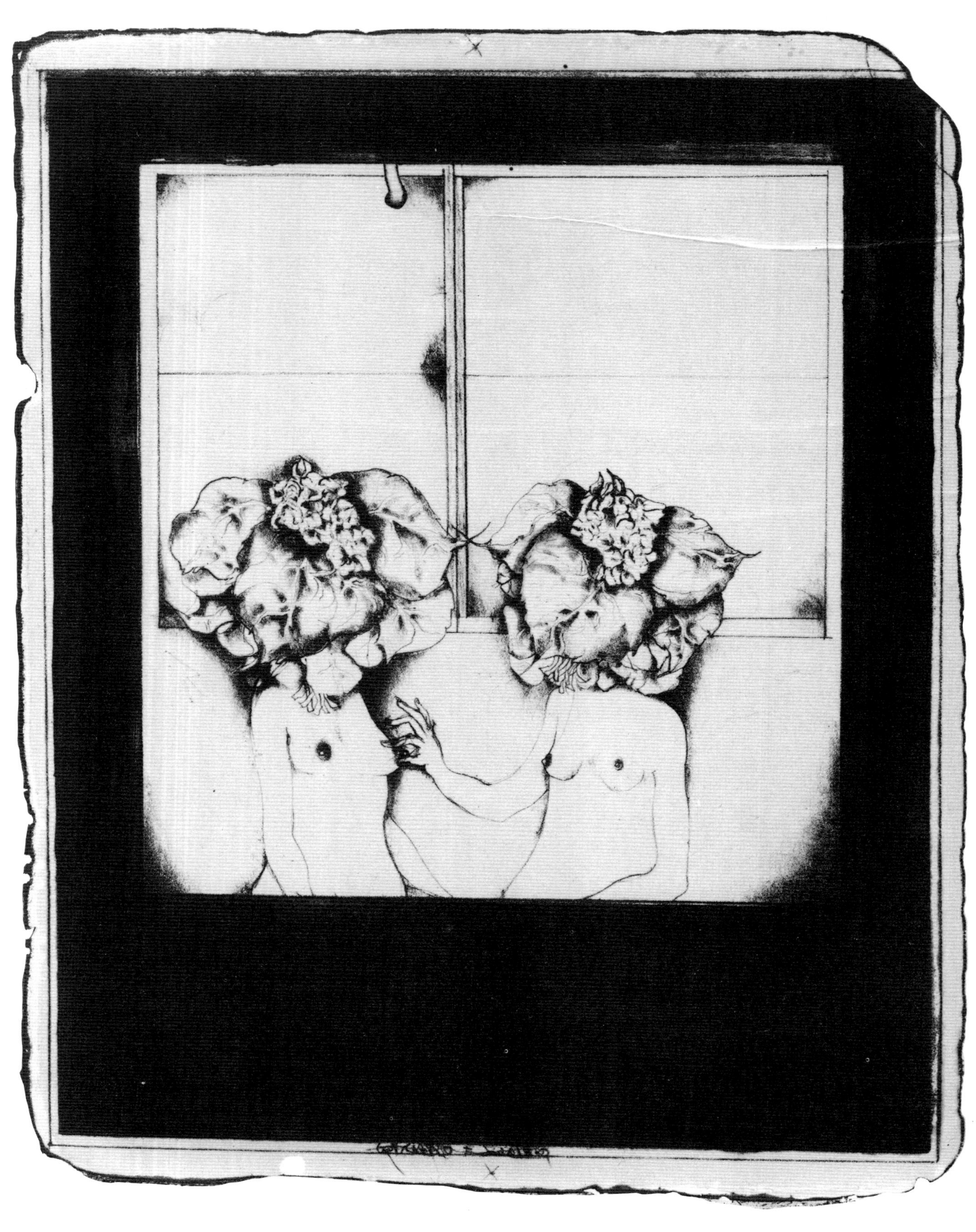

"Ommaggio al manierismo" 1965
lithograph in two colours, 41.5x32.8 cm

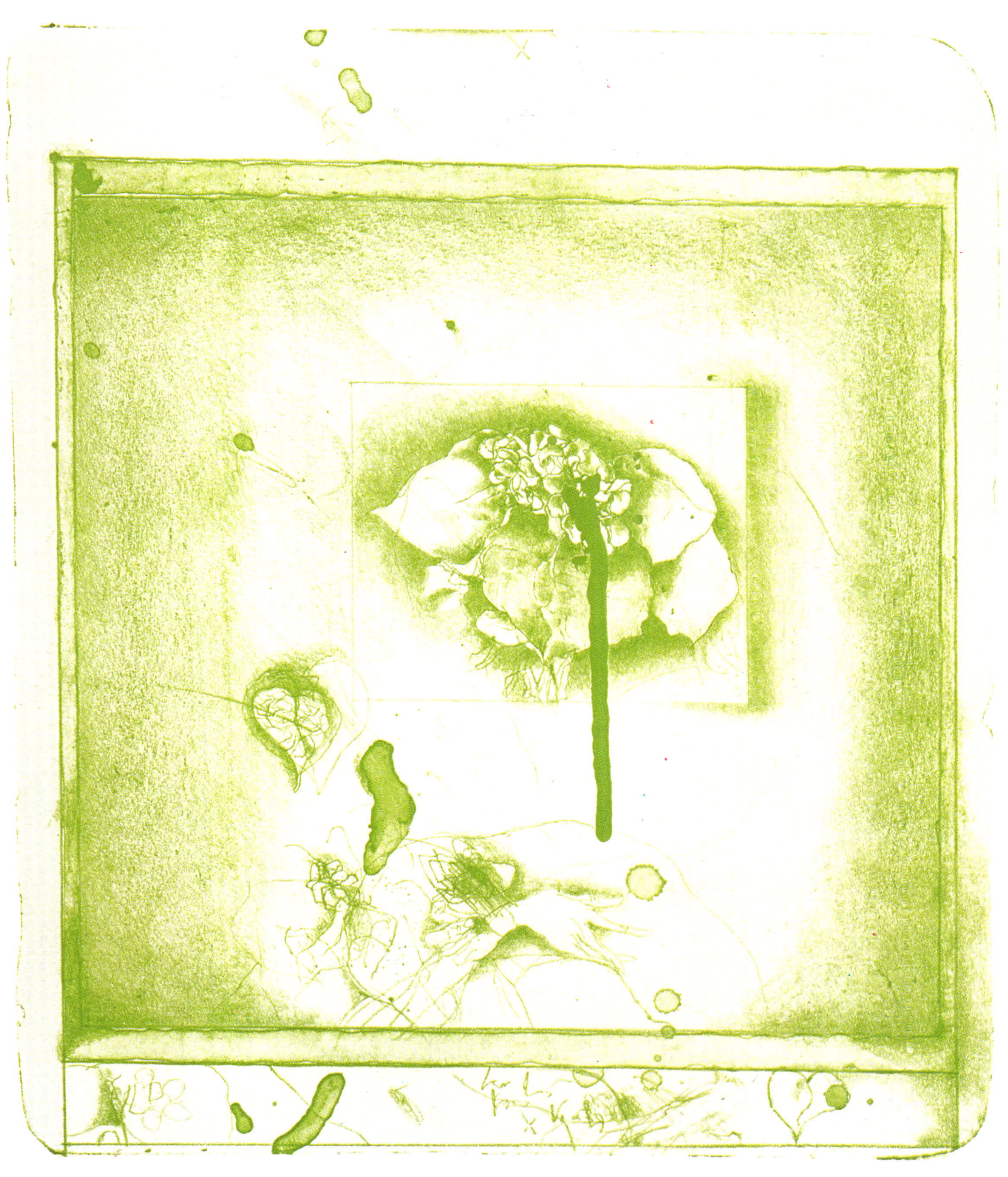

"Viole I" 1965
lithograph in one colour, 37.5x32.2 cm

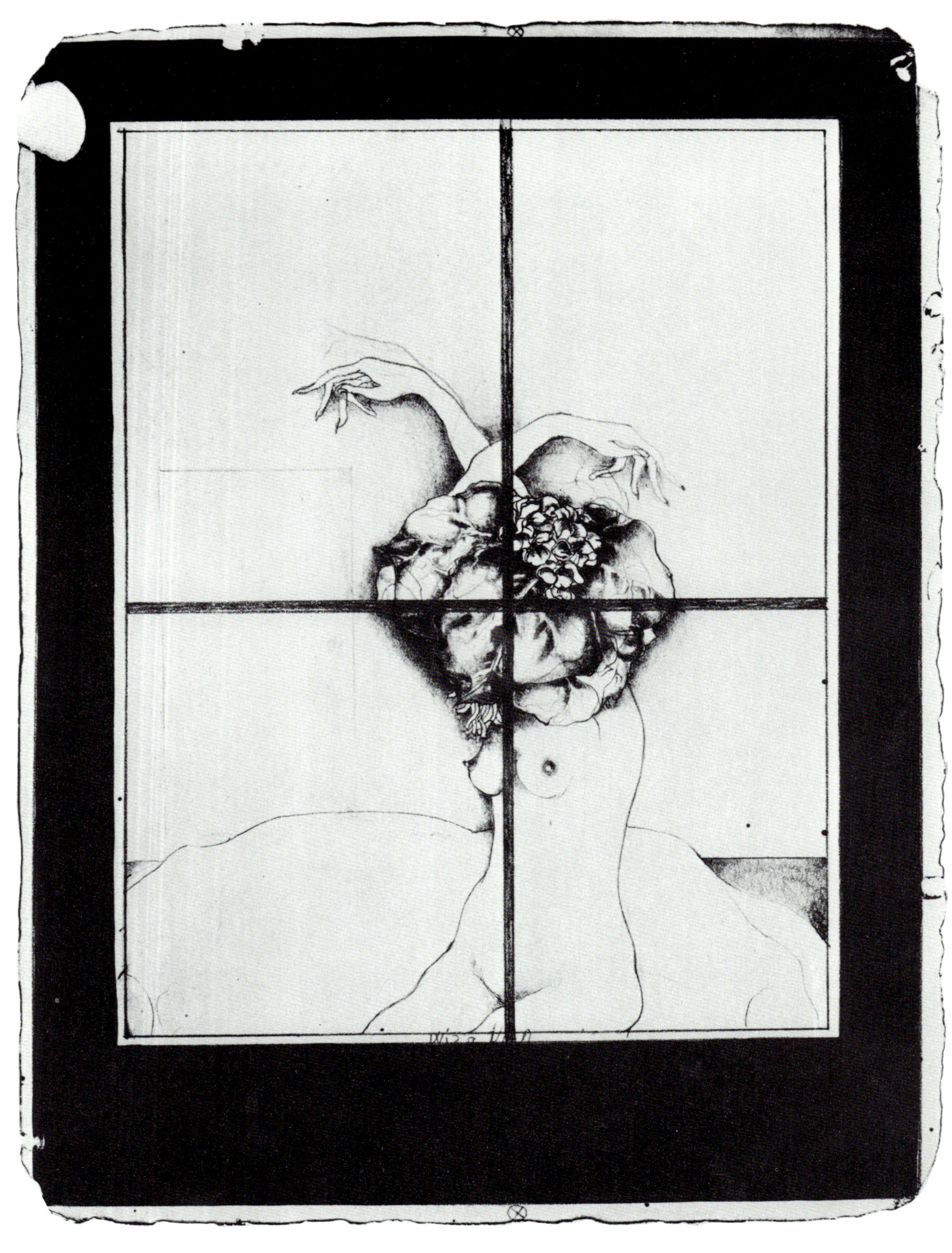

"Vis-à-vis II" 1965
lithograph in two colours, 40.5x30.5 cm

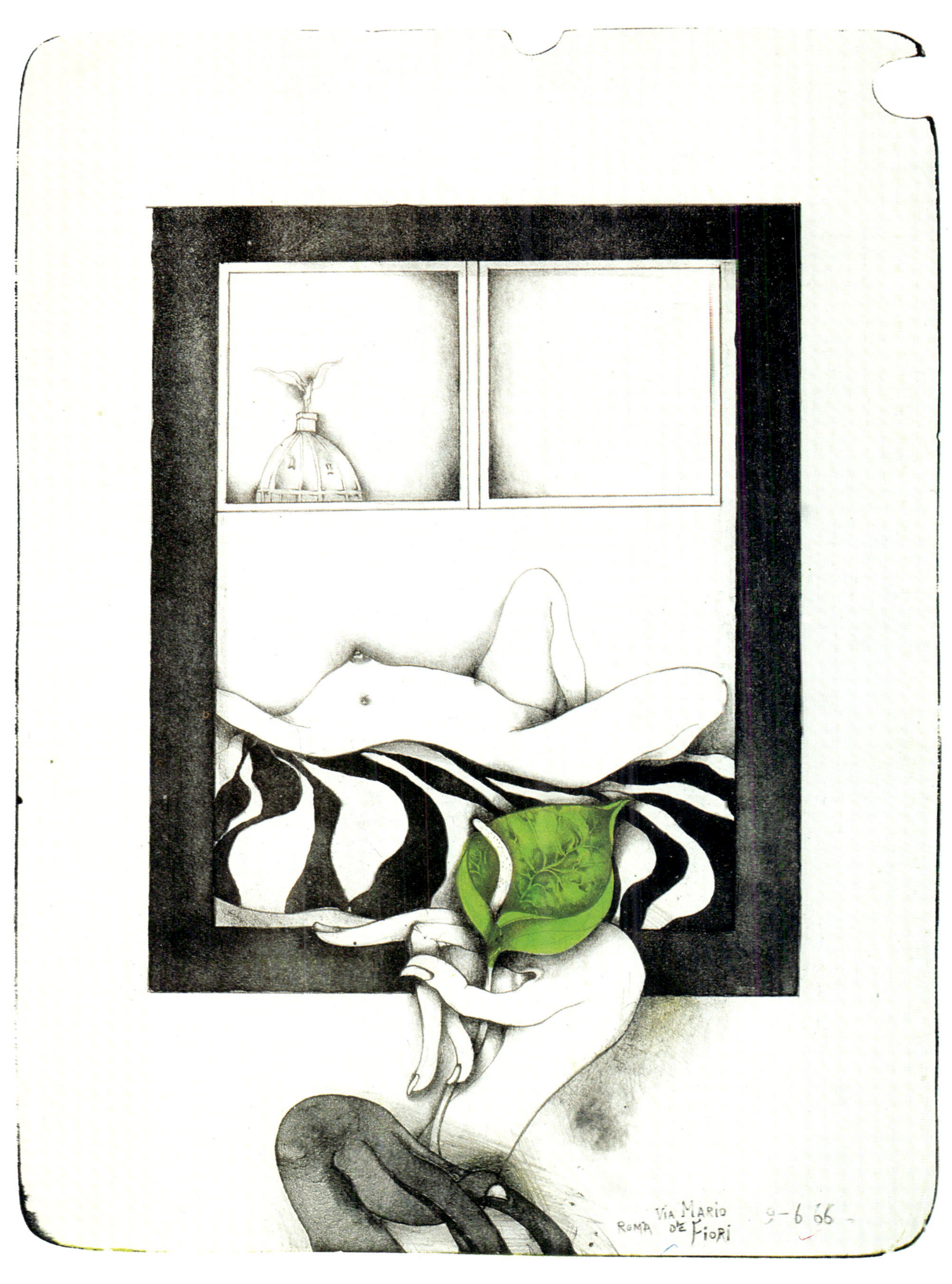

"Via Mario de'Fiori" 1966
lithograph in two colours, 63.8x47.2 cm

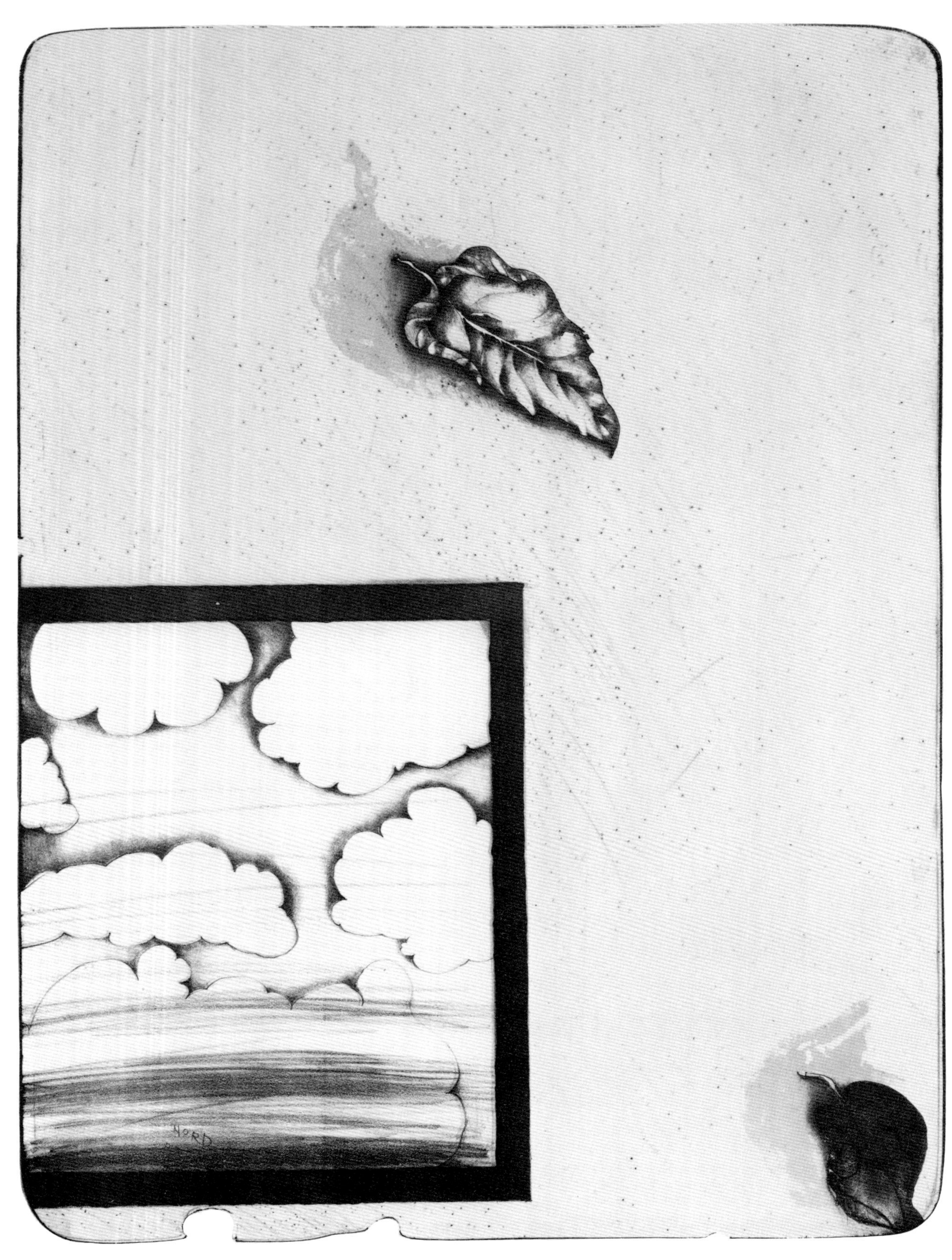

"Autunno" 1966
lithograph in three colours, 64.5x48.2 cm
"L'alarcobaleno" 1970, *lithograph in five colours, 64x48.5 cm* ▷

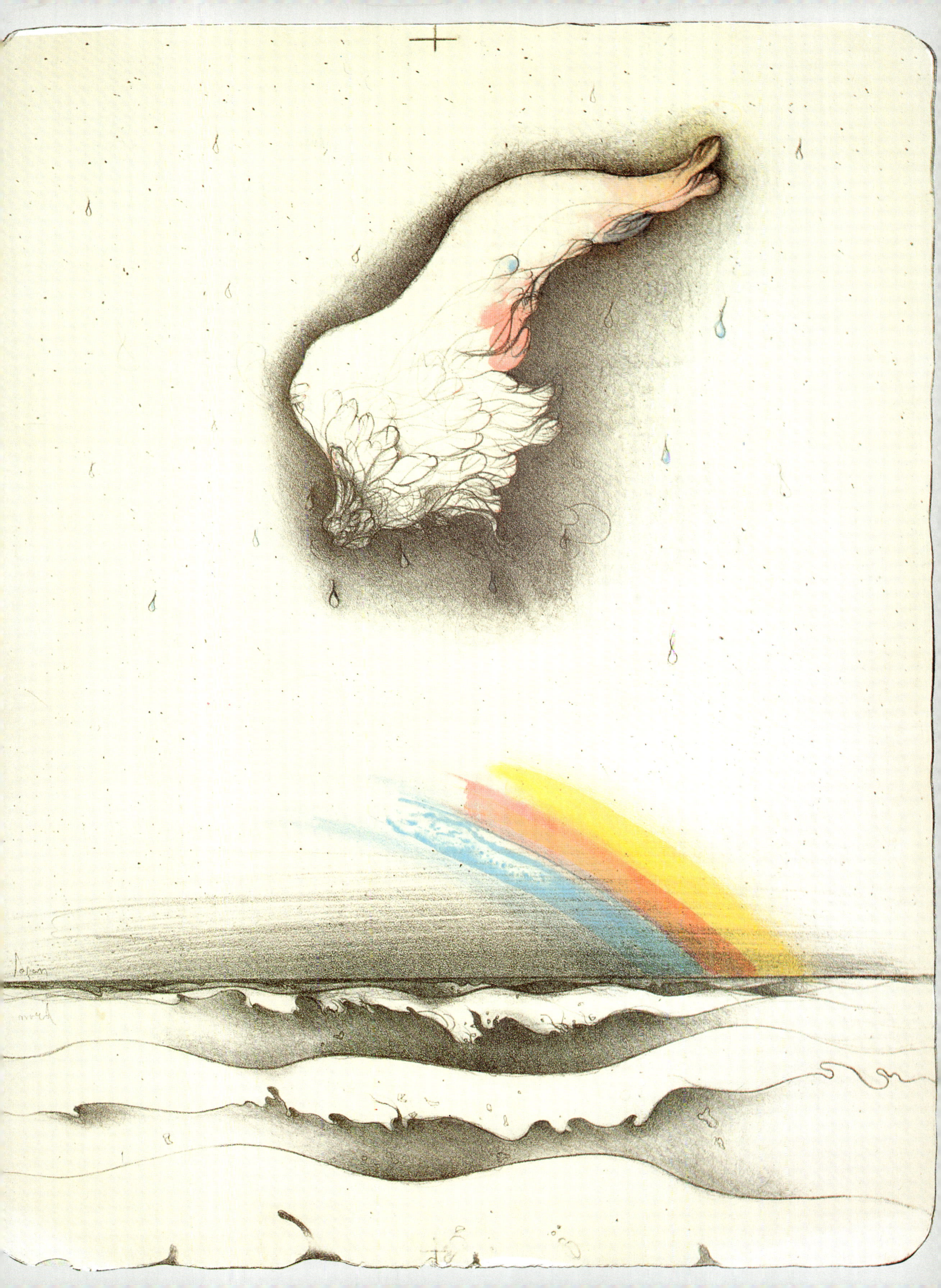

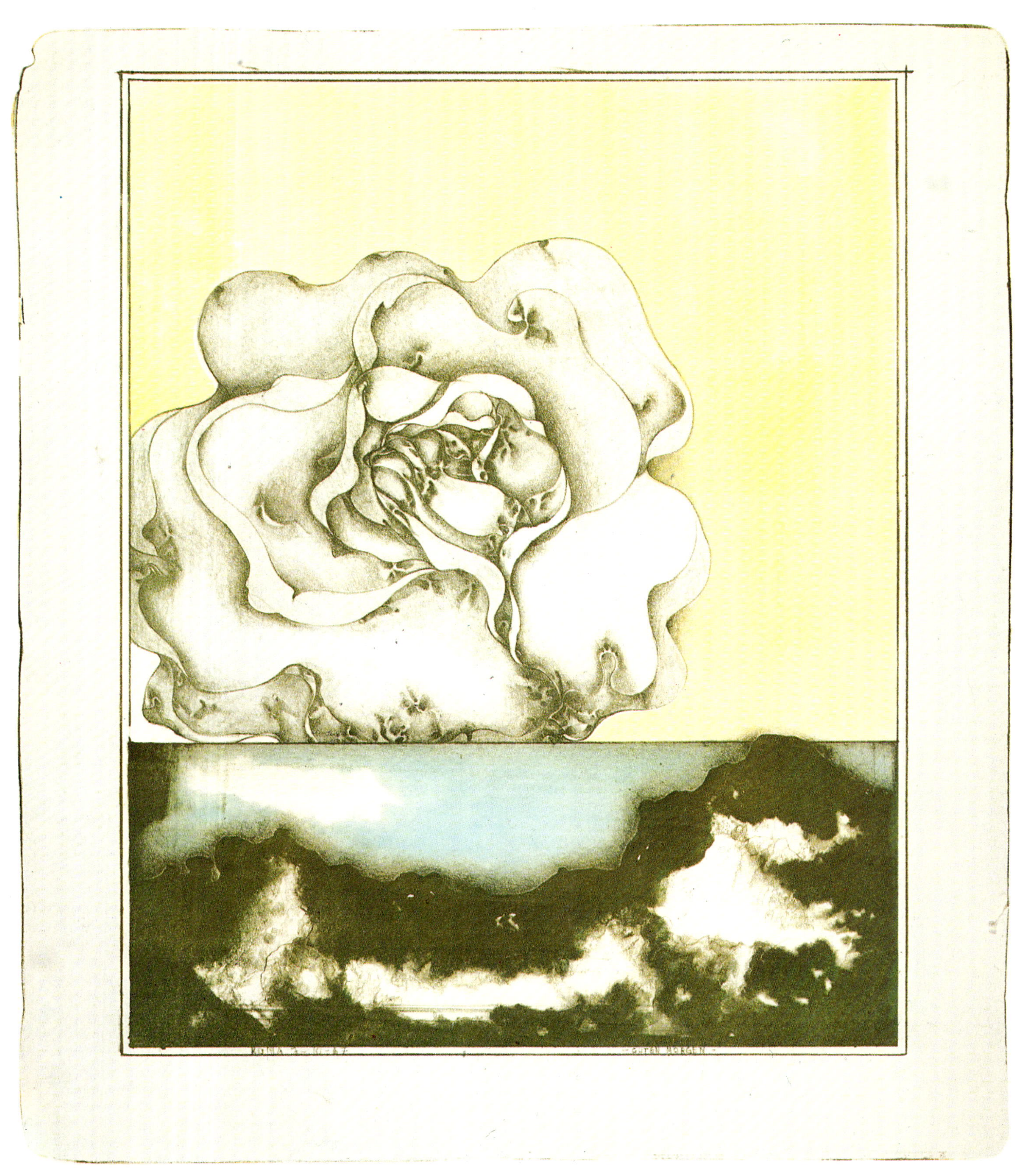

"Guten Morgen" 1967
lithograph in four colours, 58x50 cm

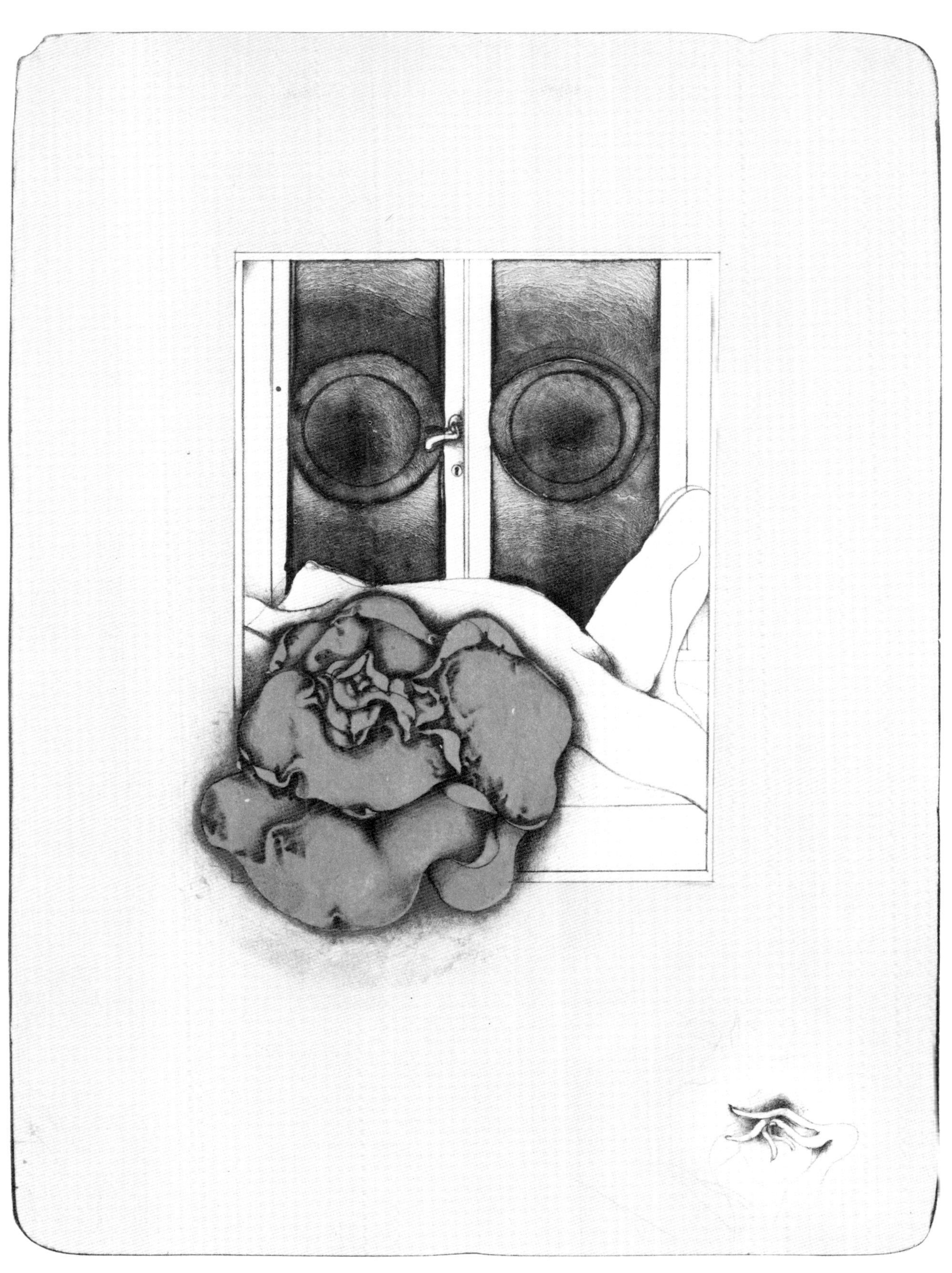

"Strangers in the Night" 1966
lithograph in three colours, 64x48 cm

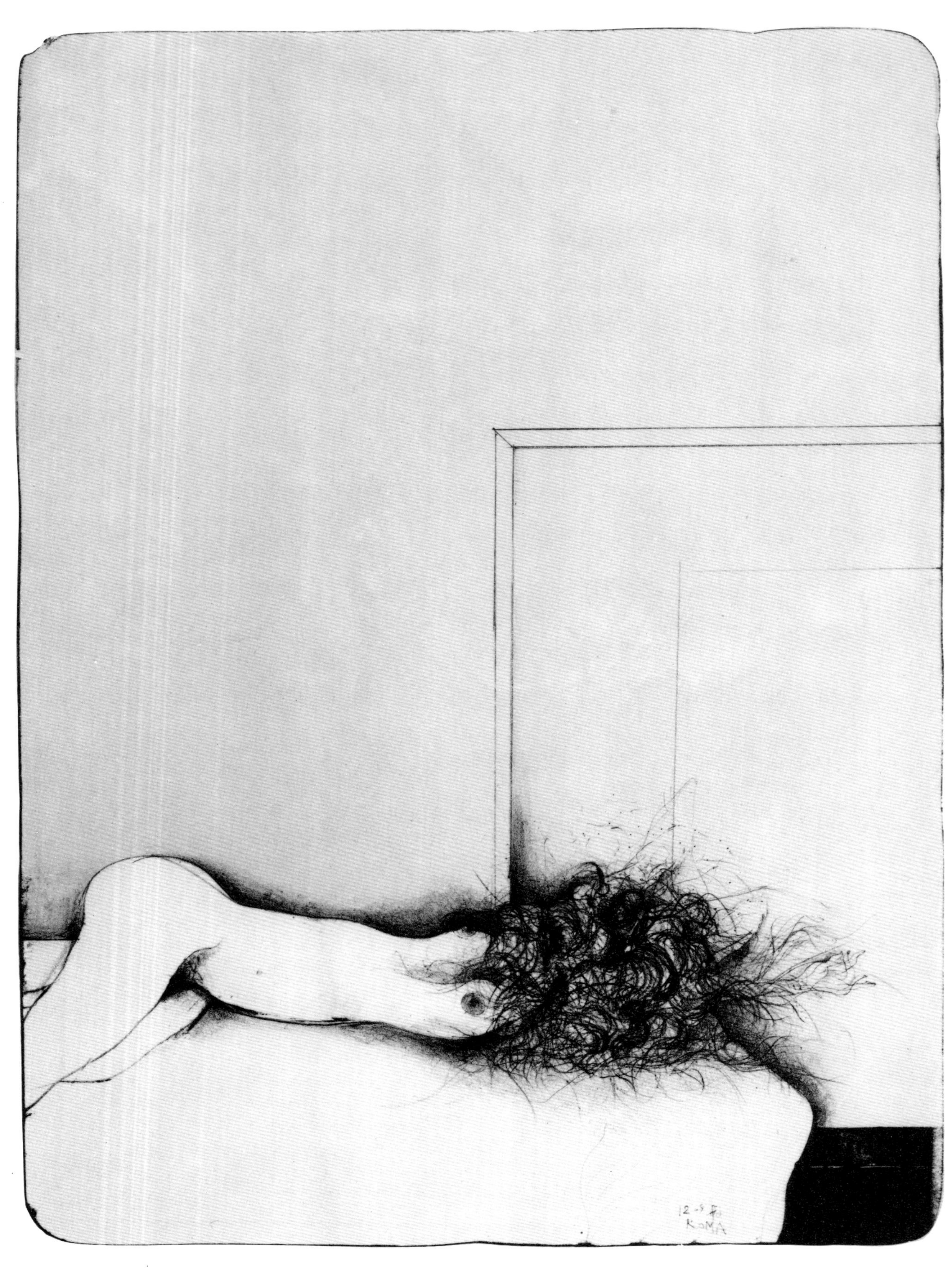

"Sogno" 1967
lithograph in three colours, 64.8x48.5 cm

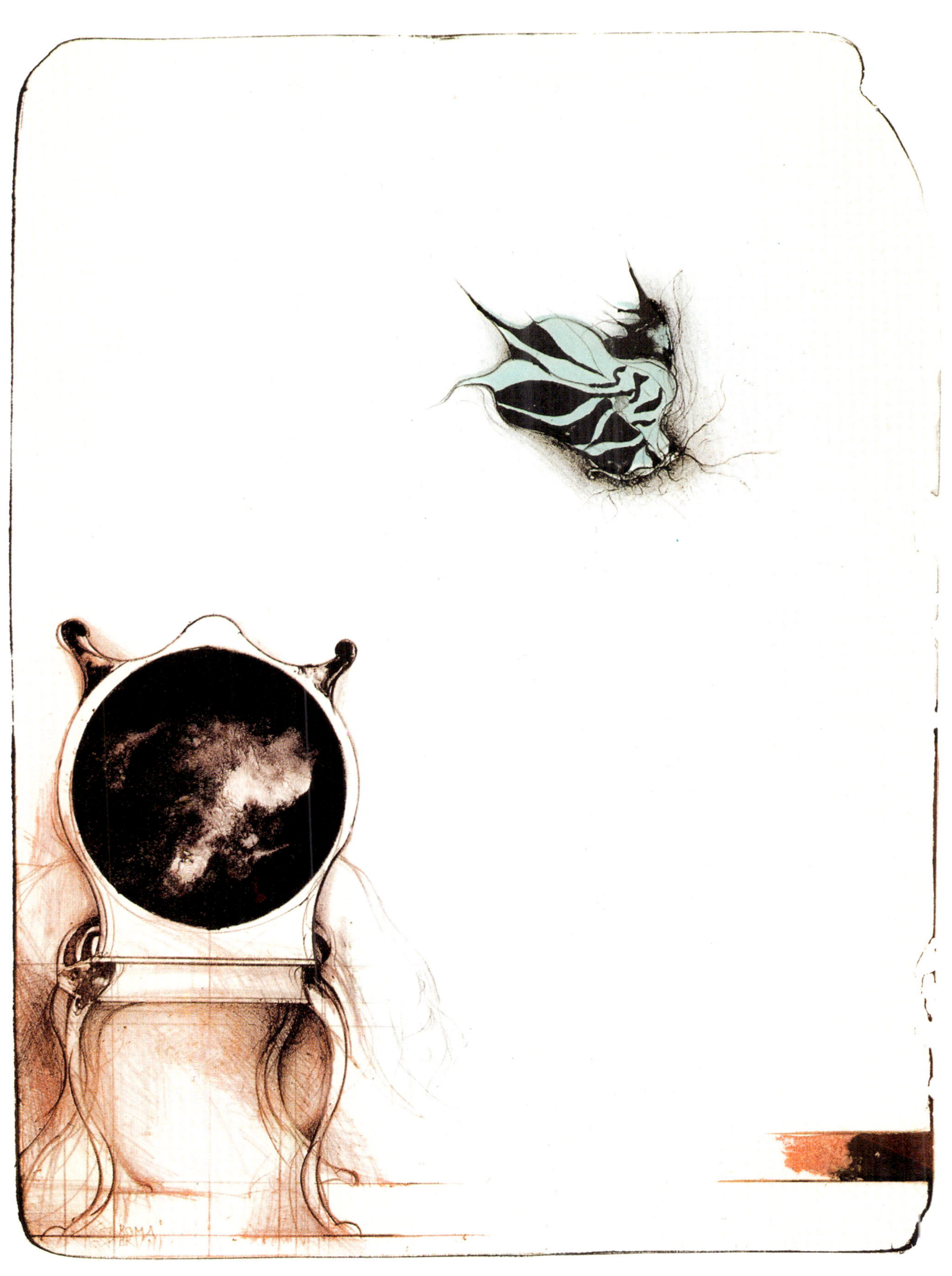

'Der Schmetterling" 1967
lithograph in four colours, 64.6x48 cm

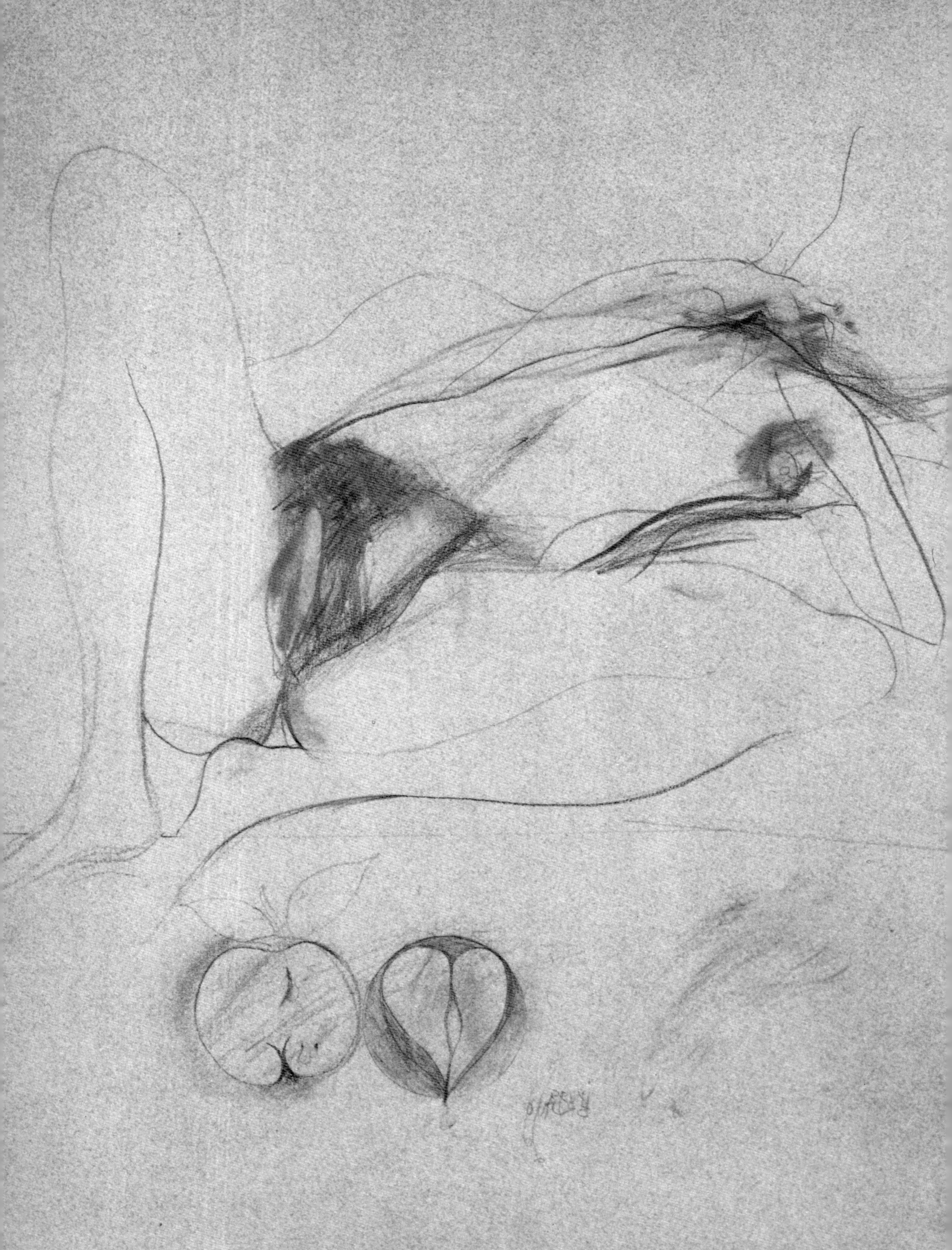

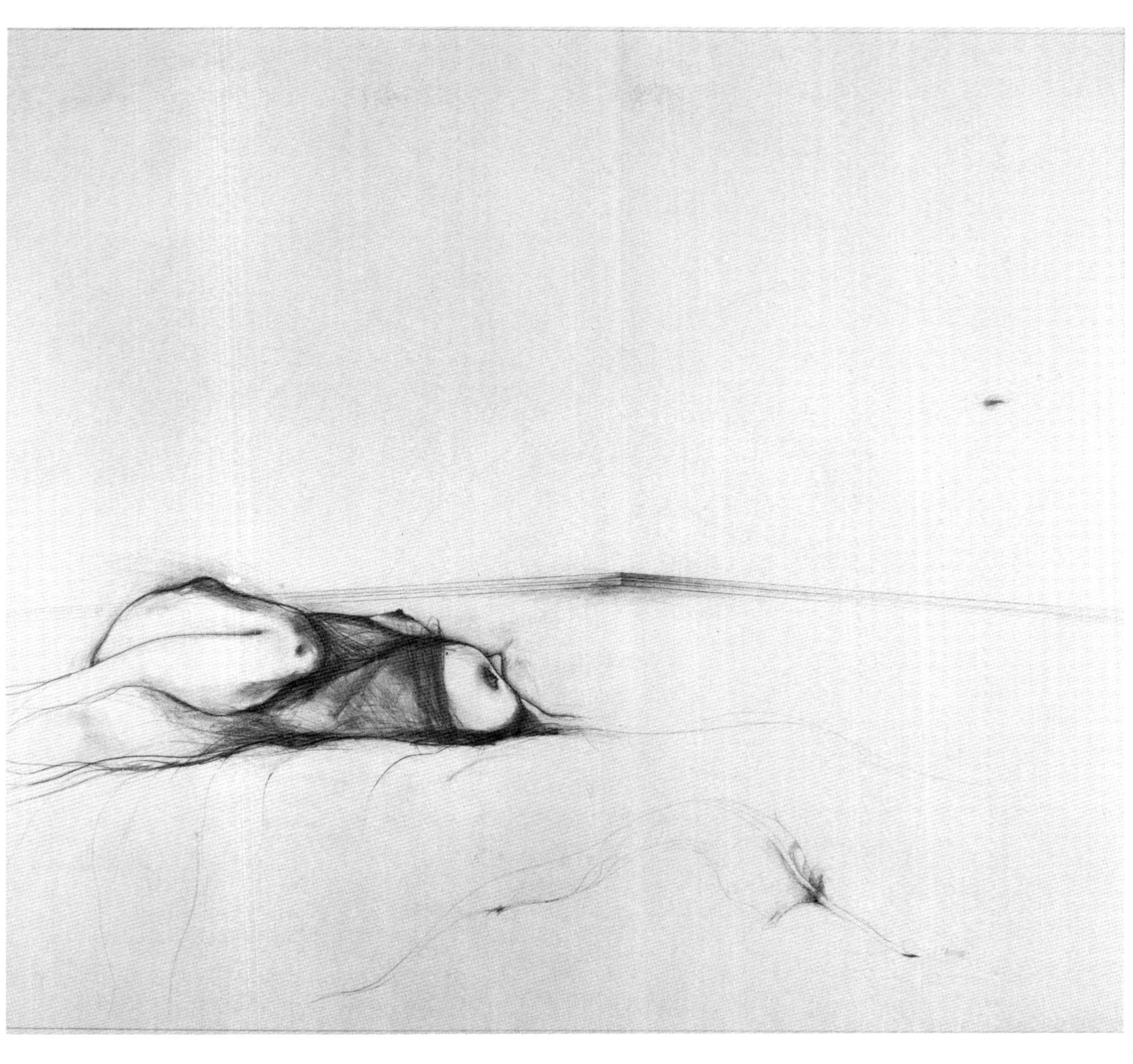

"La piuma" 1970, *pencil drawing, ca. 70x90 cm*
◁ "Without Title" 1963, *pencil drawing, 85x70 cm*

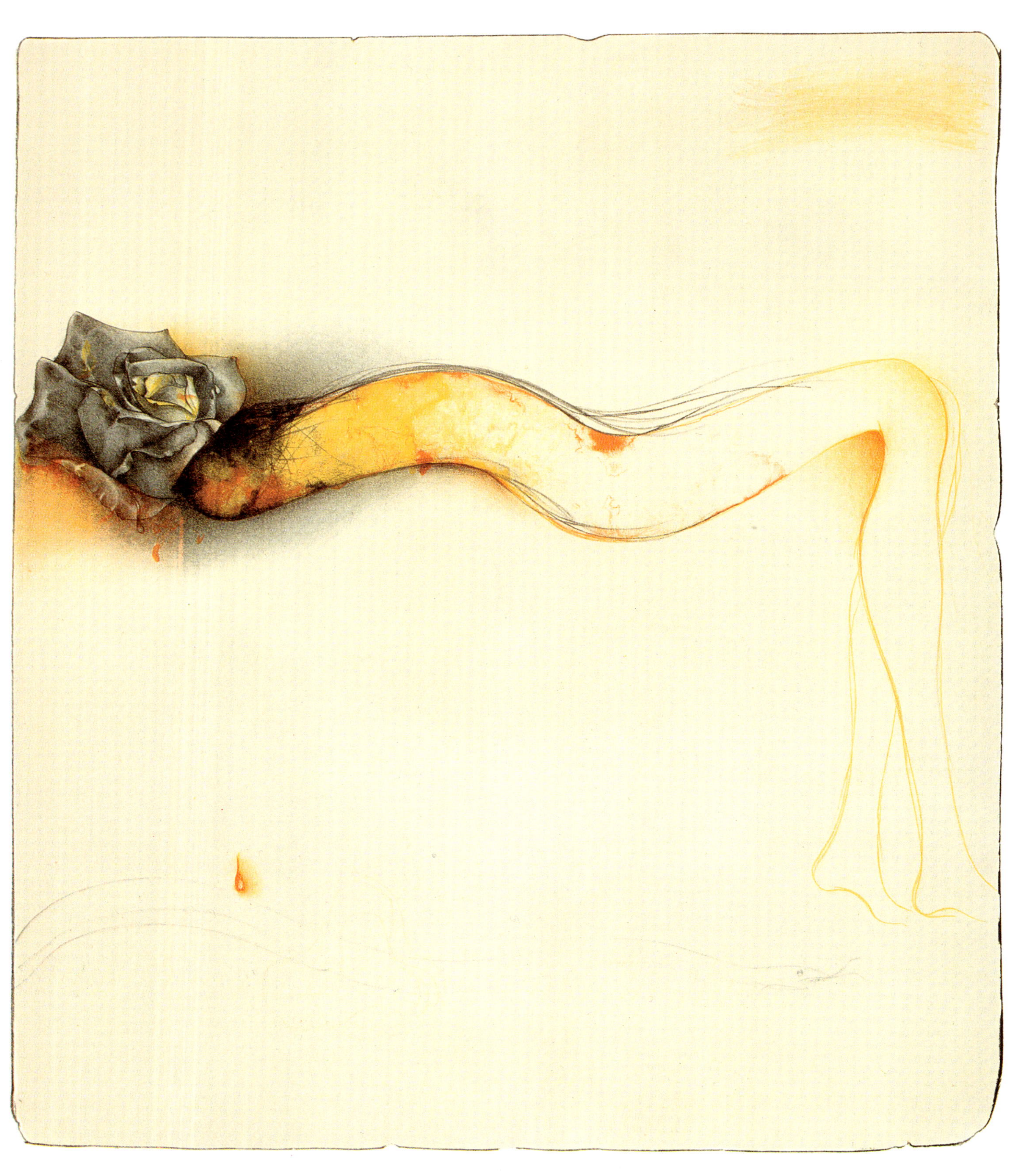

"Metamorphosis" 1970
lithograph in four colours, 71x61.5 cm

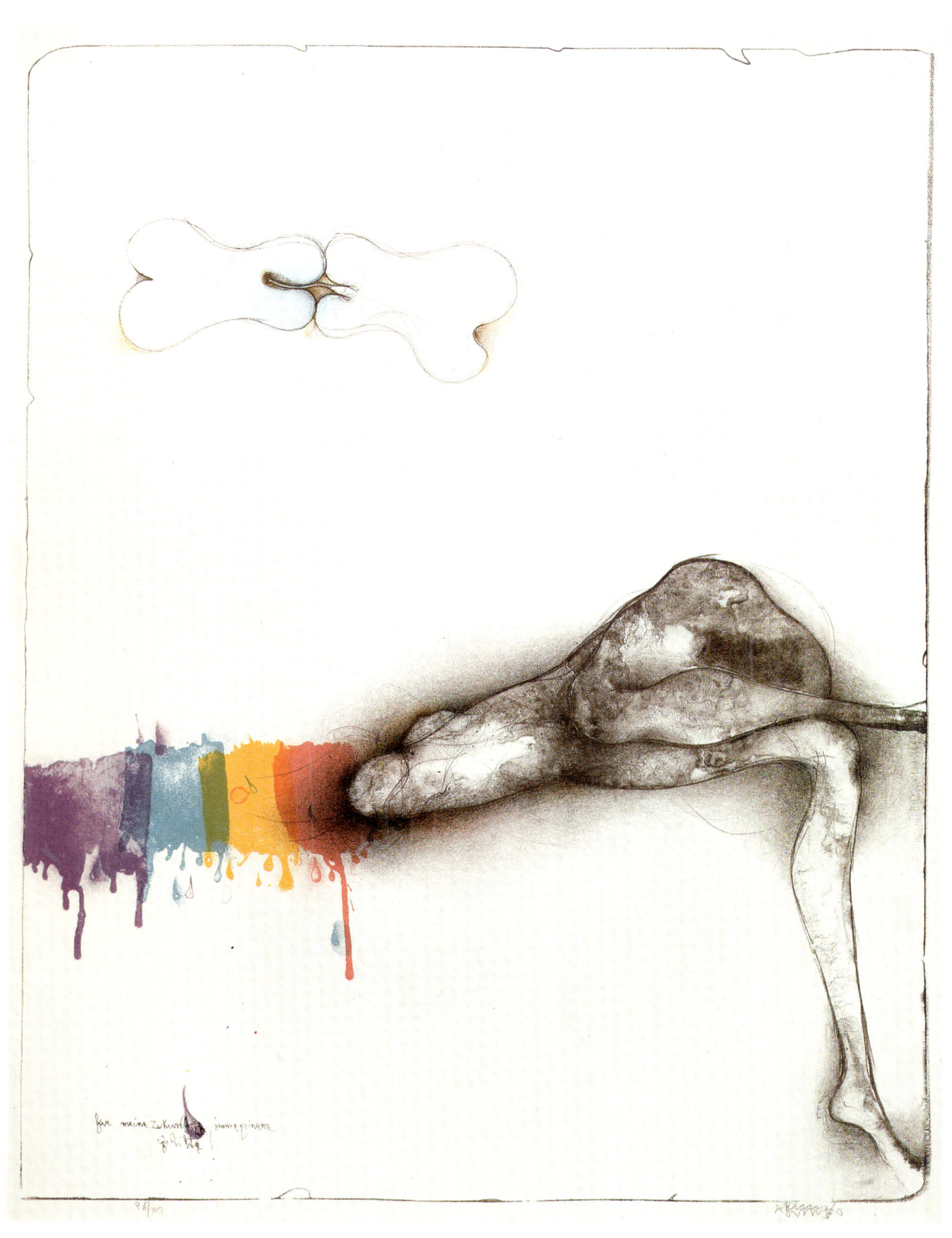

"Pensieri strani" 1970
lithograph in five colours, 85x65 cm

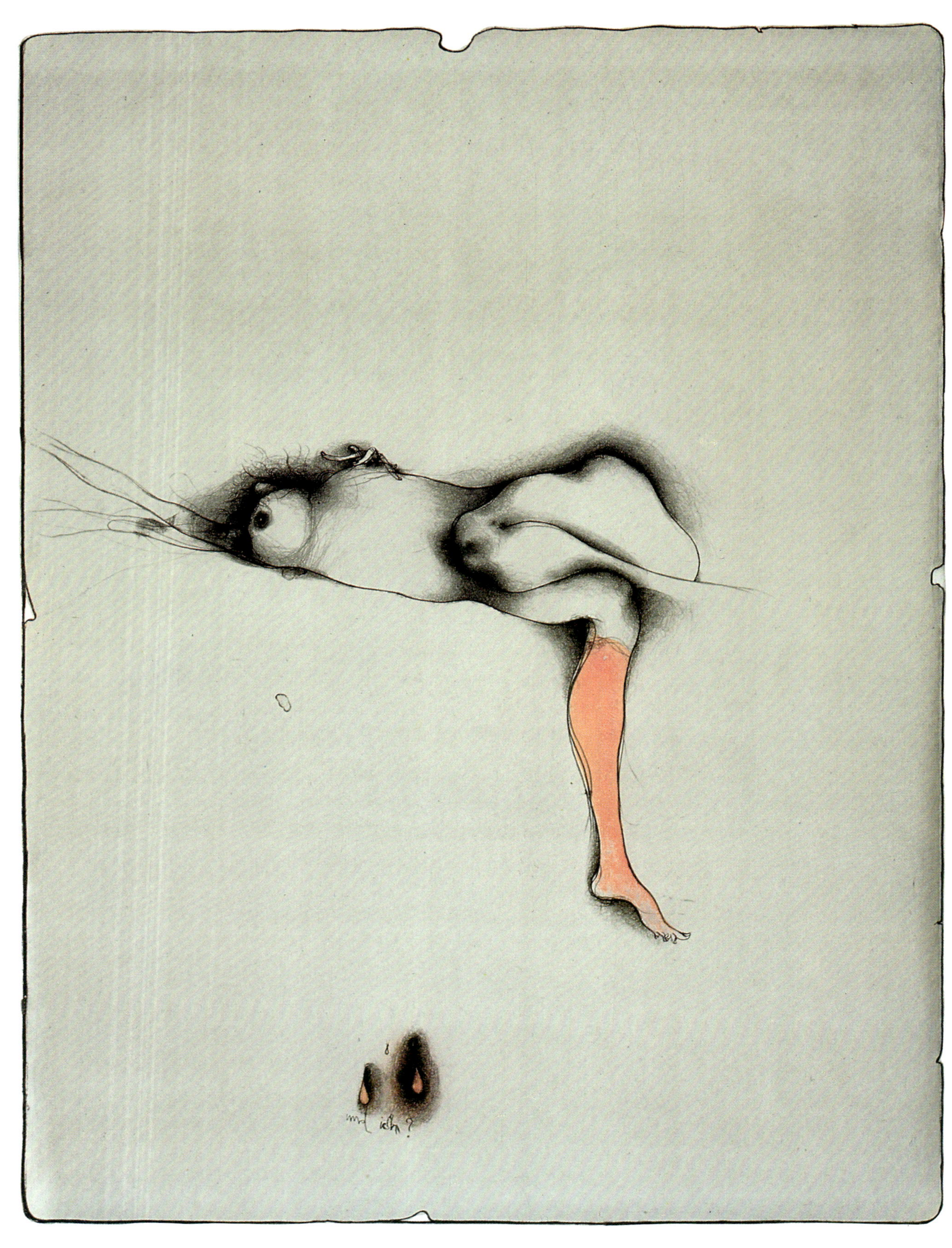

"Und ich?" 1970
lithograph in three colours, 85x64 cm

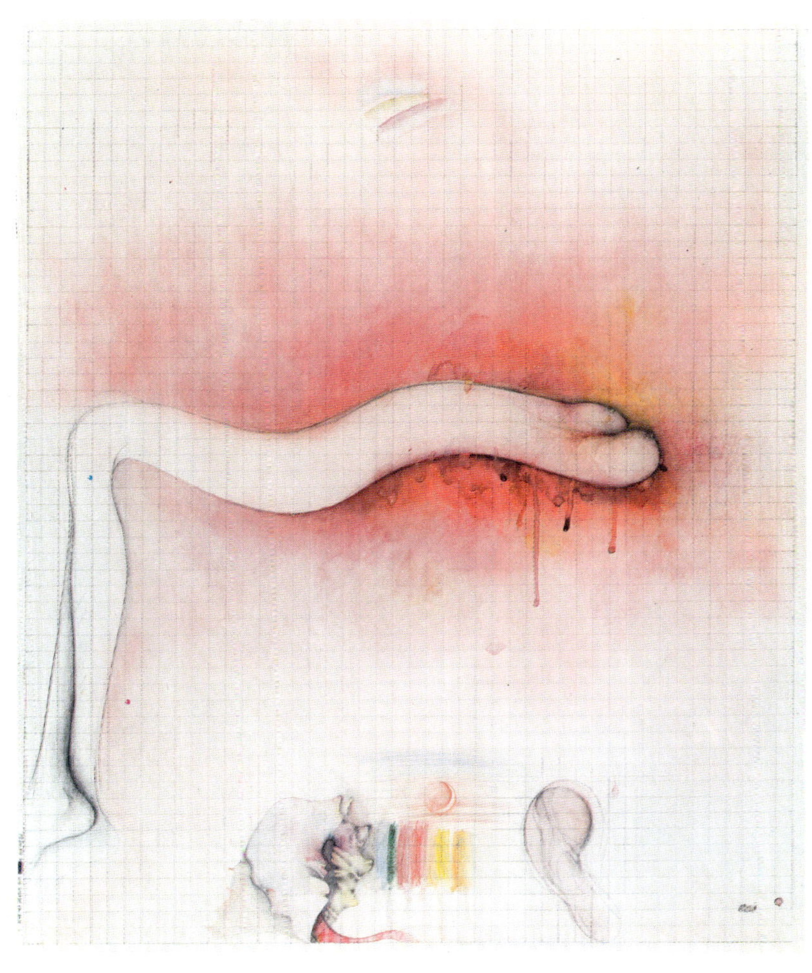

"Fräulein Penis und andere Sachen" 1971
pencil, coloured crayon and water-colour, 115.5x95 cm

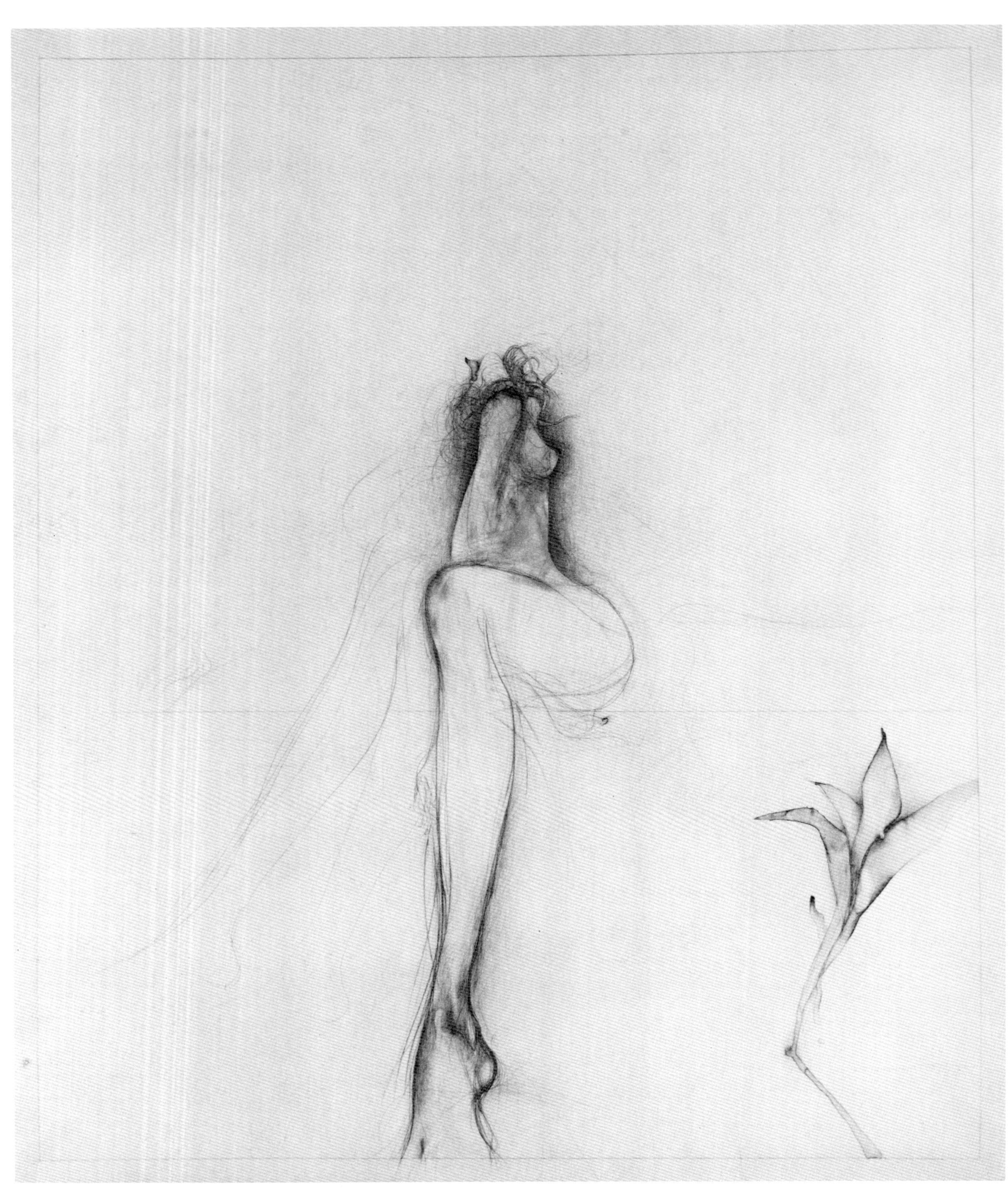

"Nudo e fiore" 1970
pencil drawing, 115x95 cm

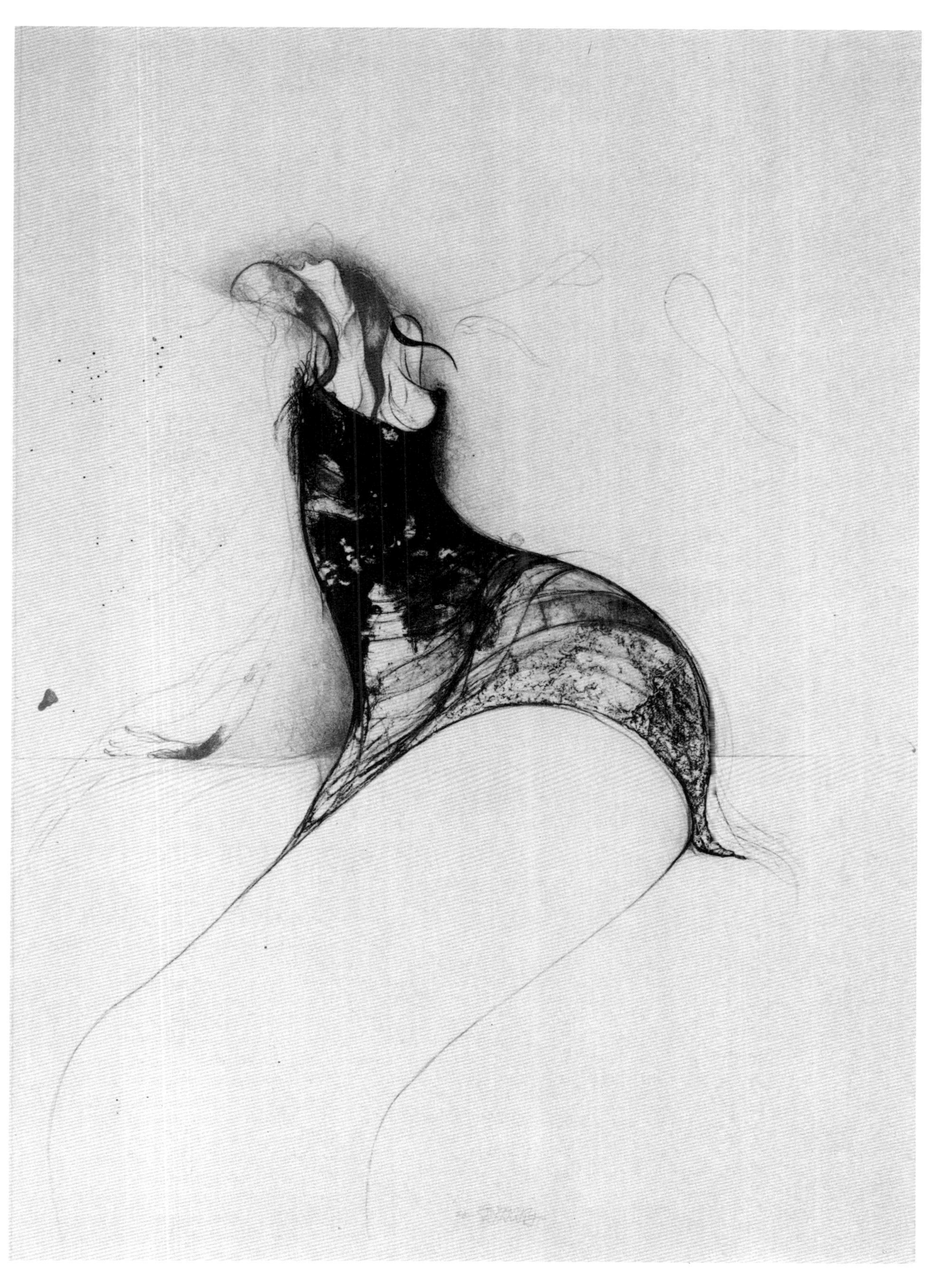

"Lach . . . lach" 1971
lithograph in five colours, 70.5x50 cm

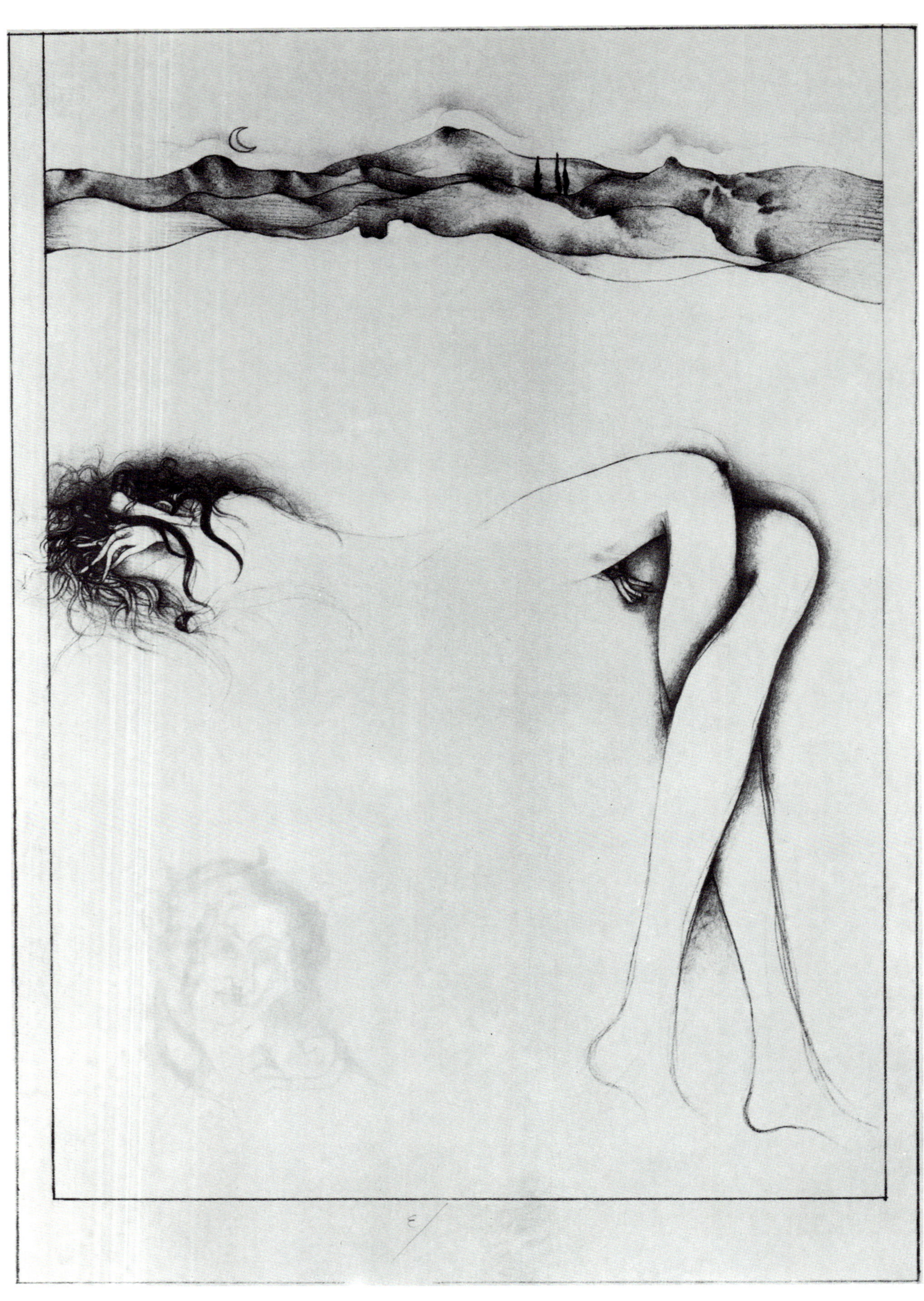

"Tra le colline toscane" 1971
lithograph in four colours, 70.5x50 cm

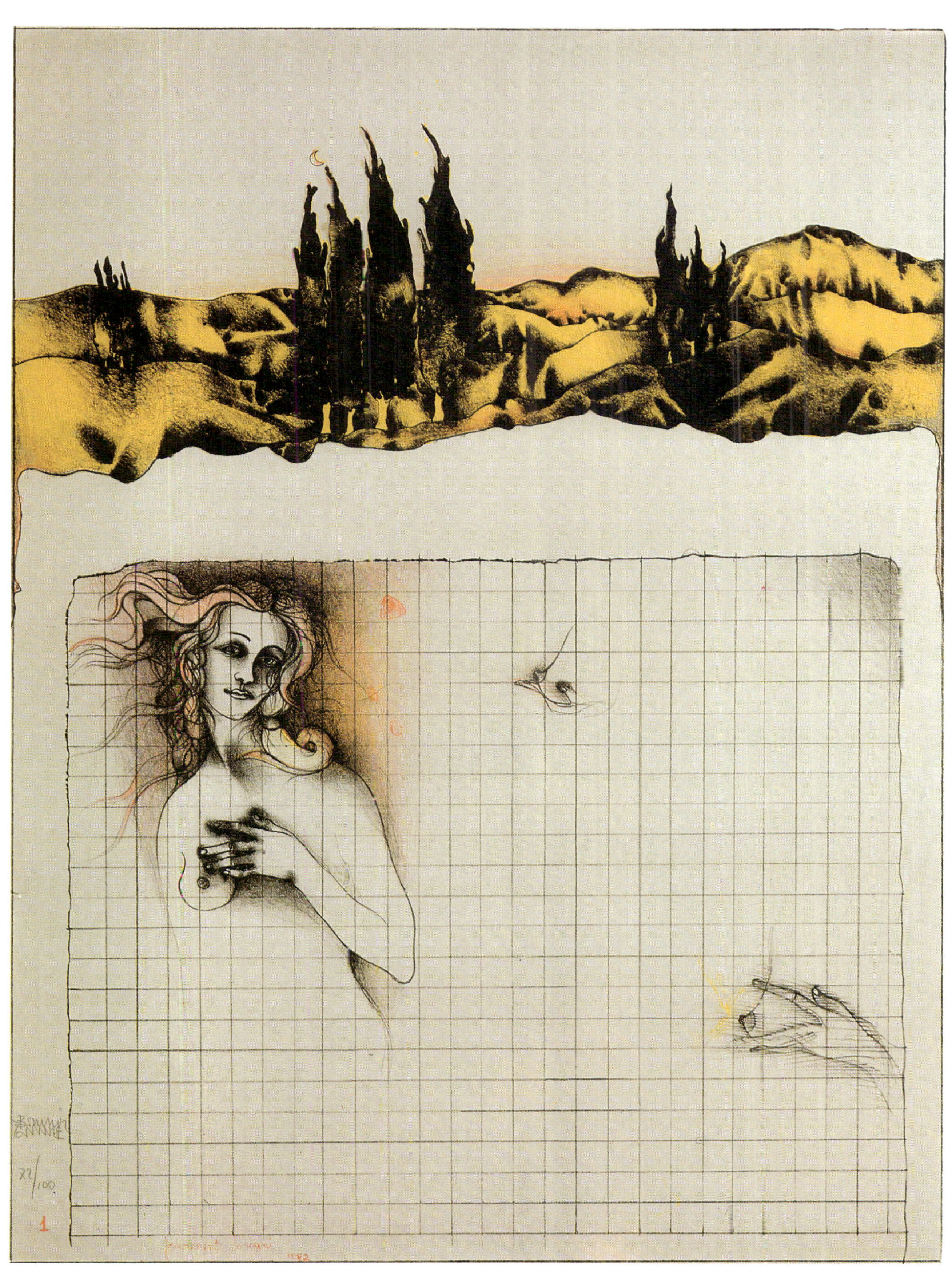

"Frammenti toscani" 1972
lithograph in four colours, 80.5x59.7 cm

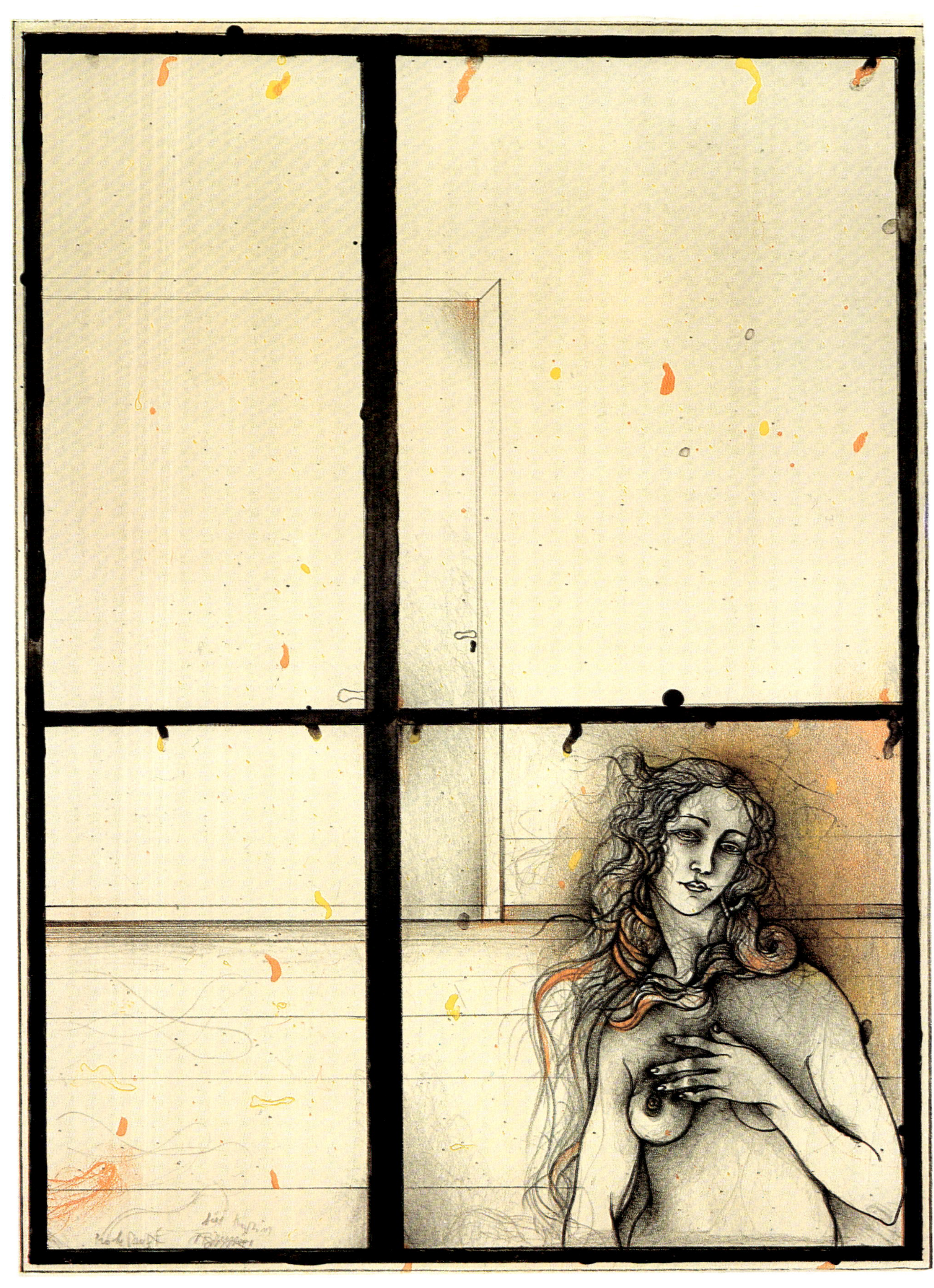

"Langweiliges Weekend der Venus in Florenz" 1971
lithograph in four colours, 69.5x50 cm

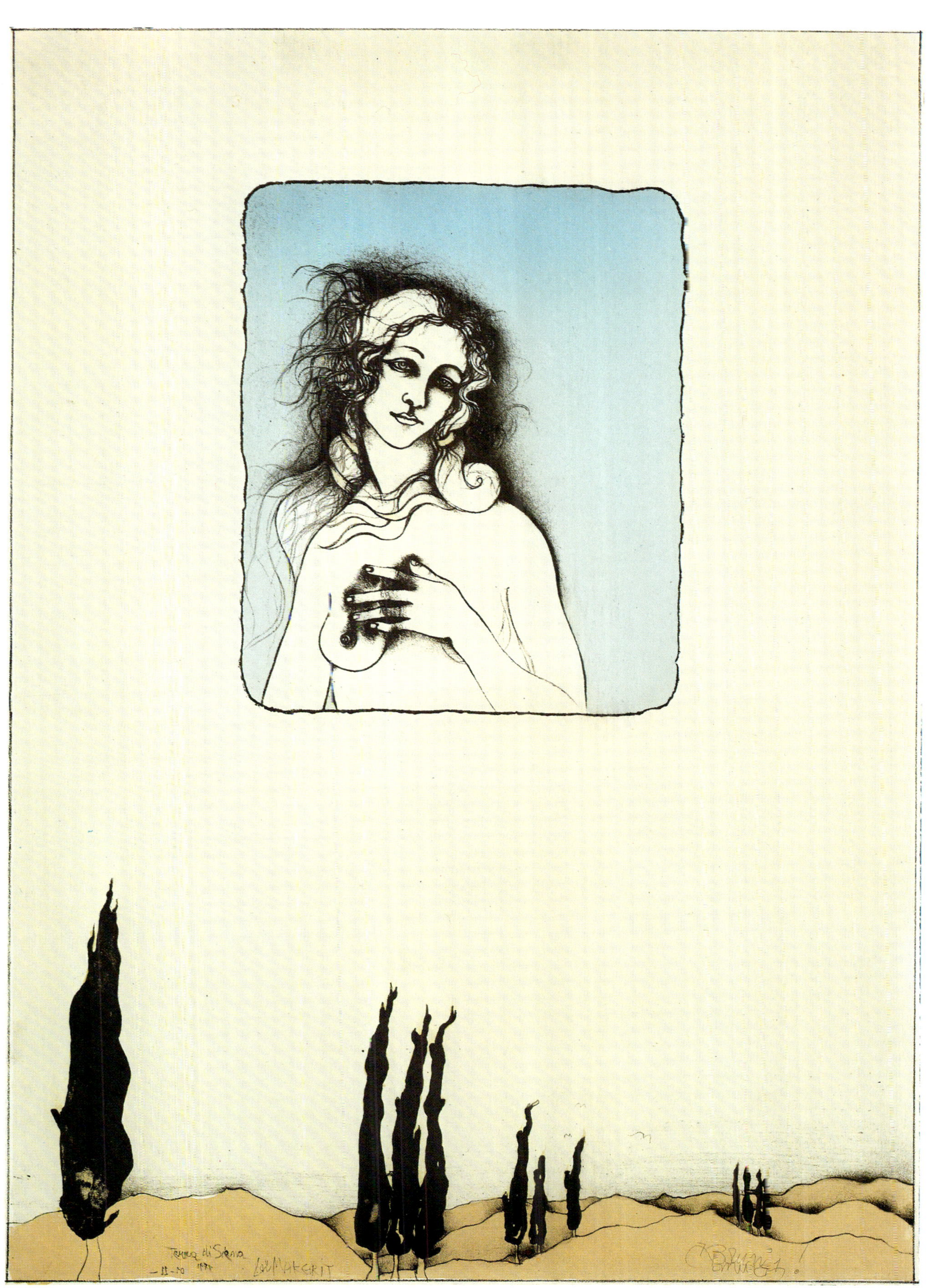

"Terra di Siena" 1971
lithcgraph in four colours, 70.5x50 cm

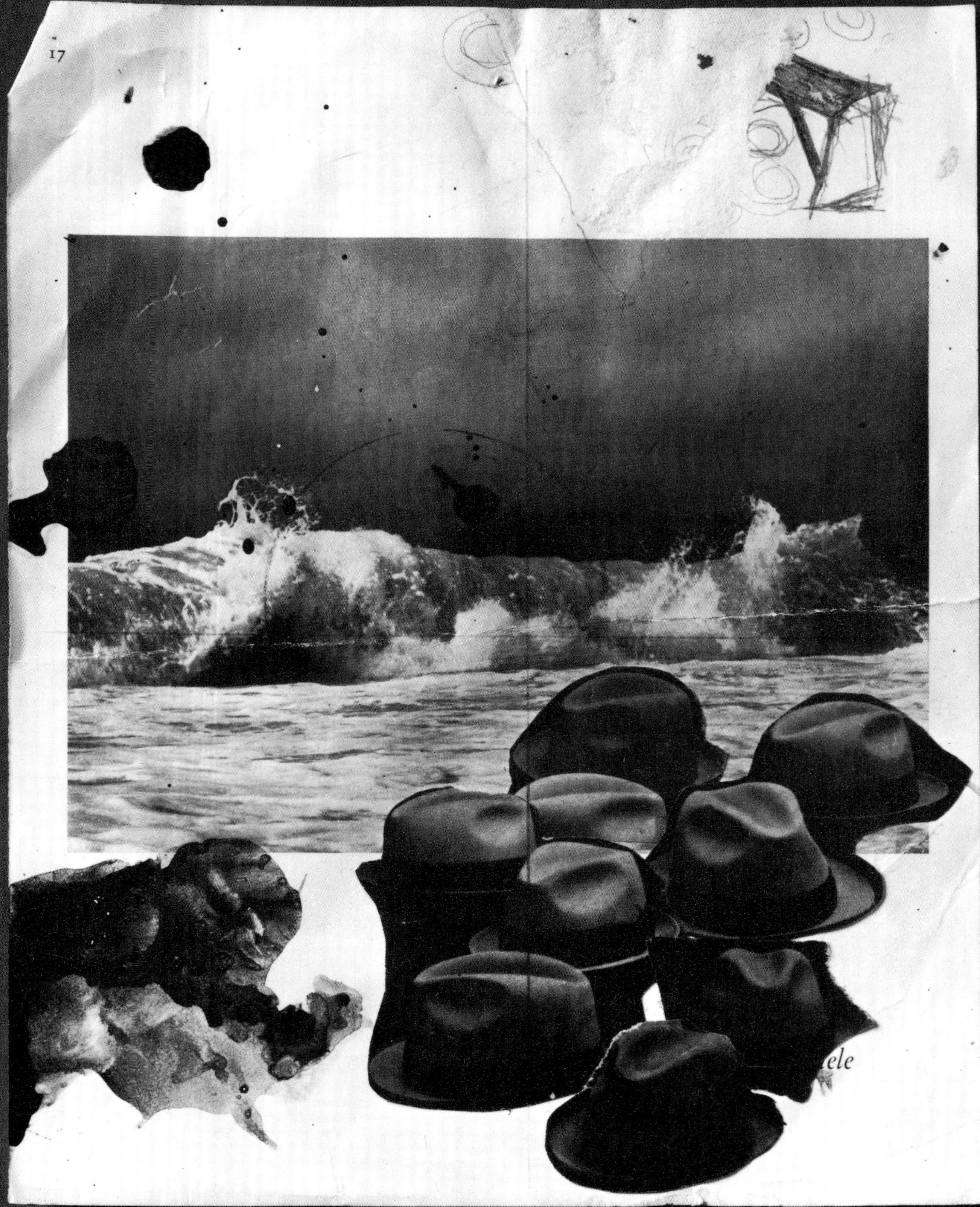
17

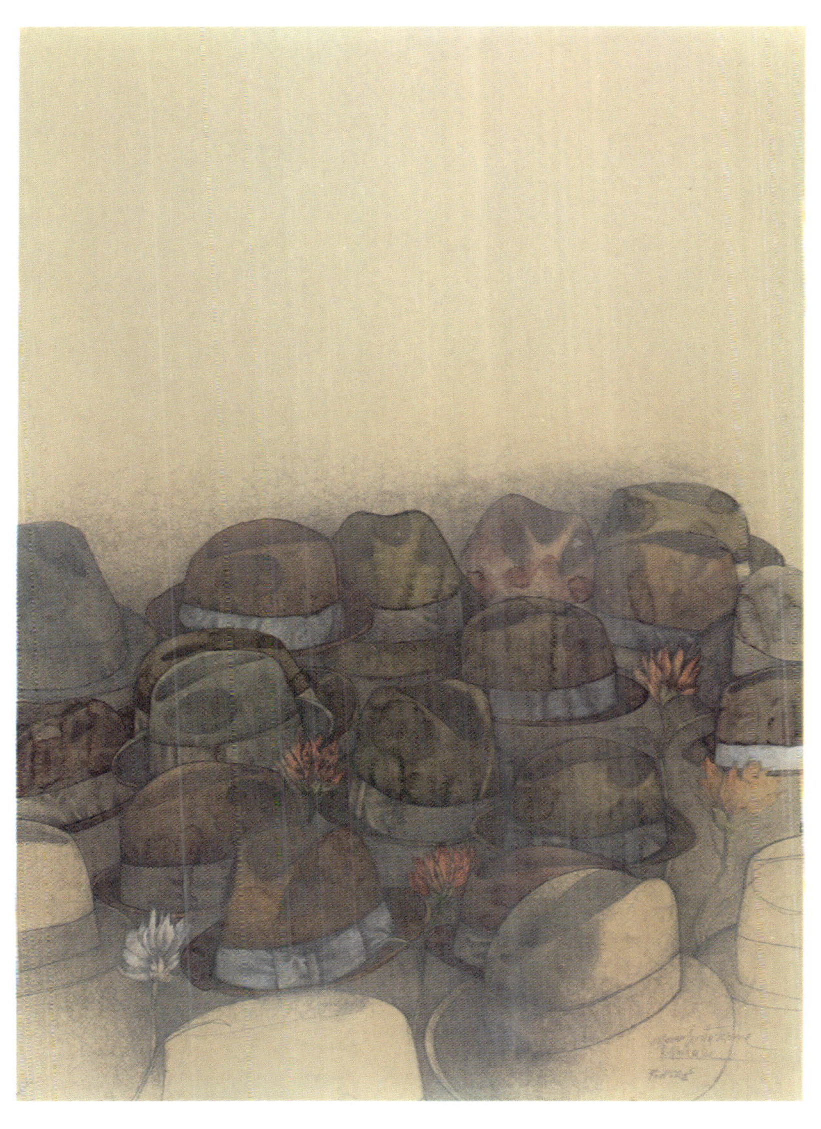

"Funerale R.L." 1972
pencil and gouache, 130x110 cm

◁ "Discusione assurda" 1973, *collage, 24.8x19.8 cm*

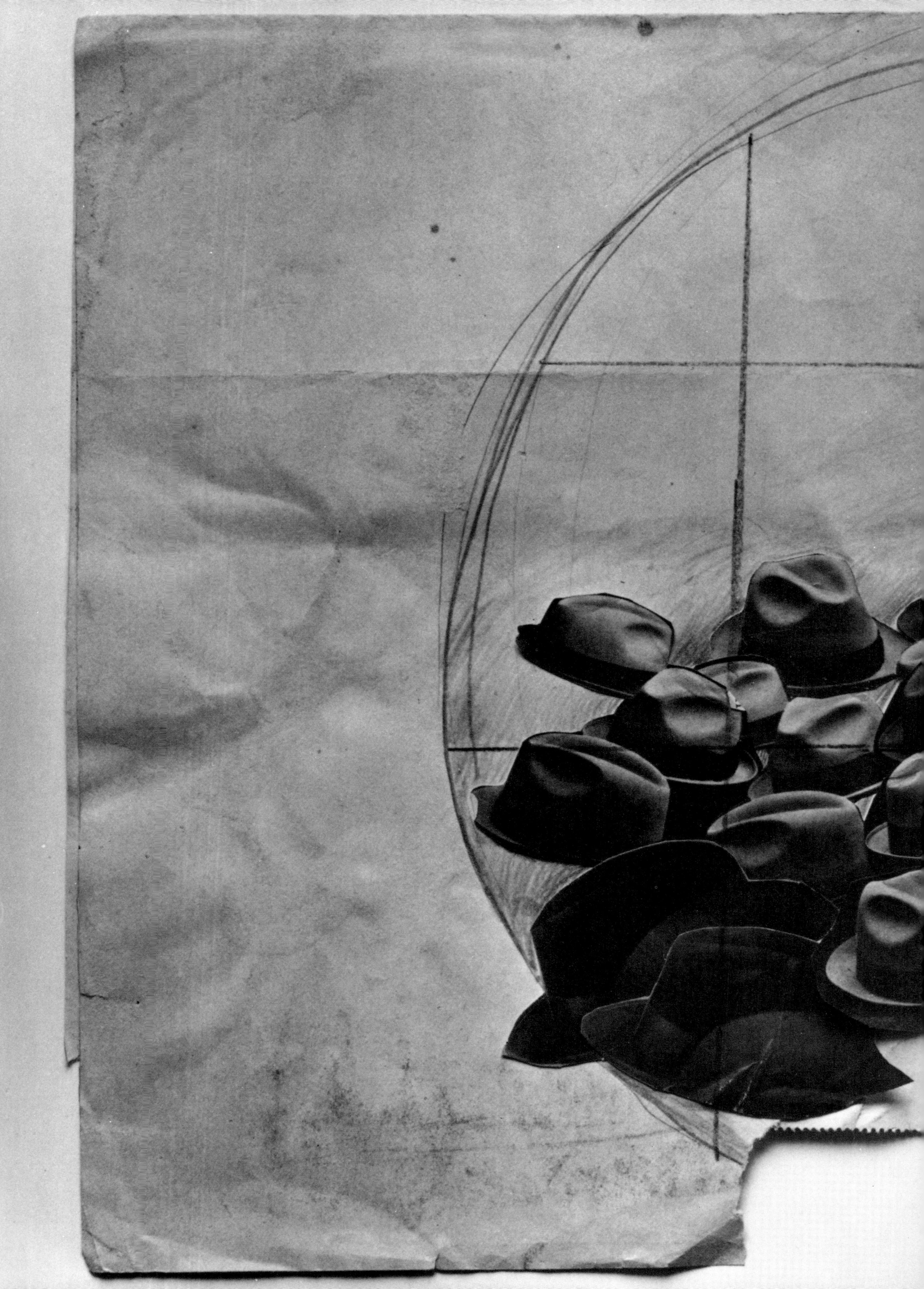

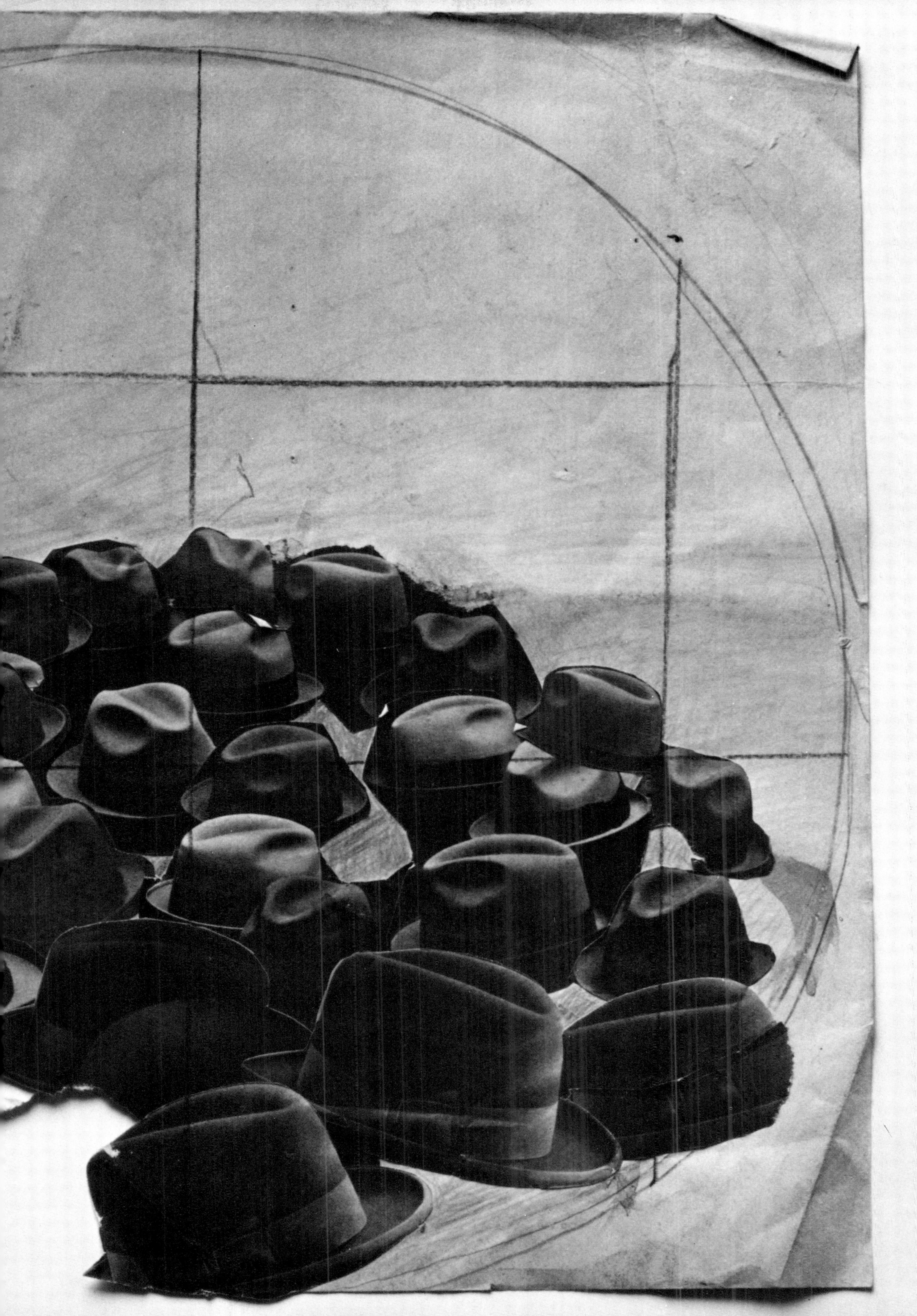

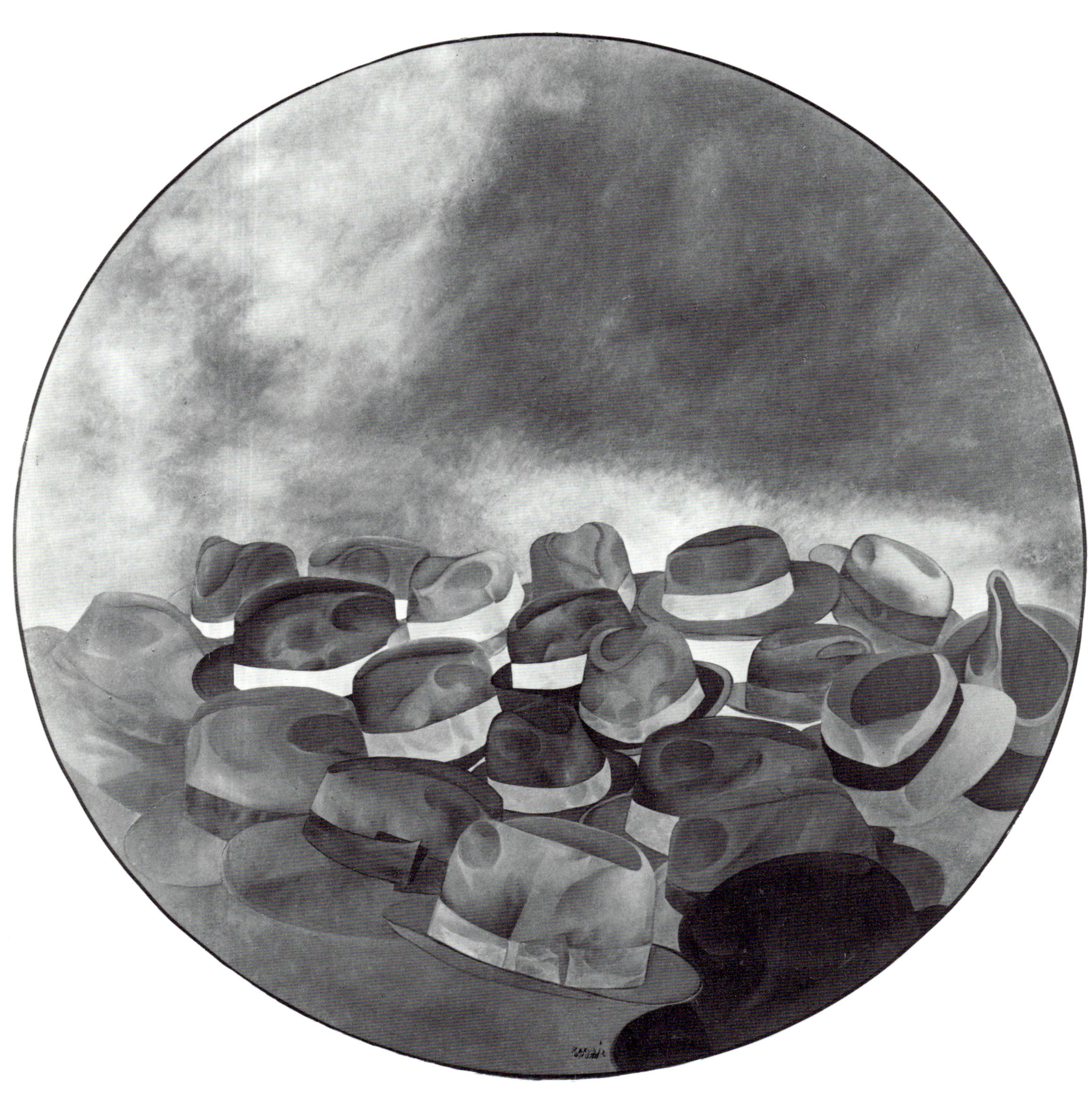

"Kundgebung" 1972, *oil on canvass, ∅ 150 cm*
◁ Working sketch, 1973, *collage and coloured pencil, 30.5x42 cm*

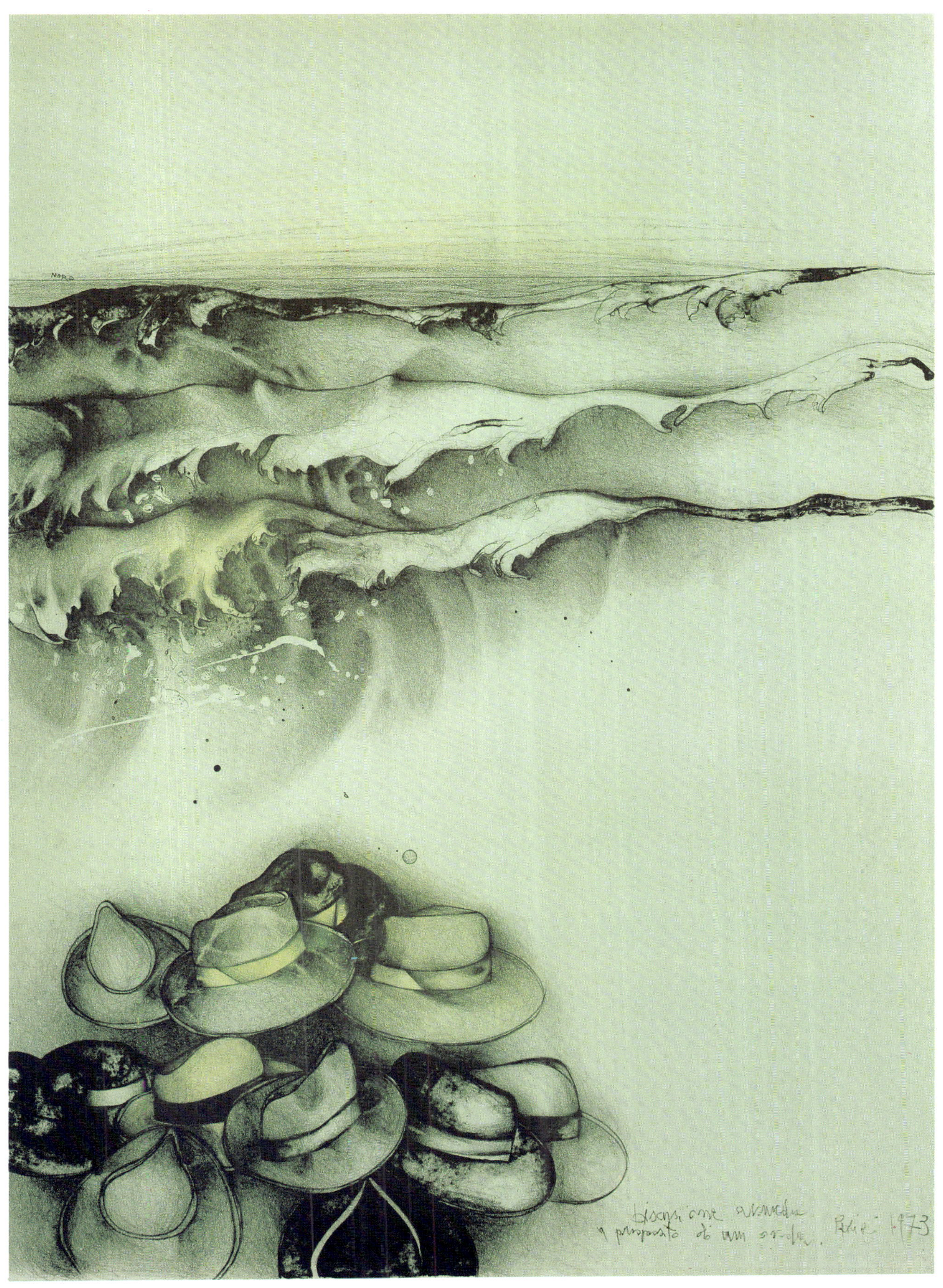

"Discusione assurda a proposito di un onda" 1973
lithograph in four colours, 75x54 cm

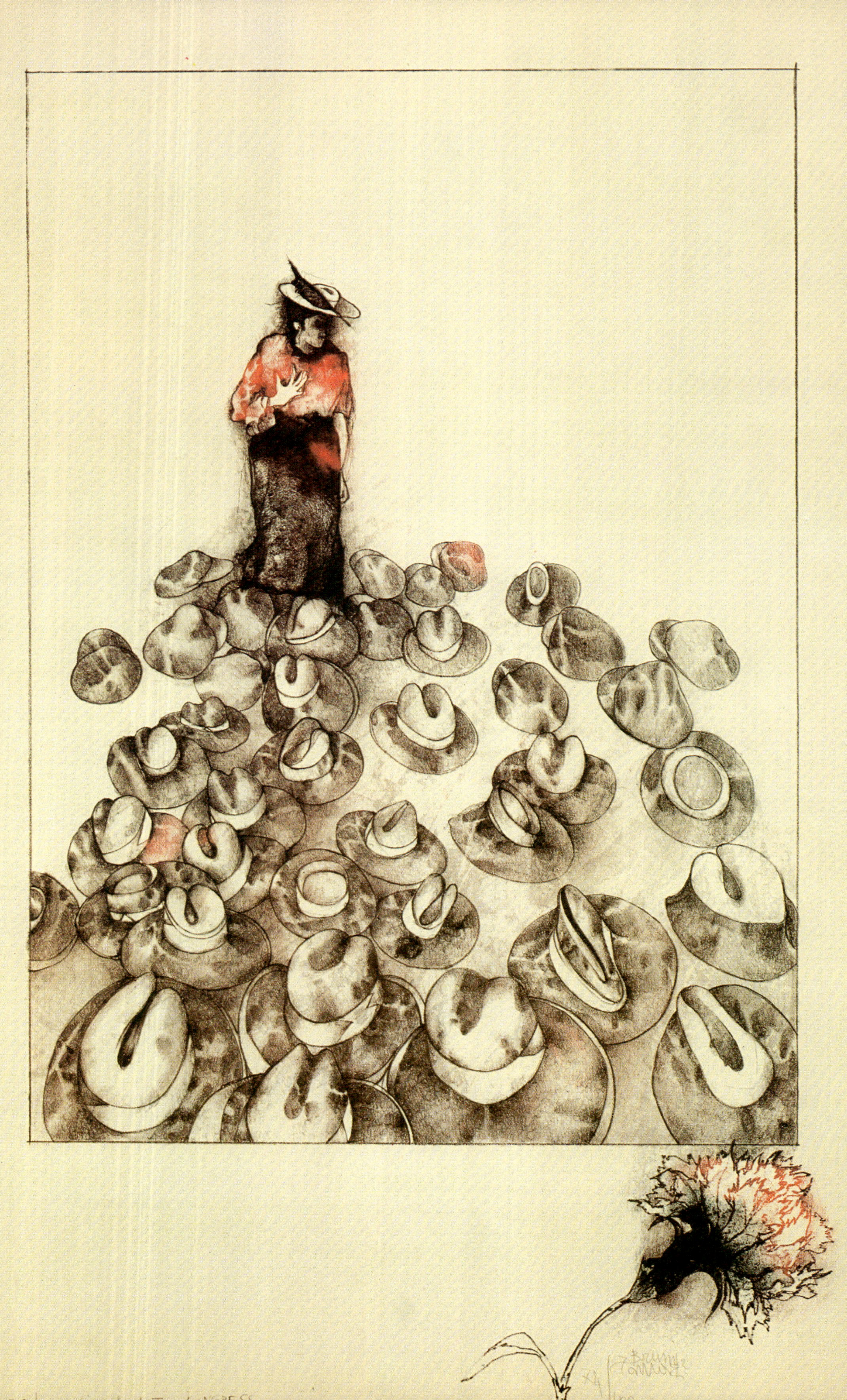

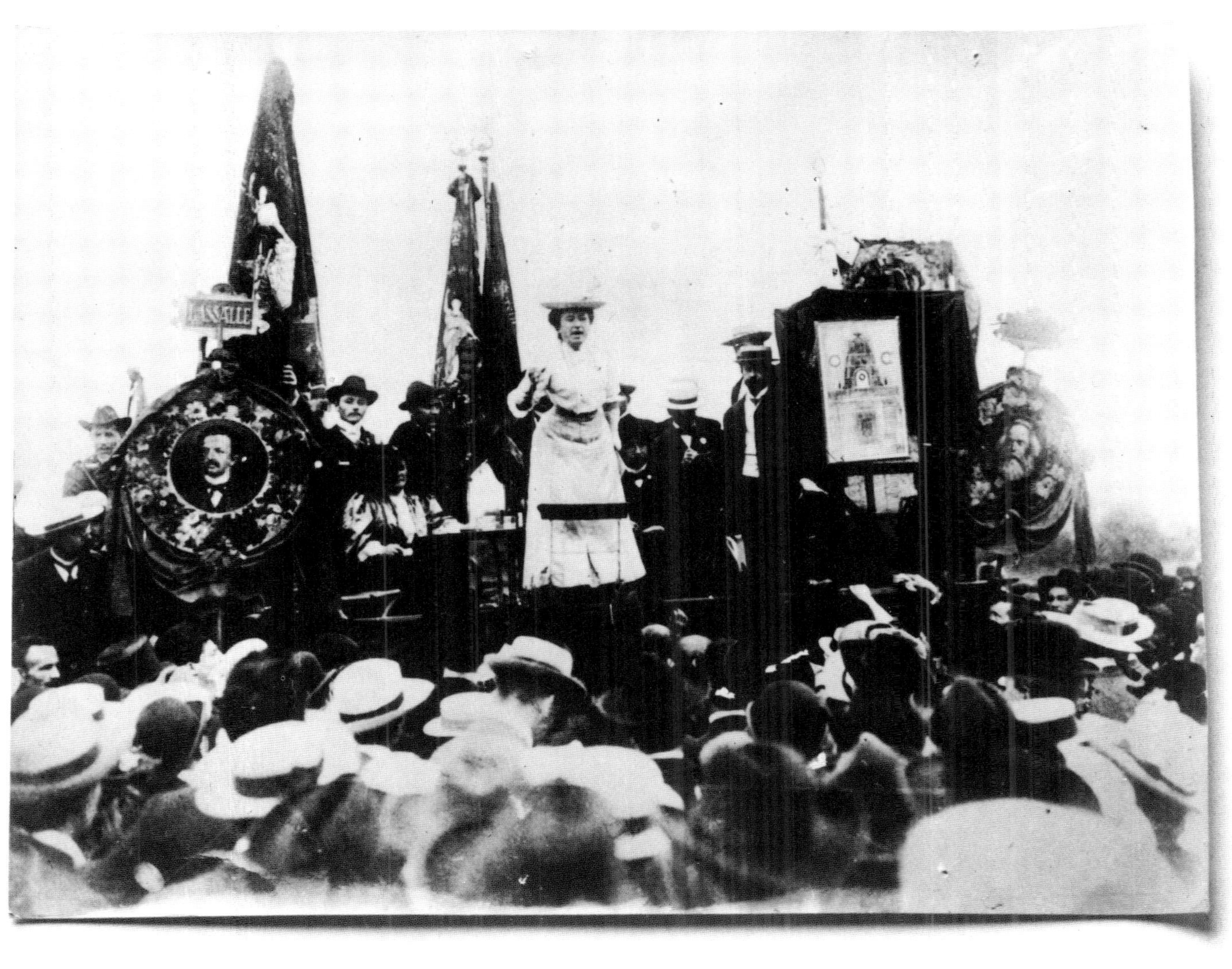

Photograph "Rosa Luxemburg", working motive
◁ "Sozialistenkongress 1907" 1972, *lithograph in three colours, 70.5x50 cm*

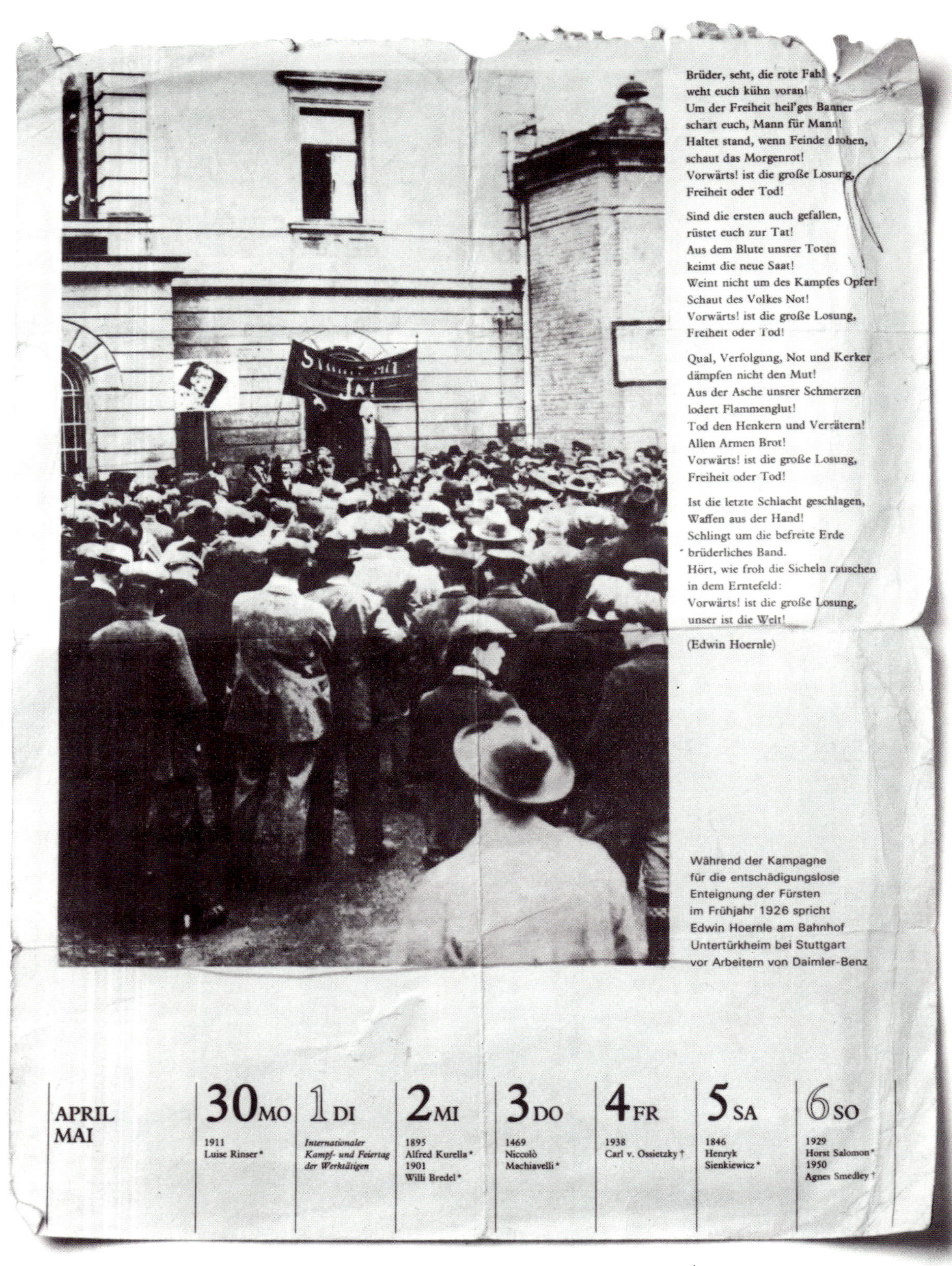

Brüder, seht, die rote Fah[illegible]
weht euch kühn voran!
Um der Freiheit heil'ges Banner
schart euch, Mann für Mann!
Haltet stand, wenn Feinde drohen,
schaut das Morgenrot!
Vorwärts! ist die große Losung,
Freiheit oder Tod!

Sind die ersten auch gefallen,
rüstet euch zur Tat!
Aus dem Blute unsrer Toten
keimt die neue Saat!
Weint nicht um des Kampfes Opfer!
Schaut des Volkes Not!
Vorwärts! ist die große Losung,
Freiheit oder Tod!

Qual, Verfolgung, Not und Kerker
dämpfen nicht den Mut!
Aus der Asche unsrer Schmerzen
lodert Flammenglut!
Tod den Henkern und Verrätern!
Allen Armen Brot!
Vorwärts! ist die große Losung,
Freiheit oder Tod!

Ist die letzte Schlacht geschlagen,
Waffen aus der Hand!
Schlingt um die befreite Erde
brüderliches Band.
Hört, wie froh die Sicheln rauschen
in dem Erntefeld:
Vorwärts! ist die große Losung,
unser ist die Welt!

(Edwin Hoernle)

Während der Kampagne
für die entschädigungslose
Enteignung der Fürsten
im Frühjahr 1926 spricht
Edwin Hoernle am Bahnhof
Untertürkheim bei Stuttgart
vor Arbeitern von Daimler-Benz

APRIL MAI	30 MO	1 DI	2 MI	3 DO	4 FR	5 SA	6 SO
	1911 Luise Rinser *	*Internationaler Kampf- und Feiertag der Werktätigen*	1895 Alfred Kurella * 1901 Willi Bredel *	1469 Niccolò Machiavelli *	1938 Carl v. Ossietzky †	1846 Henryk Sienkiewicz *	1929 Horst Salomon * 1950 Agnes Smedley †

Calendar page, working motive
"Manifestazione popolare" 1972, *lithograph in two colours, 76x56 cm* ▷

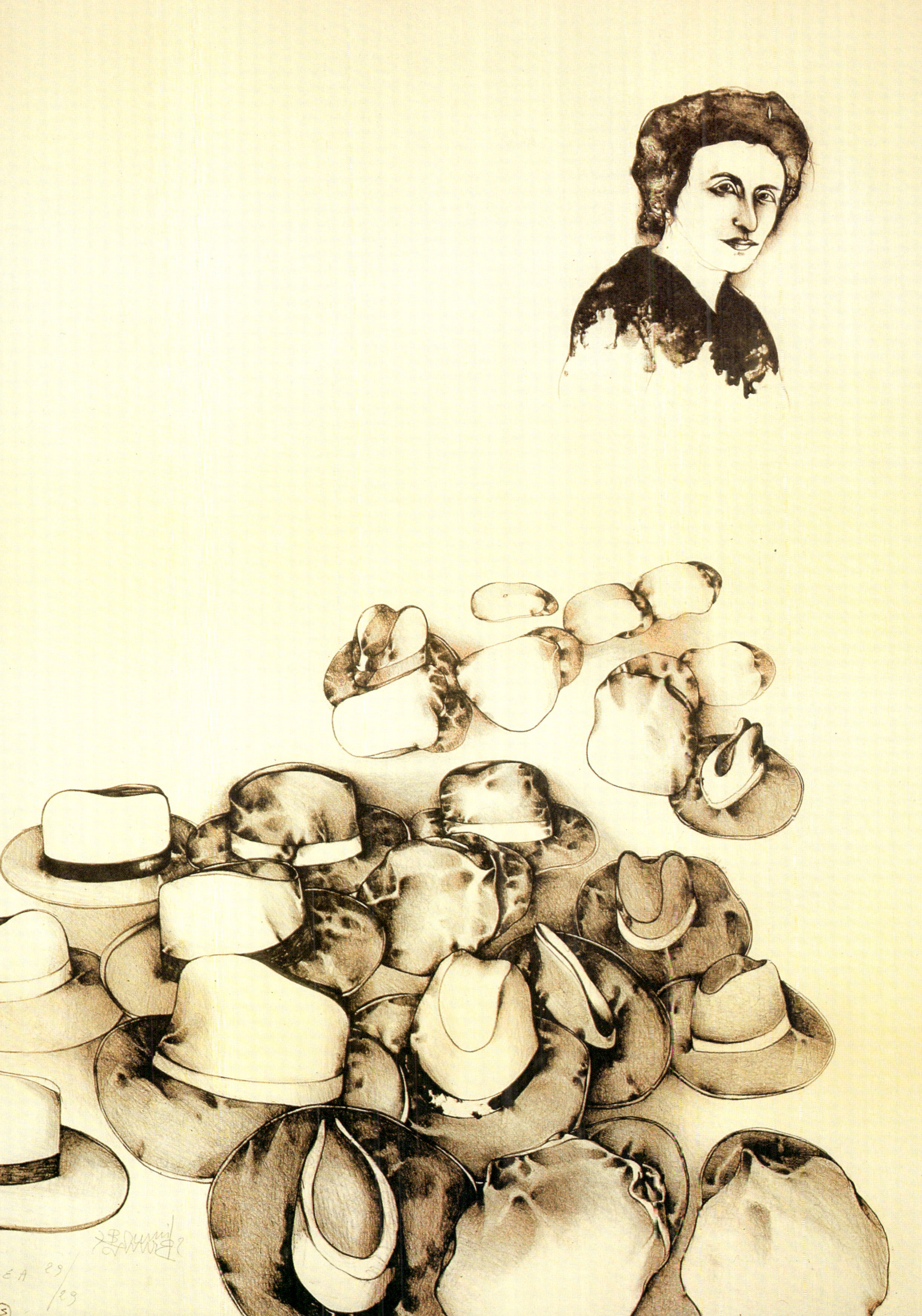

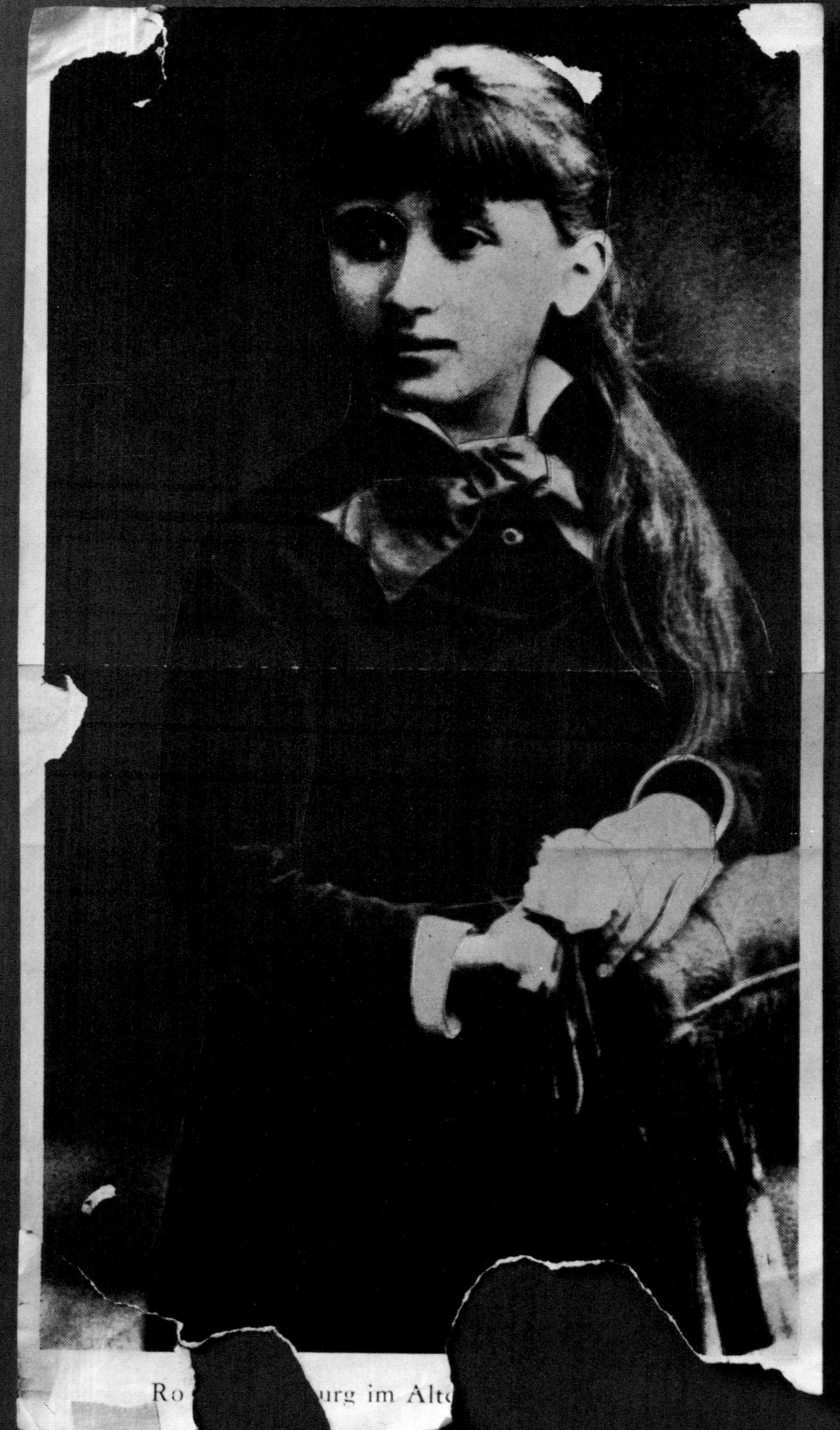
Ro urg im Alt

Hans-Harald Müller

The Position of the Rosa-Luxemburg-Cycle in the Graphic Work of Bruno Bruni. The Attempt of an Encirclement.

1. *"... could I live only to paint for two years –, that would swallow me up. I would not be any painter's apprentice, nor would I ever ask anybody for advice, only learning while painting and asking you. But these are mad dreams. I cannot do it, for no dog needs my pitiful paintings, but the people do need my articles ..."*

Rosa Luxemburg, from a letter to Konstantin Zetkin. August 22, 1908.

I.

The Rosa-Luxemburg-Cycle was created in 1972, at the same time as the suite, "Frammenti Toscani" (1972), which is related in motif to the earlier suite, "Venus by Botticelli" (1971). The eight lithographs of "Venus by Botticelli" and the "Frammenti Toscani" present an adaptation of Quattrocento painting styles combined with historical and contemporary allusions: the figure of Venus passes through obvious visual and conceptual changes. For example, the painting, "David's Hand," relates to various *studi fiorentini;* in "Terra di Siena" the figure of Venus is moved from the center of the picture and is replaced by a cartouche in the style of later centuries.

The Rosa-Luxemburg-Cycle focuses on stages and situations from the life of the most influential theoretician and pioneer of democratic communism. It is completely heterogeneous in theme and subject matter to "Frammenti Toscani" of the same period and this similarity suggests a question about the relationship of Bruni's graphic work to those *sensibel nachempfundenen Marginalien* (Renato Guttuso). For example, in "Frammenti Toscani," what is the relationship of social and political themes to the aesthetics and artistic technique? Does Bruni try to present the life and work of Rosa Luxemburg in contemporary terms and not in the past, while in other lithographs he appears to deal with subjects and art historical adaptations *alla ricerca del tempo perduto?*

◁ "Rosa Luxemburg" newspaper clipping as working motive

II.

2. *"I once saw a painting of Lady Hamilton in an exhibition of French painters of the 18th century; I do not remember who the painter was, and only remember a heavy style, a robust, provocative beauty that did not appeal to me. I prefer a more delicate type of woman. I still remember clearly a picture of Madame de Levallière in the same exhibition painted by Lebrun in a silver-grey tone that highlighted the transparent face, the blue eyes and the light dress. I could hardly break away from the painting in which I saw incarnated, the entire refinement of pre-revolutionary France – a truly aristocratic culture with a slight touch of decay . . ."*

Rosa Luxemburg, from a letter to an unknown adressee. April 9, 1915.

A first approach to the question about the relationship of social and political themes to aesthetic refinement in Bruno Bruni's work may be found, without doubt, in the genesis of the work itself.

The early etchings and lithographs from 1961 to 1964, as listed in the catalogue of 1976, are social sketches and, with only a few exceptions, they concentrate on body posture, physiognomy, gestures of the figures and their relation to one another. These graphics reflect the daily life of its protagonists not without critical, social intentions as in the lithographs "Nella stanza" and "Murder" (1963). The abstract, nervously expressive etching "Algeria" (1962) is an exception in this sequence of critical sketches. It is an aesthetic and problematic hymn that incorporates political allusions to the former French colony and the later socialist Republic of Algeria.

Only in 1965 does the influence of the famous *Hamburger Schule* of Wunderlich, Janssen and many others begin to dominate the work of Bruni who, at that time, was a student of Gresko. And at the same time we find many adaptations of elements, techniques and topics from Surrealism ("Tra le nuvole" and others), Mannerism ("Omaggio al Manierismo), Pop Art, and Art Nouveau ("Floreale"). For instance, Bruni's preference for combined images of the body and organic elements, perfectly executed for the first time in "Donna-fiore" in 1965 and still featured prominently in his recent drawings, graphic designs and sculptures.

A series of lithographs, also from 1965, documents that Bruni's continuing interest in critical, social topics has remained constant throughout this period of aesthetic differentiation, of the cult of refinement, of intellectuality, and of sensuality: This interest is seen in the series "Oratori" and "Oratore" where the gesticulating figure of Janus gives a political speech that has different rules for what is said and what is done; and finally, in "Cardinale" where the two-faced priest blesses his congregation differently in each room. This polemic and anti-clerical theme, first introduced in "Cardinale," was varied in the lithographs "Dal balcone" and "Concilio ecumenico" of the Amor-Roma collection (1973-74).

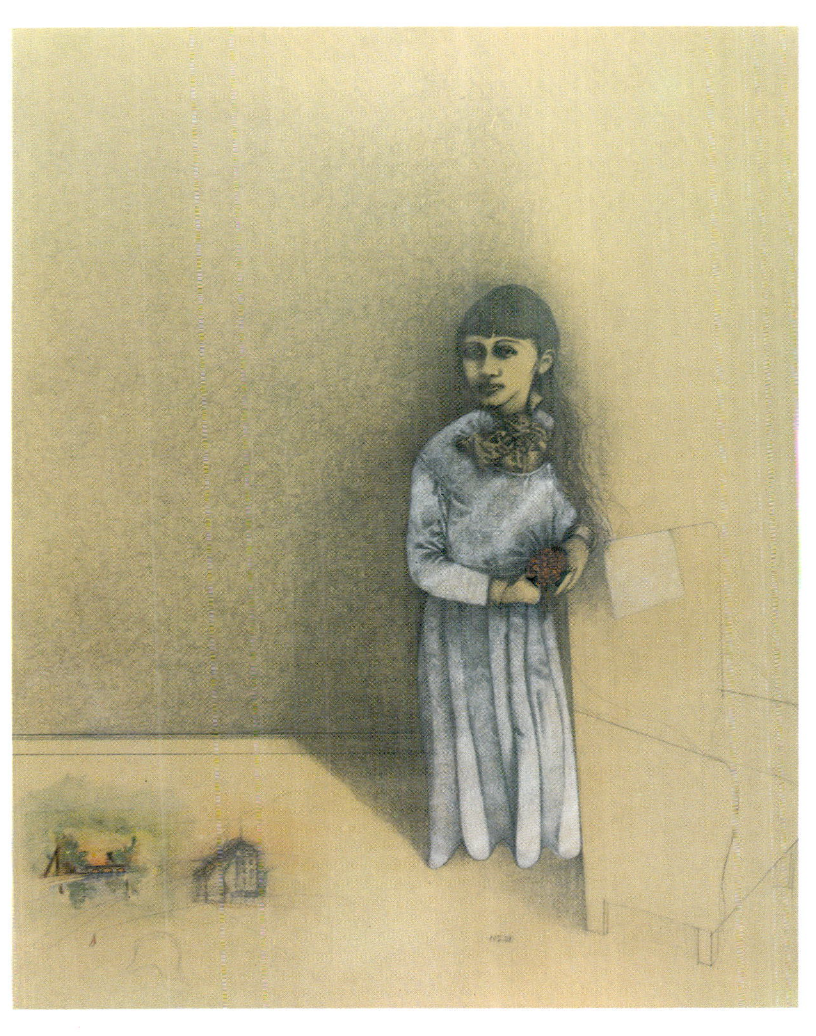

"Rosa a dodici anni" 1975
pencil, crayon and gouache, 105x84 cm

These remarks are necessarily limited to a few superficial observations about the development of Burno Bruni's graphic work, but they demonstrate that Bruni's work was characterized primarily by aesthetic differentiation and stylistic refinement and that, until the 1970s, it reflects co-existing interests in aesthetic refinement and in critical social topics.

III.

3. "You are wrong to think that I am generally against modern poets ... It is true: I am a little afraid of their excellent and skillful control of form and poetic expression and, at the same time, lack of greatness and nobility. This discord leaves my soul untouched so that the beautiful form becomes a grimace. They usually reflect wonderful moods. But moods do not make human beings ..."

Rosa Luxemburg, from a letter to Sophie Liebknecht, November 24, 1917.

4. "Romain Rolland is not unknown to me ... I read his "Jean Christopher in Paris" in a German translation. I am afraid to hurt you, but I want to be, as always, quite honest. I thought the book was very forthright and pleasant, but rather more a pamphlet than a novel, not an actual work of art. I am inexorably sensible in this respect, the most pleasing purpose cannot replace genius."

Rosa Luxemburg, from a letter to Hans Diefenbach. August 28, 1917.

In contrast to the increased aesthetic and technical refinement that characterized the development of Bruno Bruni's work up to the beginning of the 1970s, his Rosa-Luxemburg-Cycle is dominated by an almost timid restrain in the use of obviously existing skills. Bruno Bruni's Rosa-Luxemburg-Cycle is also further away from the outdated method of *agit-prop-art,* however inspired by social realism with its persuasive and expressive technique, than it is from the subtle sensualistic, manneristic graphics of the same period. The Rosa-Luxemburg-Cycle is not an attempt to convert this socialist theoretician into a monument, not a loud glorification of the victim of German post-war militarism, not a secularized hagiography that tries to create political idols. In this cycle, the image of Rosa Luxemburg is not merely transferred to the present but is shown in a historical context. The element of admiration is reduced to an interest in physiognomy, in gestures, in details that, often become symbols, in the interrelationship of various moments of a life that is important not only for its political greatness. The political motivation expressed in the Rosa-Luxemburg-Cycle nas no desire to teach or to convert, nor the need to show an "aphoristic, political morality in pictures" (Brecht). This motivation may be felt - independent of subject - in the subtle coexistence of picture and title that demands information from the spectator, while at the same time providing it.

Bruni's Rosa-Luxemburg-Cycle consists of twelve lithographs: six belong to the Rosa-Luxemburg collection; three to the collection "Quaderno di appunti;"

and another three single pieces are associated with the Cycle by means of title and subject. The entire Cycle refers to stations in Rosa Luxemburg's life and makes most careful use of the few still existing photographic documents. The first image, a study in physiognomy, is entitled "Dodici anni, 1882" and shows Luxemburg as a child from a well-off, educated family. The lithograph, "Il piccolo fiore dei proletari" provides a variation of the first picture of the cycle and, at the same time, relates to later physiognomical studies in which both imagery and title allude to the recuring motif of flower metaphors. Indeed, Rosa Luxemburg herself was well aware of these floral associations when she changed her name from 'Rosalia' to 'Rosa'; she even sometimes signed letters to intimate friends as 'Rosetta.' This first picture of the Cycle prefigures imagery seen in "Rosa Luxemburg a 12 anni" (from the collection "Quaderno di appunti") by including the faint background image of the bridge over the Landwehrkanal from which Luxemburg was thrown by her killers in 1919.

The second picture in the Cycle, "Zitadelle zu Warschau, 1906" shows Rosa Luxemburg in prison as the result of her illegal activities for the Socialist Party of Poland. These activities, performed under a phony name and in extremely dangerous circumstances after the first unsuccessful Russian Revolution of 1905, offered a kind of interruption to Luxemburg's "revolutionary journey." It is no coincidence that the identity of Rosa Luxemburg – face, profile, finger prints, prisoner No. 317 – is marked on the facing prison cell. For this was neither the first

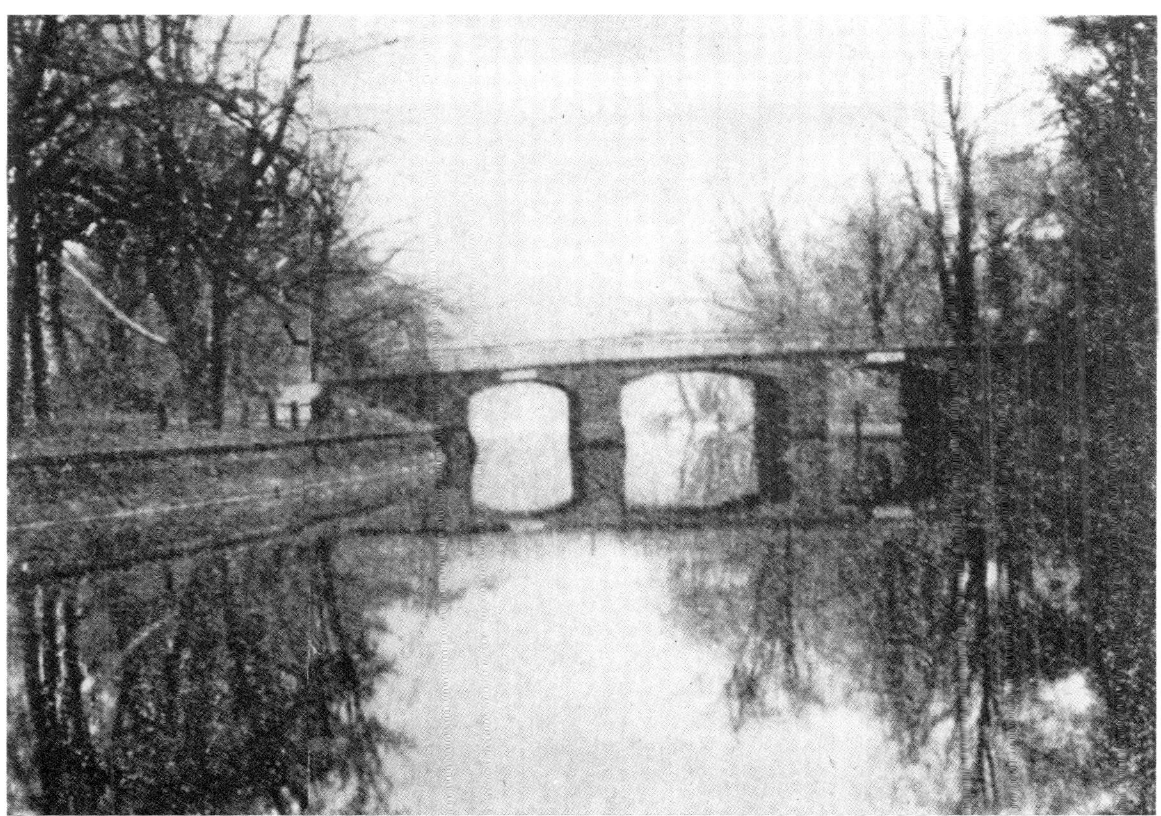

"The -Landwehrkanal- at Berlin" working photo

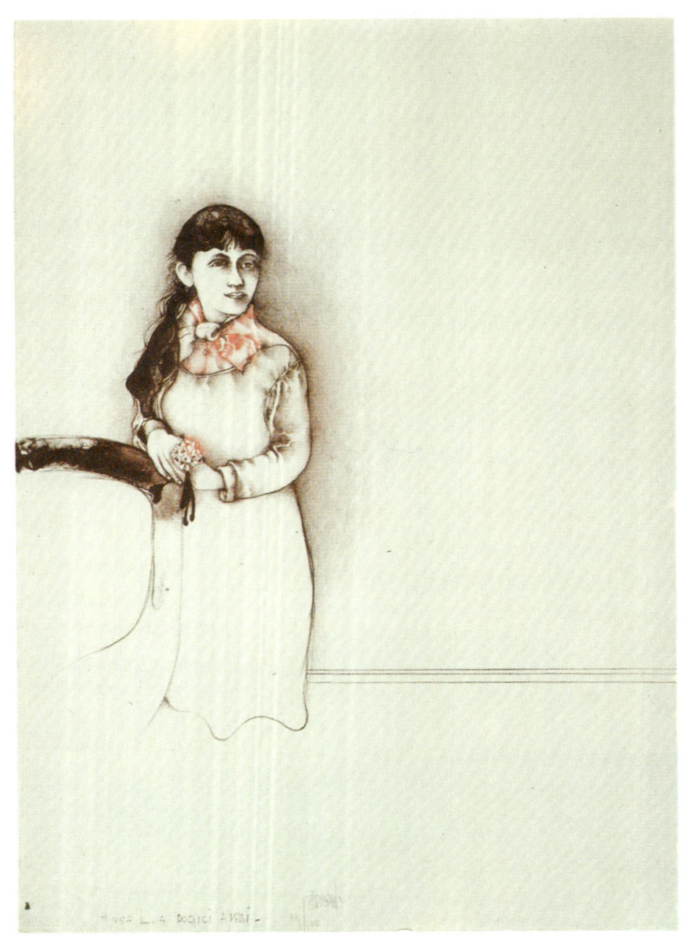

1

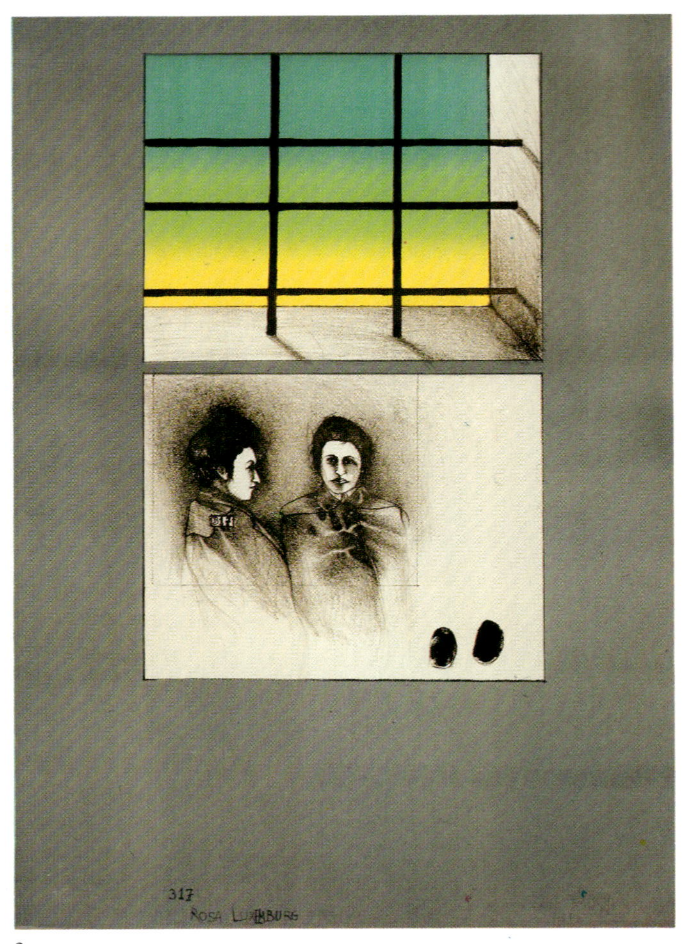

2

"Rosa Luxemburg" 1972
series of six coloured lithographs in size 70.5x50 cm

1 "Dodici anni, 1882"
2 "Zitadelle zu Warschau, 1906"
3 "Sozialistenkongress, 1907"
4 "Rosa Luxemburg"
5 "Berlin, 9. November 1918"
6 "Ermordet, 15. Januar 1919"

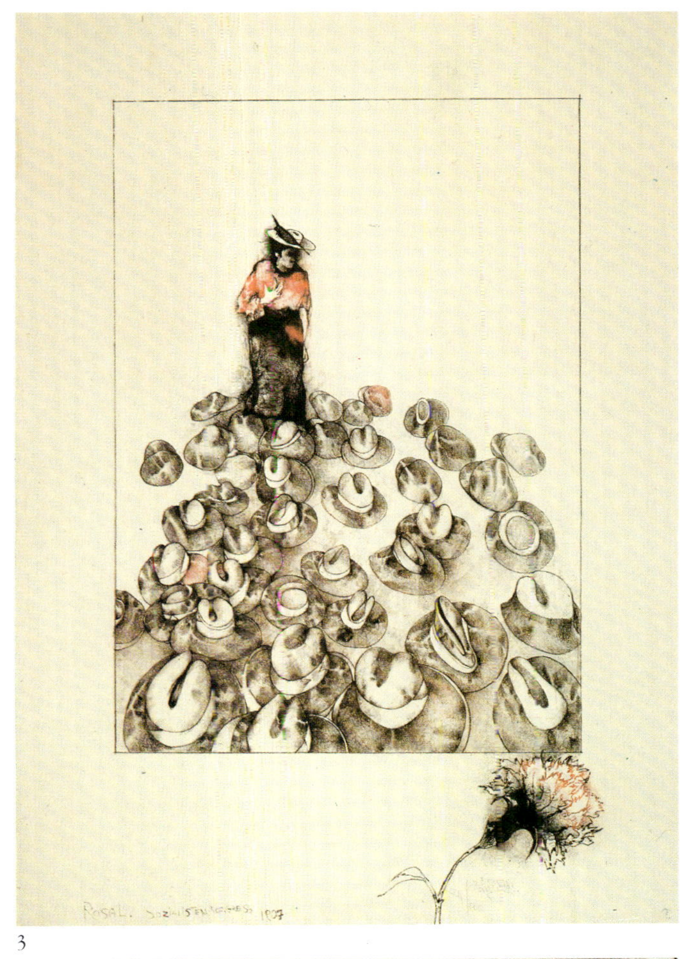
3

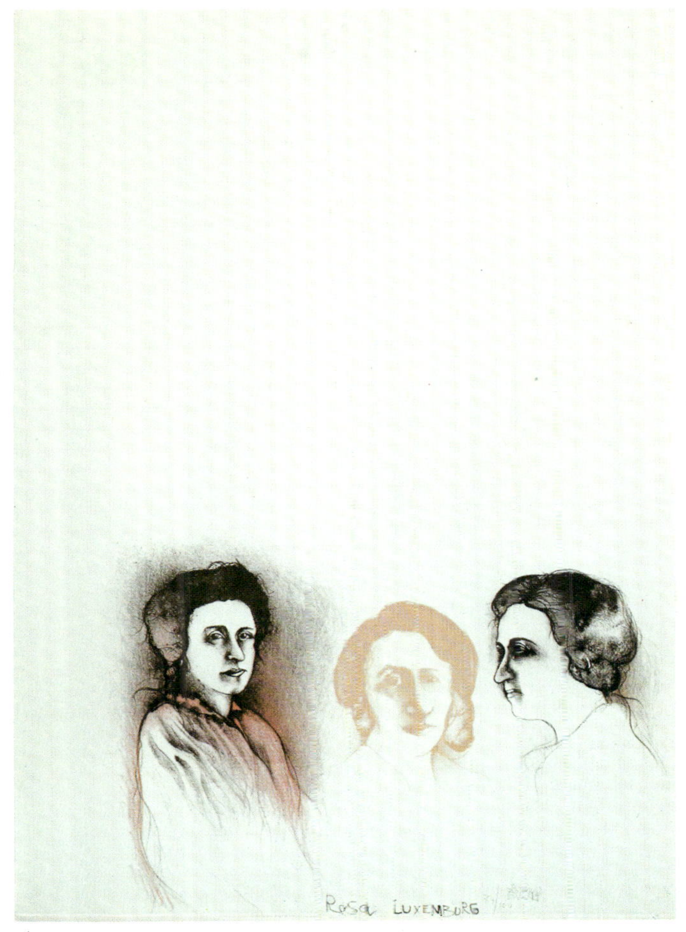

4

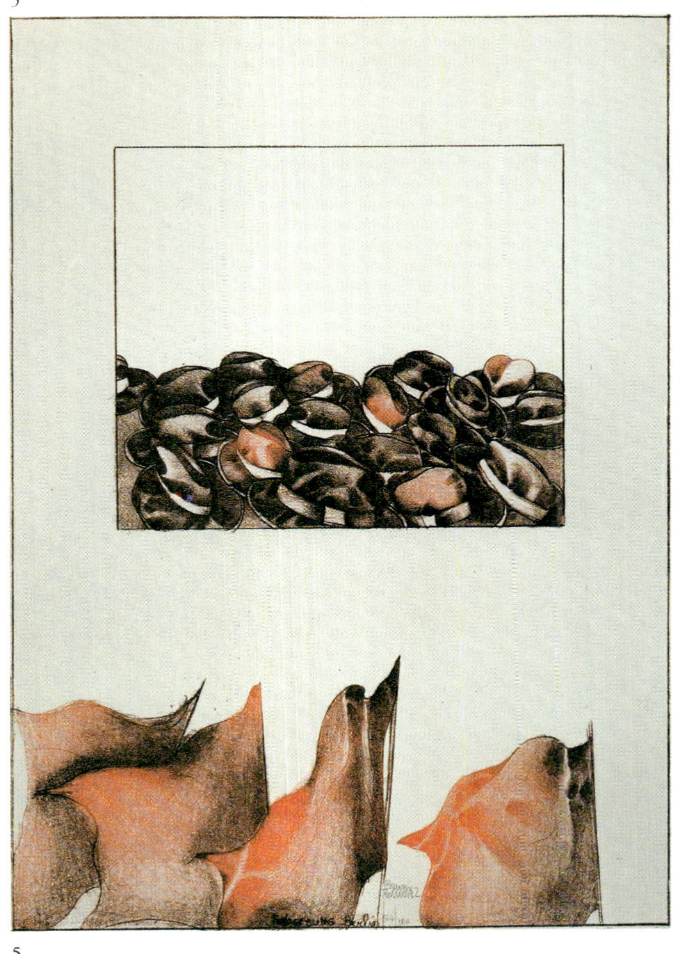
5

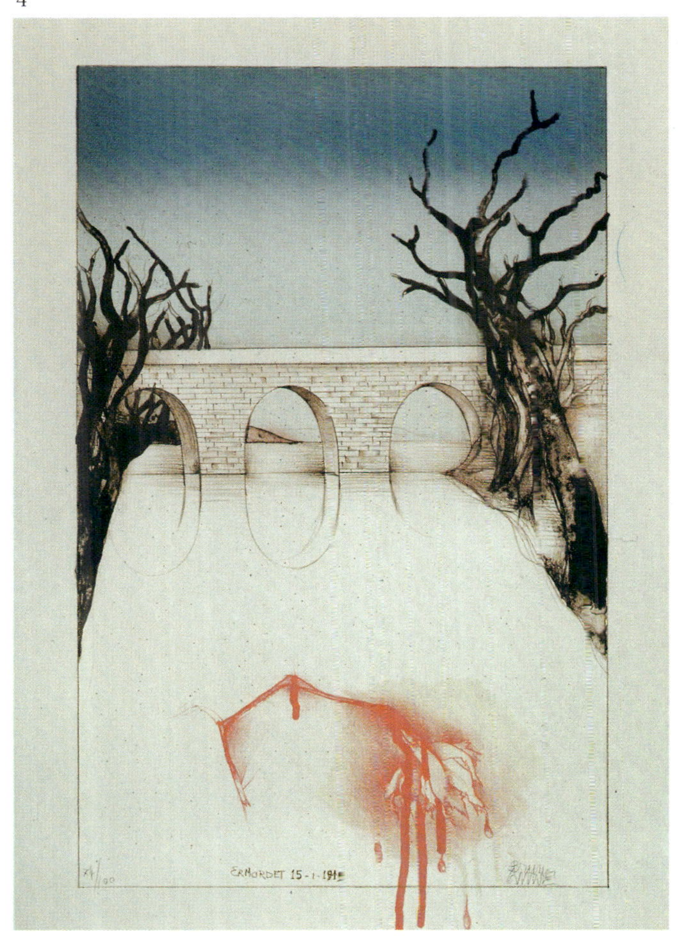

6

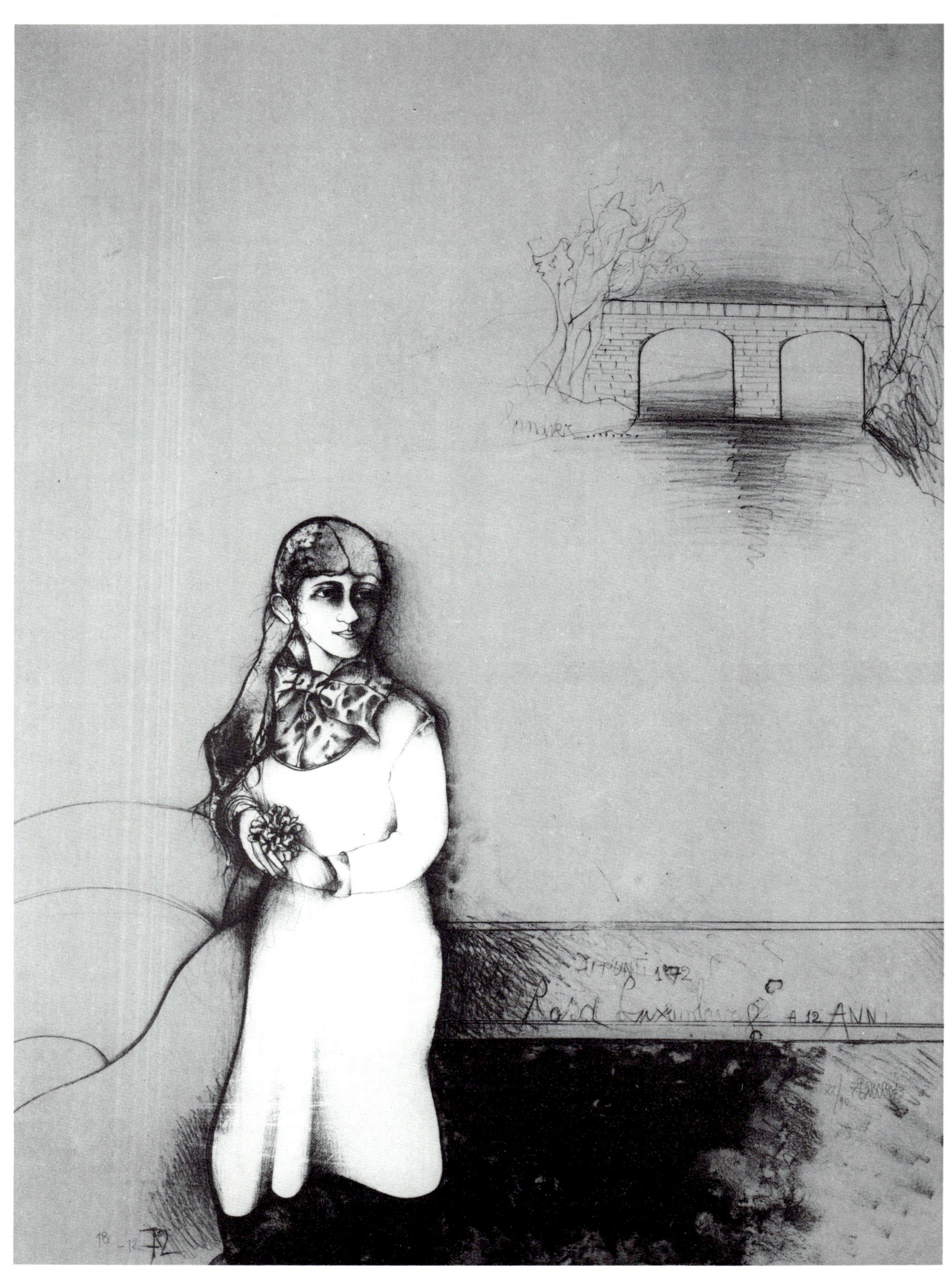

"Rosa Luxemburg a 12 anni" 1972
lithograph in four colours, 74x54,5 cm, out of the portfolio "Quaderno di appunti"

nor the last imprisonment suffered by this famous theoretician and practical pioneer of the working class. Rosa's longest stay in prison, from 1915–1918, was without trial and without sentence. Though many of the letters from this period are still unpublished, they document that despite the conditions of imprisonment, extremely dangerous and destructive to identity, Rosa Luxemburg remained confident about the victory of the proletariate. Her strong personality, talents and interests enabled her to comfort and encourage friends who were becoming desparate outside of prison. She wrote to Louise Kautsky from prison, January 26, 1917:

"And everone who writes to me sighs and complains (. . .) Loosing oneself in the misery of daily life is completely incomprehensible to me and I cannot stand it. Look, for example, how with a certain calmness Goethe was always master of circumstances. Imagine what he went through in his lifetime: the great French Revolution that must have looked to him like a bloody and totally senseless farce; and a series of wars from 1793 to 1815 during which time the world seemed like a madhouse. During this time he pursued his studies about the metamorphosis of plants, the theory of colors, about a thousand things, with tremendous calm and spiritual balance. I don't expect you to write poetry like Goethe, but his ideas about life – the universalism of interests, the inner harmony – everyone can accomplish or at least try to. Should you say: Goethe was not a political fighter, then I say: a fighter must be above things even more or else he will become mixed up with every minor matter (. . .)"

The picture, "Zitadelle zu Warschau, 1906" is a dialectic: the identity that was to have been destroyed by the prison experience was, instead, strengthened; the condemned became a judge of our times.

The third picture in the Cycle, "Sozialistenkongress, 1907,' shows one of the high-points of Rosa Luxemburg's political career, just one year after her release from the Warsaw prison. At the International Socialist Congress in Stuttgart she holds the mandates of the German, the Polish and, upon Lenin's request, the Russian Socialist parties. Here, the concept of the picture applying the 'picture-in-a-picture' composition and resumpting the flower metaphors of the "fiore dei proletari" is problematic: the "citoyenne Luxemburg", as Jean Jaurès approvingly calls her, is surrounded by a sea of hats, symbolic of the bourgeoisie. A modification of this image is seen in "Manifestatione popolare."

"Rosa Luxemburg," the fourth picture in the Cycle, is simply a study of Luxemburg's face, presented without political symbols or historical references. These three faces of Rosa Luxemburg at different ages and conceived in different styles shows an intense effort on the part of Bruni to create an enduring image of a multifaced revolutionary personality; one that belongs to three different cultures and nationalities.

The fifth picture of the cycle, "Berlin, 9. November 1918," uses the same "picture-in-a-picture" composition that we saw in "Sozialistenkongress, 1907."

The 'picture' shows the hats of the bourgeoisie in the foreground contrasted by an image of the apparently victorious red flag the somber red color of which (the entire Cycle has very muted colors) looks discouraging. November 9, 1918, the day that Rosa Luxemburg was released from prison after three years, was also the day of the November Revolution, the political triumph over the empire. During the party meeting of the KPS(S), in December 1918, Luxemburg warned against overestimating the importance of that victory: "We must not pursue the illusions of the first phase of the November 9 Revolution, nor repeat them; it is not enough to overthrow the capitalistic government, only to replace it with another one." The two aspects of the November 9 Revolution, referred to by Luxemburg, are reflected in the conception of the picture.

"Ermordet, 15. Januar 1919" is the last picture of the Rosa Luxemburg Collection. In a striking contrast, it destroys the illusions of the apparently victorious red flag presented in "9 November": here there is no movement, everything is rigid, decline is inevitable. In this image we see dead scenery: the Landwehrkanal and Lichtenstein Bridge where the militaristic mob threw Rosa Luxemburg's body after torturing her in the Eden-Hotel. Rosa Luxemburg has been killed, the "fiore dei proletari" destroyed: "The icecold wind of a long reactionary period blew over the flower field of great and fertile ideas." (Paul Frölich)

Whereas the Rosa-Luxemburg-Cycle documents important phases of Rosa's life, the so-called "Quaderno di appunti" (note-book) tries to interpret the image of Rosa Luxemburg without using incidental sketches from her life. Each of the three pictures in the series implies a prognosis and a fact: portraits of her youth are combined with later studies. In each picture, Luxemburg's entire *vita* is integrated with the menacing symbol of the Landwehrkanal. In "Studi su Rosa Luxemburg" and "1919" Bruni accomplishes too pretty a composition that partially misrepresents the image of Rosa Luxemburg: In the "Studi su Rosa Luxemburg" a portion of the picture is darkened to symbolize the imminent tragedy; in "1919", the date is written on a black amorphous spot, as a momento.

IV.

5. "I was particularly fascinated (in Gerhard Hauptmann's novel, Emanuel Quint) by one problem that I have never found described before, but have experienced deeply in my own life: the tragedy of the person preaching to the masses who feels that every word leaving his lips becomes instantaneously coarse, rigid, and distorted in the minds of the audience. And, to this personal distortion, the preacher is surrounded by pupils who shout: "Show us the miracle. You taught us the way. Where is your miracle?" Hauptmann's description is ingenious. Hänschen, one should never complete one's judgement of people: they can always surprise you in a bad way, but thank God, also in a good way."

Rosa Luxemburg, from a letter to Hans Diefenbach. March 5, 1917.

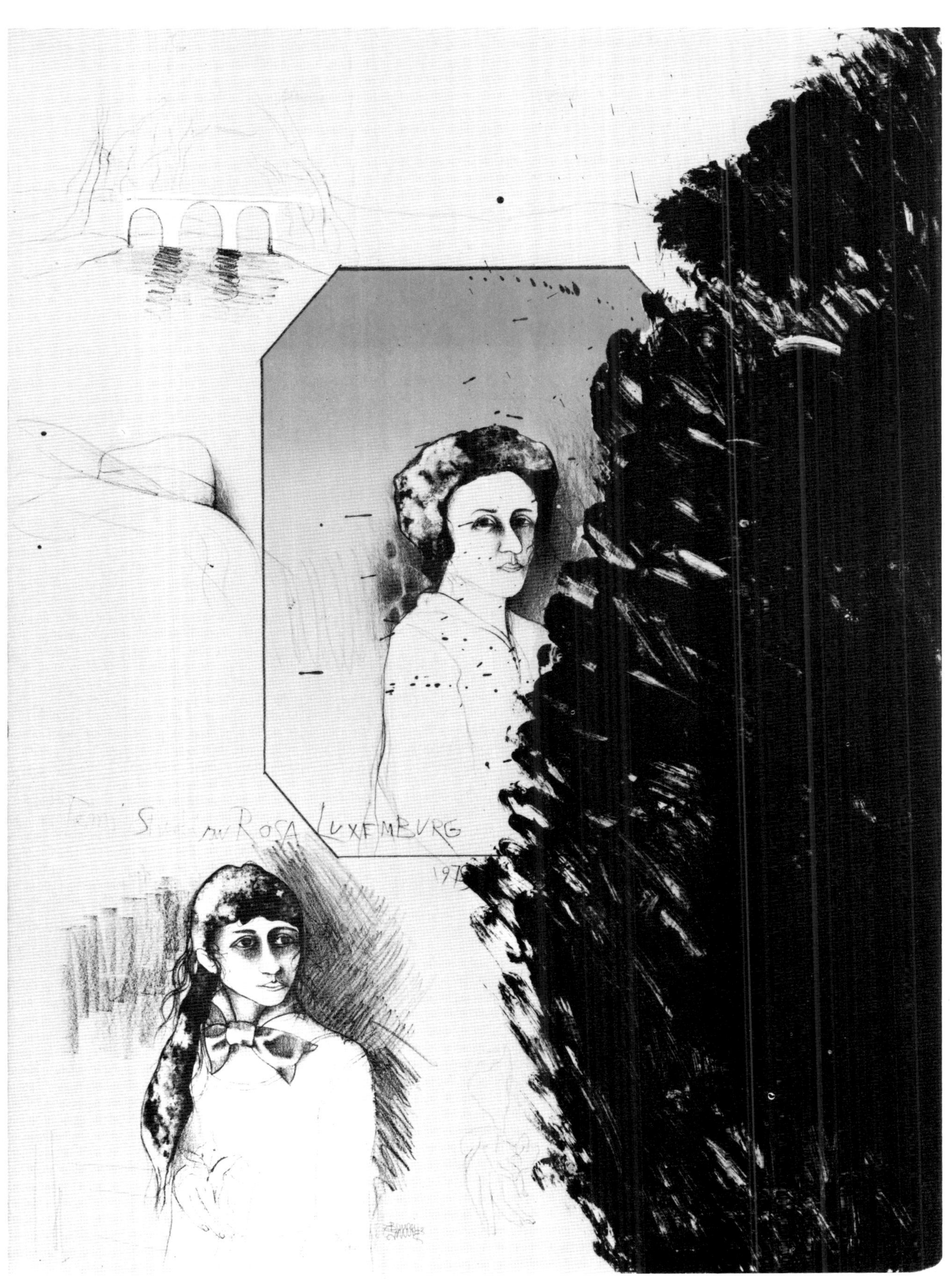

"Studi su Rosa Luxemburg" 1972
lithograph in five colours, 74x54,5 cm, out of the portfolio "Quaderno di appunti"

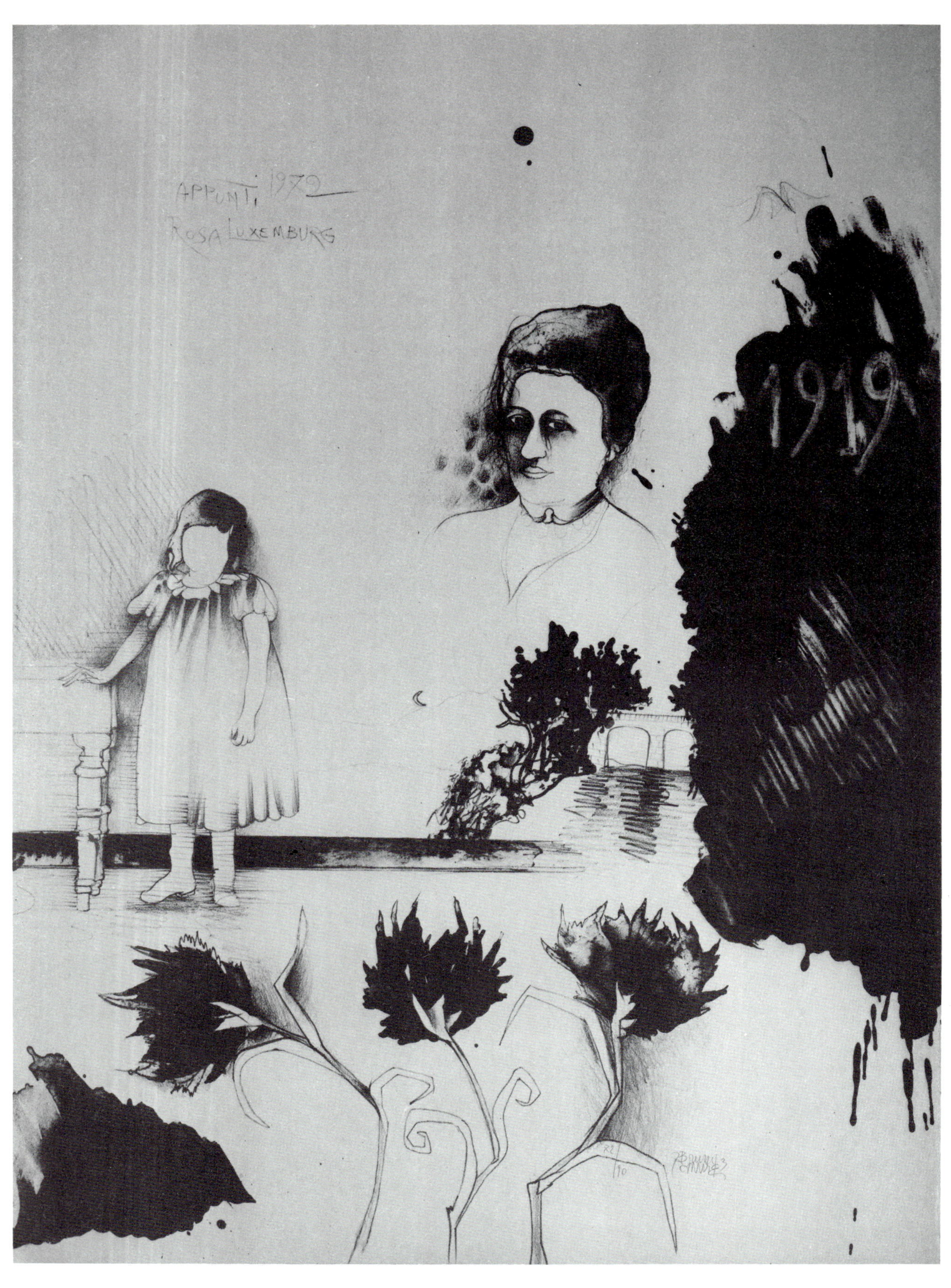

"1919" 1972
lithograph in three colours, 74x54,5 cm, out of the portfolio "Quaderno di appunti"

Bruno Bruni's Rosa-Luxemburg-Cycle is neither an attempt to make politics more aesthetic nor art more political. Instead, the biographical concept of the Cycle, with complementary picture and title, encourages independent evaluation of each domain. Before Bruni, it had been the purpose of political art to blur this borderline by artistic identification.

The pictures in the Rosa-Luxemburg-Cycle are memorabilia, attempts at precisely recollecting a political biography and a universal revolutionary personality. This process of precise recollection requires the medium of contemporary aesthetic intercession, as well as a reflective distance from the object of recollection. Otherwise, the result would be merely contemplative.

Except for the portrait of "Antonio Gramsci" (lithograph, 1977), Bruno Bruni never dealt directly with social political themes after the completion of the Rosa-Luxemburg-Cycle.

Working photo, polaroid ▷

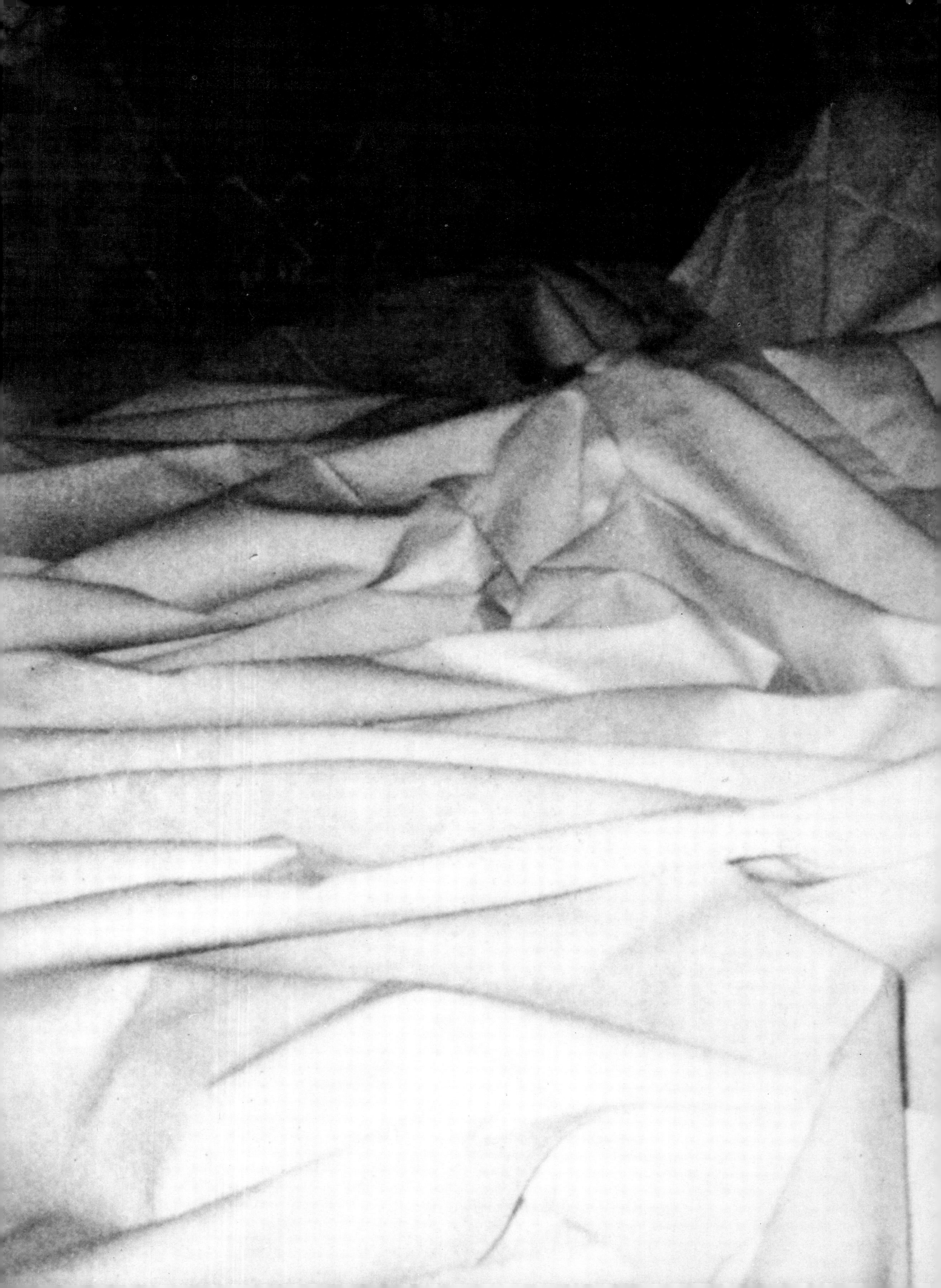

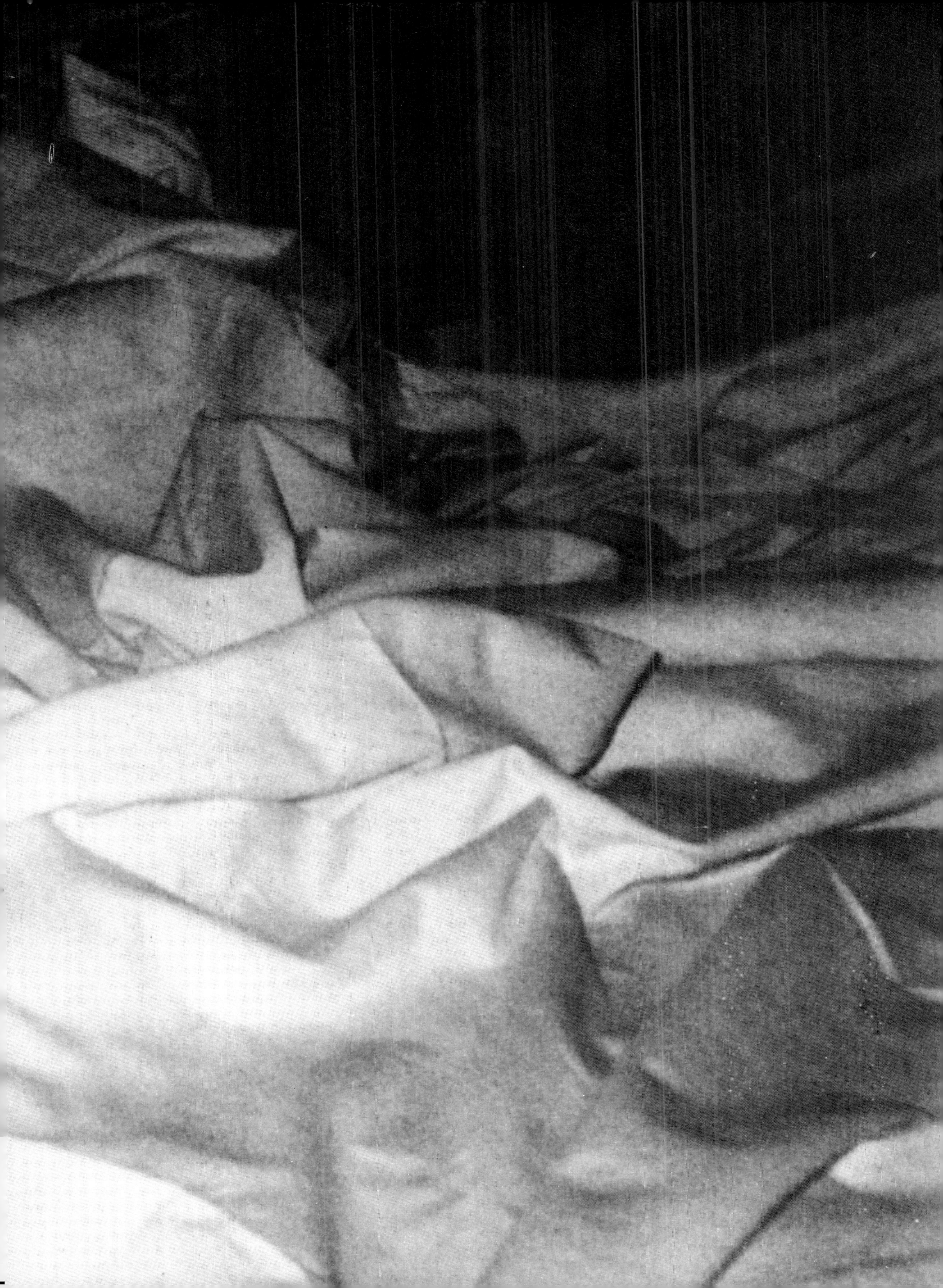

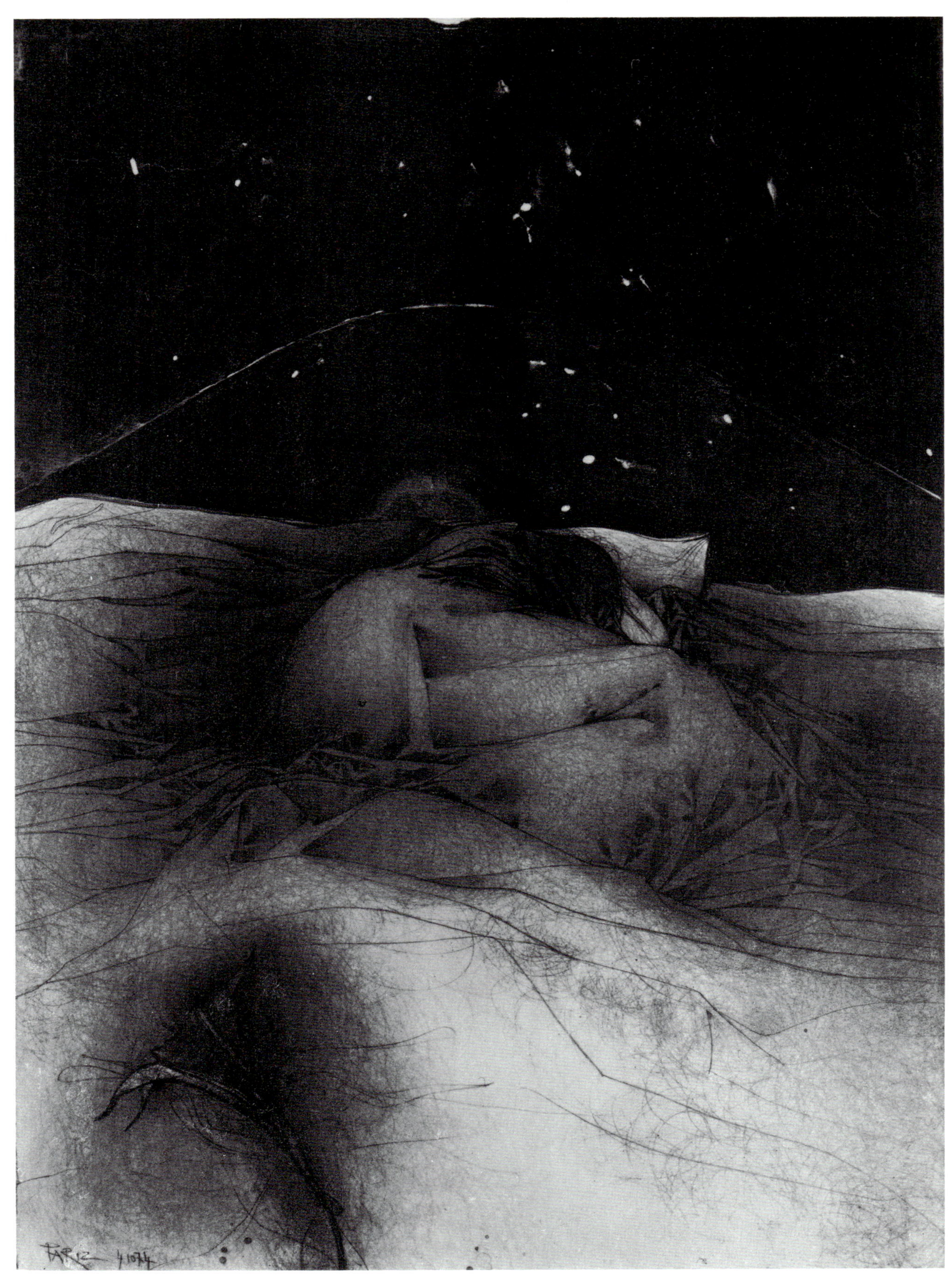

"Sotto le coperte" 1974
lithograph in four colours, 76.7x56.5 cm

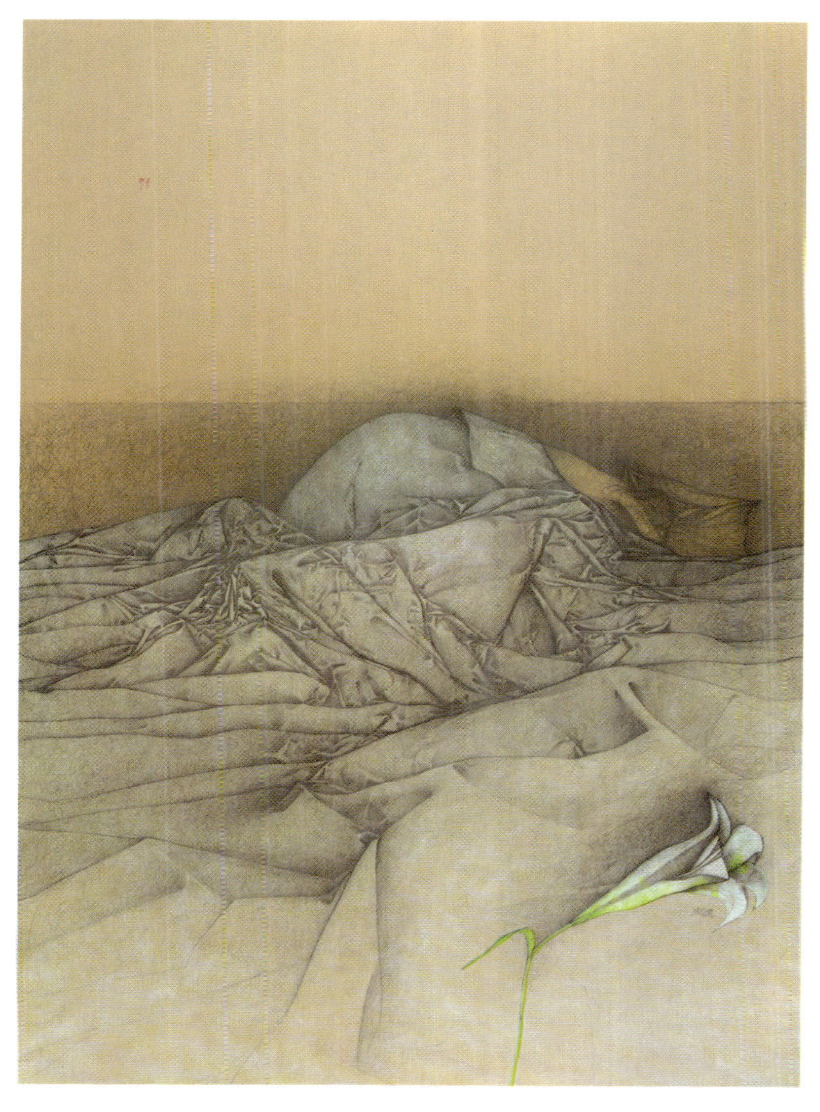

"Sotto le coperte" 1975
pencil and gouache, 109x80 cm

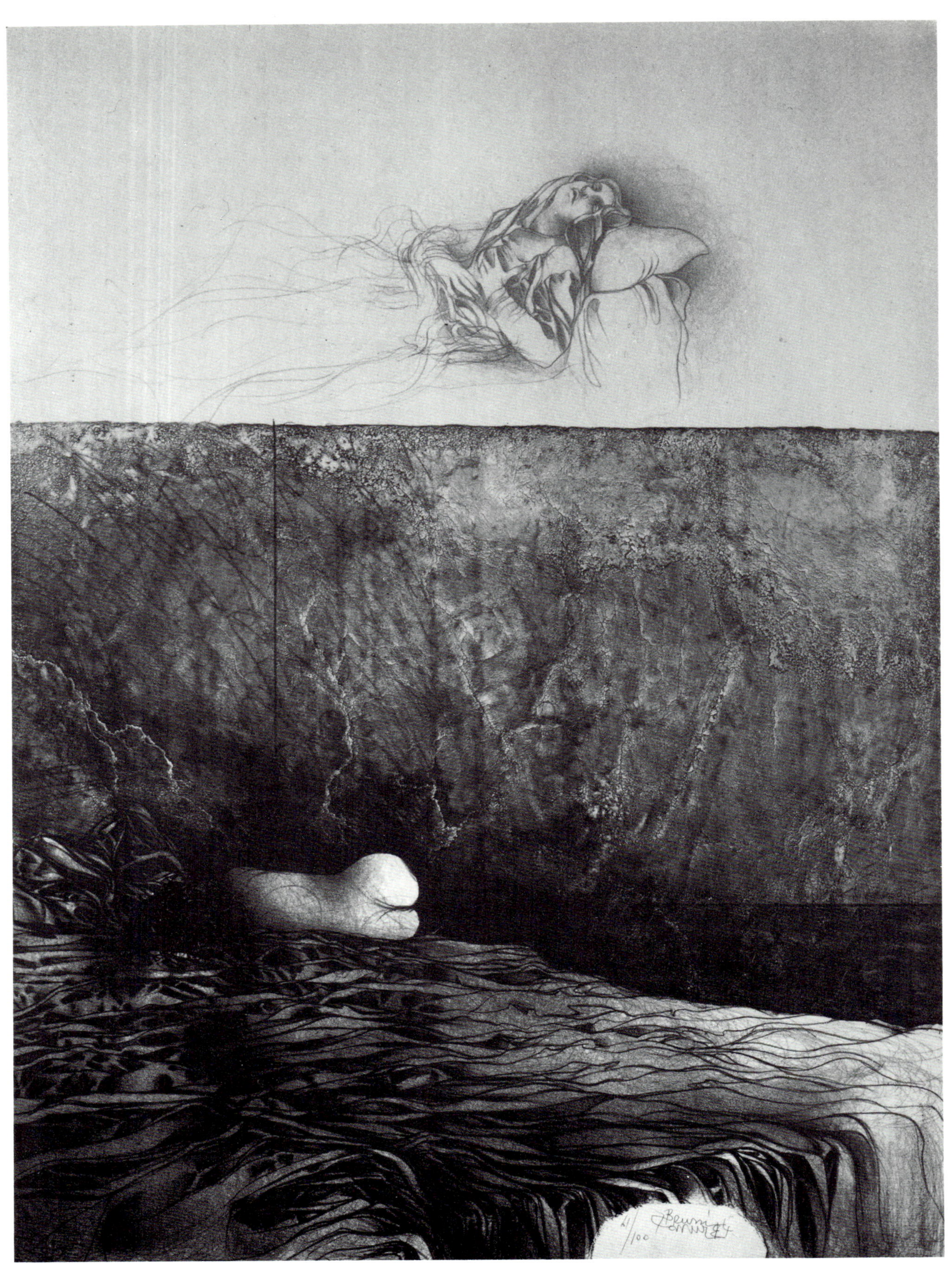

"A touristic visit to Rome" 1974
lithograph in four colours, 80x60 cm

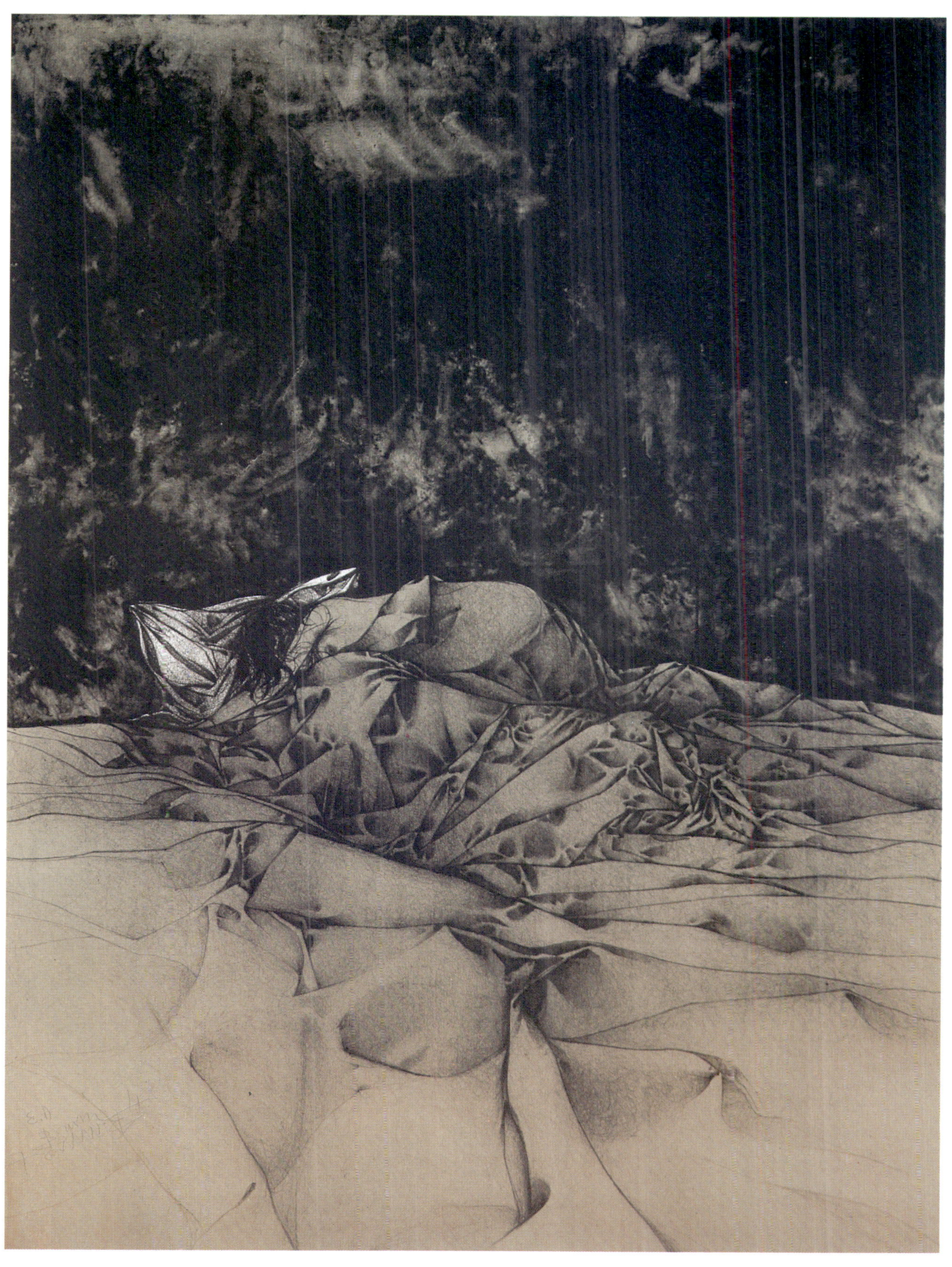

"Mit Bett und Kissen„ 1974
lithograph in three colours, 75x56 cm

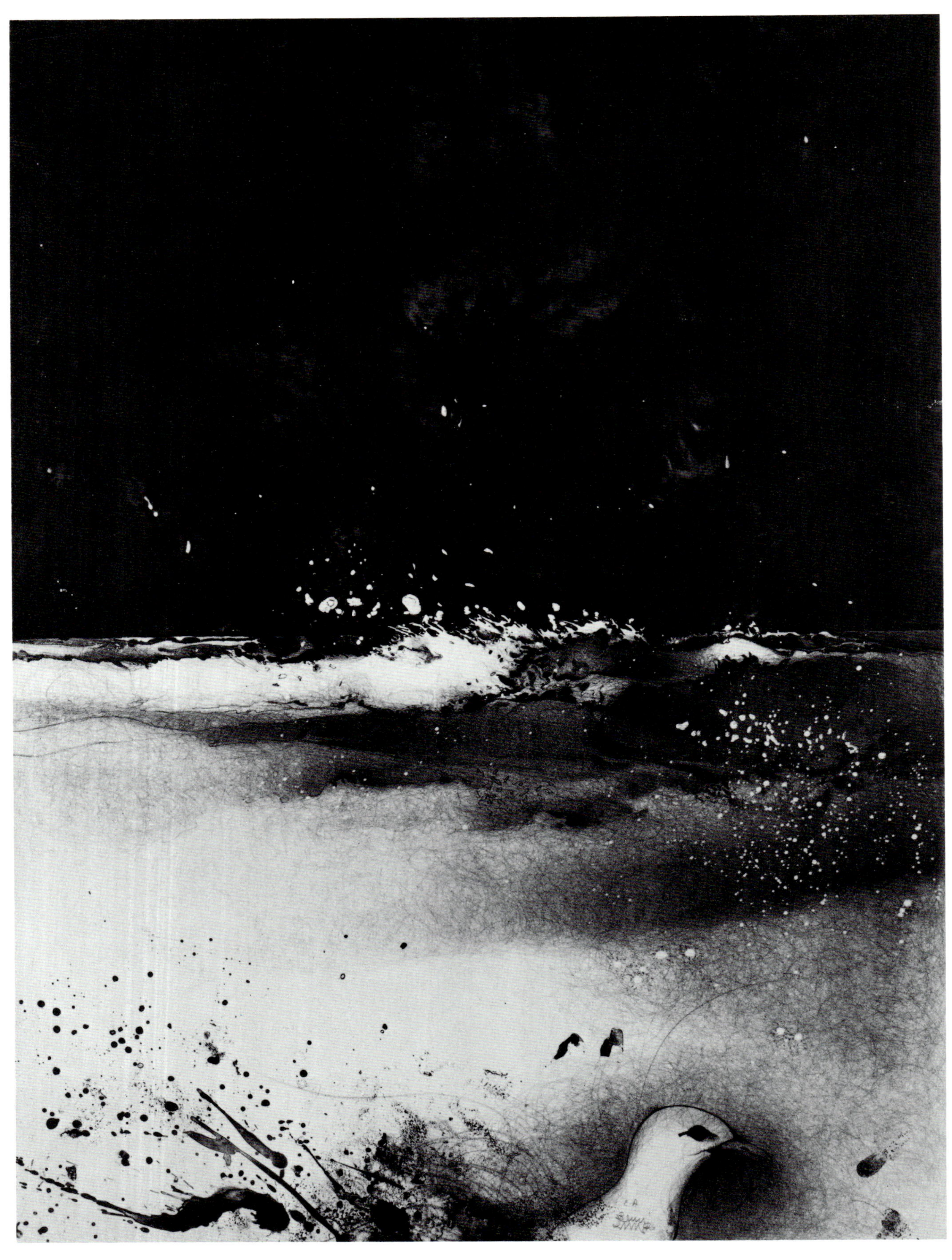

"Paesaggio nord" 1974, *lithograph in four colours, 75x56 cm*

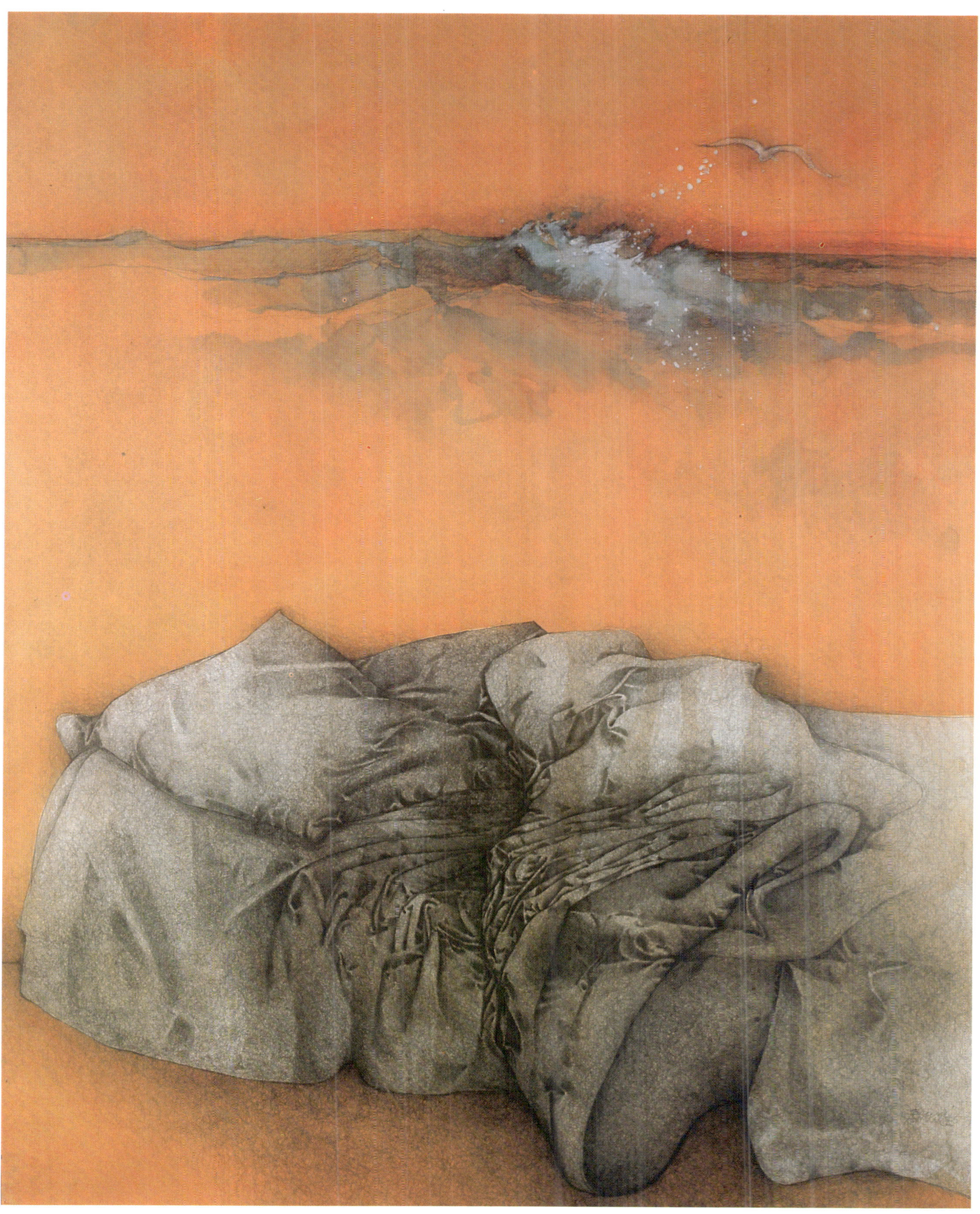

"Melancolia" 1976, *gouache, 106x85 cm*

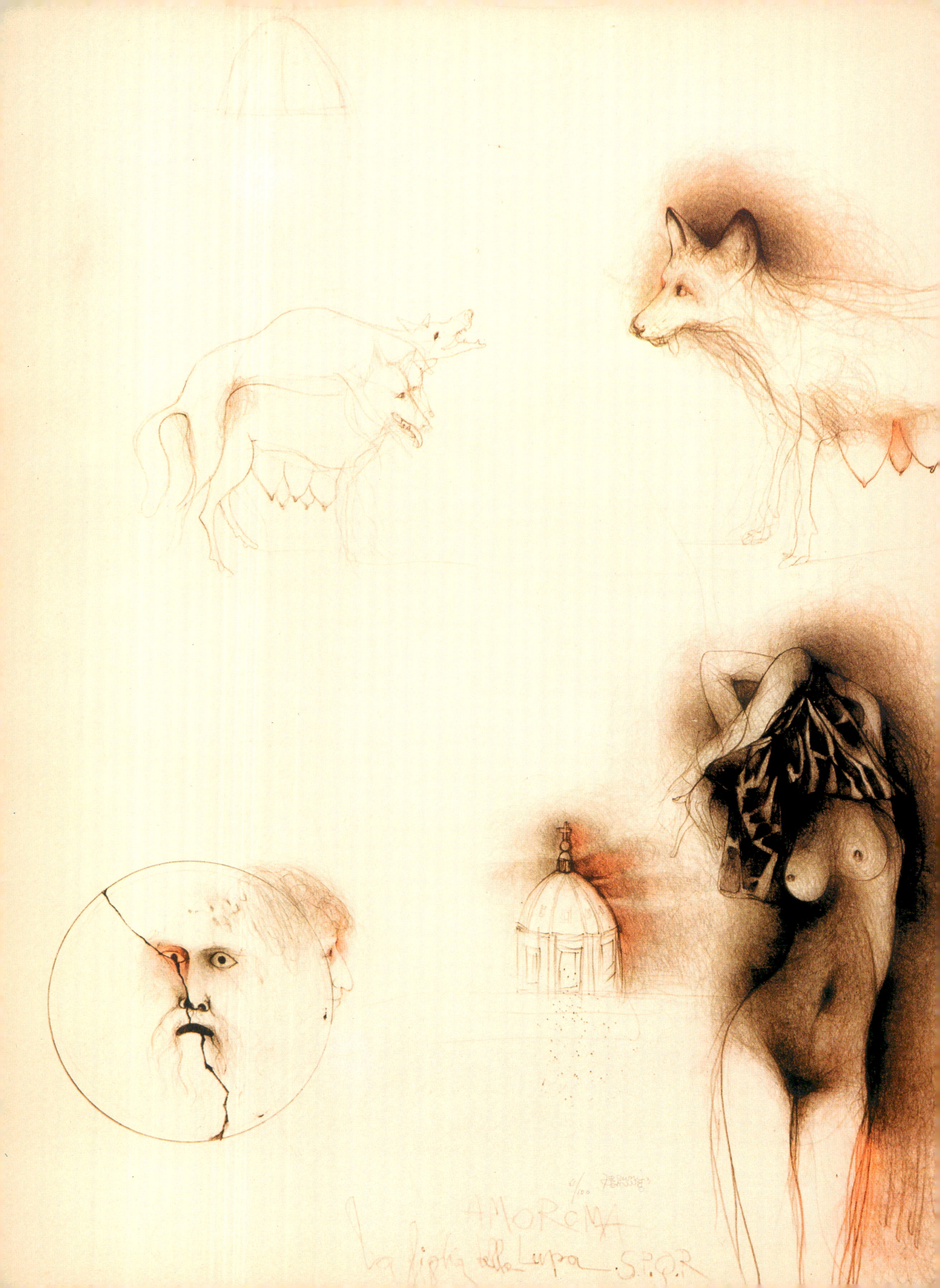
AMORoMA
La figlia della Lupa S.P.Q.R

Max Bense

The Lithographs of Bruno Bruni

Beauty asks that one renounces being carefree.
Robert Walser.

Art does not exist alone in the imagination of an artist. For an artist is a perceiving, thinking human being whose background, education, will power and freedom to make decisions determine the spiritual organization of his work, be it naive, superficial, subtle or profound. The process of the development of art, rather than its final form, depends on these qualities which eventually produce the artistic "existence." Its ultimate fascination derives from the sensitive and rational, or the engaged and artistic, moments of a creatively determined personality. Thus, one can well imagine that any kind of development, beginning with the pre-creative conscious up to its final creative expression depends upon permanent and reinforced observation that not only transforms eye and hand into one instrument, but also finally integrates imagination and realization into one single thought.

I am testing these hypotheses as I look at a few of my favorite lithographs by Bruno Bruni in which I find exactly the above mentioned transition from the pre-creative fascination to the independent creation. I am trying to communicate what I "like" through what I "perceive" and what I can "judge," and to legitimate it into a profound aesthetic organon.

It is clear that Bruni's kind of painting and drawing represents the antithesis of naive, visual expression or, to put it another way, to the naive painting that cannot belong to any spiritual organon, because it does not have any spiritual organization.

One should not misunderstand: despite the casual appearance of this kind of a composition, everything is quite well organized and, after longer observation, one can always find a hidden determination in the experimental form of the graphic design. The artist is the first to interpret the assembly of objects and the signs that he creates are the signs of his aesthetic reality. In my

◁ "La figlia della lupa S.P.Q.R." 1973, *lithograph in three colours, 80x60 cm*

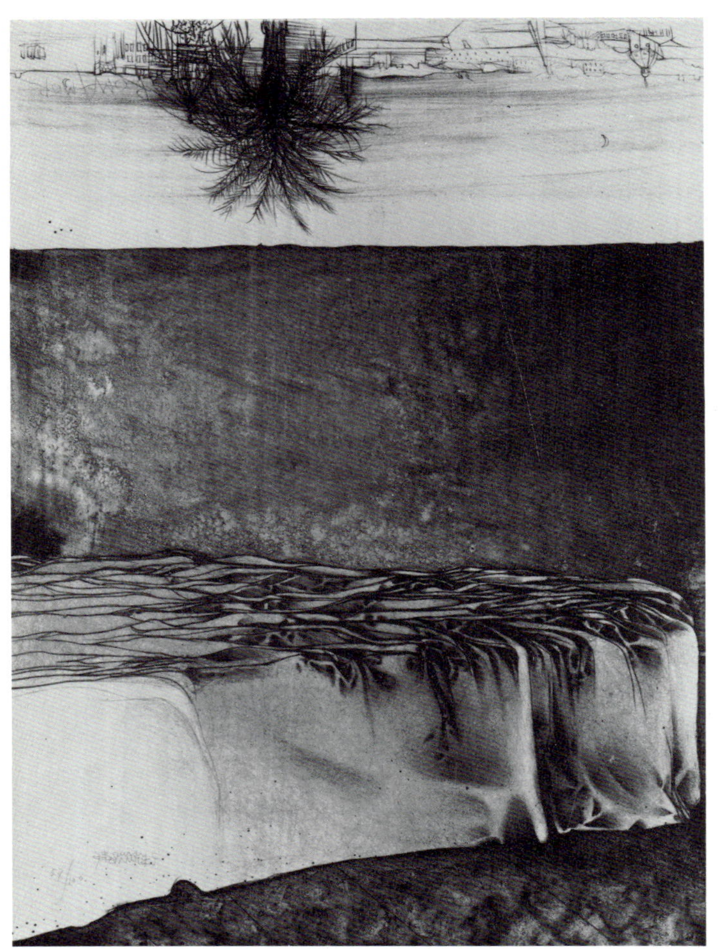

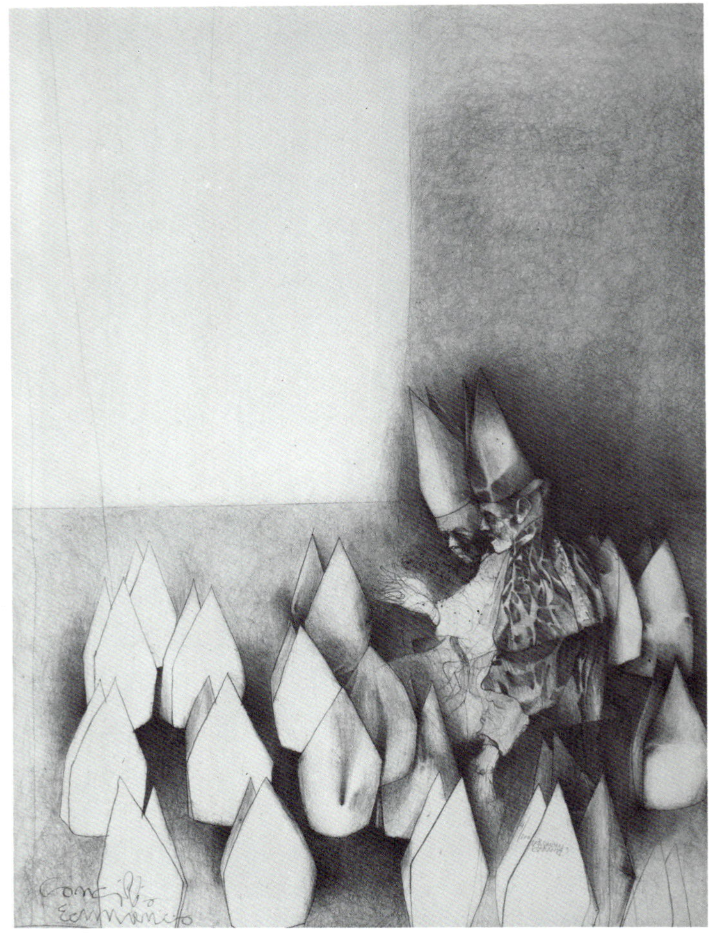

"Without Title" 1974
lithograph in three colours, 80x60 cm

"Concilio ecumenico" 1973
lithograph in five colours, 80x60 cm

analysis, I refer, in particular, to three pictures which, in various ways, incarnate the idea of "aesthetic condition," in the sense of theoretic aesthetics.

I want to add that, generally speaking, the focus of the aesthetician lies in determining the proof of the aesthetic condition of the artistic object; whereas, the work of the art historian centers on the proof and evaluation of originality of creative independence.

Of course, I can only judge as an aesthetician. I am interested in two pictures, in particular: one has a mythological subject, the other refers to the Roman landscape. The first picture is entitled, "La figlia della lupa" (The girl with the female wolf). The signature on the lithograph is combined with another hand-written inscription that sounds like a poetic wordgame:"AmoRoma" can be read backwards and transformed into "RomAmoR". This inscription is also found near the signature of the second picture, mentioned above.

Though it appears to be an informal and improvised composition, "La figlia della lupa" has a specific subject that produces its aesthetic condition. There appears to be no immediate connection between the cupola of St. Peters Church in the lower portion of the picture, the rigid round face of Luna or Zeus that has a crack, at the left, and the faint image of Bruni's face half-hidden under a bush of frizzy hair. To the right of the cupola we see a very slim, stretched, Modigliani-like female nude with a wolf above her shoulder. More wolves approach from the right and left toward the center of the picture; only their heads are defined. Further up at the left, is another, very faint image of a cupola.

The objects seem to be composed as individual pictures rather than as parts of a single picture. They represent a complete 'discrete' world of objects, though they can be assembled by anyone who knows mythology. To interpret these objects one must associate, and the associating mind is free. Of course, this kind of a picture has its "dispositio" (that has been a requisite since antiquity). However, here the composition is arranged in an empty space and its elements - the independent separate images - have no possibility of being translated into real space, but only into platonic space of non-reality. Therefore, a homogeneous perception of the composition is impossible. The perspectives that might be constructed to relate the objects - written signs, reliefs or architectual allusions - can only be imagined.

The second picture in this discussion proves, to a lesser extent, the inner disposition of the intended and the represented world, where the aesthetic reality is likely to fall apart and be destroyed. It is also signed twice with the usual signature and the above mentioned inscription "RomAmor" - a symmetrical permutation of the word from the first picture.

But this lithograph develops a totally different composition that limits the freedom of the creative, reflective critic. The 'decentralizing' composition changes to a 'stratigraphical' one. The integration of the separate images into one complete picture is accomplished by layering the images on top of one another. It is possible to distinguish five, more or less distinct, horizontal units of different subject, material, structure, color and hue. At the bottom of the picture is a Roman landscape – a sketch of a city with towers surrounded by nature, vanishes into the back. In the direct foreground the inevitable palm tree is shown close-up, its black and green colors a strong contrast to the beige color of the sky.

Again, a kind of black-green wall stops the landscape at the bottom of the picture; it has a homogeneous texture and hangs like a curtain of rain. At the top, the wall dissolves into light green waves and draperies that have a rhythmical structure. This structure continues upward in a wave-like motion until it is again transformed into a vertically shaped wall that is as light as fabric and is folded on the left. Again this wall is stopped at the right by a dark penetrating green wall of triangular patterns.

There are five levels which refer to different subjects; their connection must be determined by the creative, reflective critic: the painter and the viewer.

Finally, the third picture by Bruni shows a parade of cardinals and bishops and is entitled, "Concilio ecumenico." Again, it shows a different arrangement of objects. Unlike the 'decentralizing' and 'stratigraphical' compositions previously discussed, we now have a composition of parallel perspective that condenses the objects into the lower right corner of the picture. At the right, an endless number of clergymen, inducted by two figures with half-dead faces, are imperceptibly replaced by the symbols of the purple hat. This takes place in front of a few bare walls that appear empty like catacombs. Often in Bruni's pictures we find extremely compact image areas, compressed into one corner of the picture. In this example, the cardinals stay to themselves.

It seems to me that as we consider the possible compositional types, the preconscious origin of art becomes apparent. It is not a question of copying images, but rather that images and ideals are created for possible perception. Everything that seems to be experimental and temporary in those lithographs, turns out to be a symbol. In any case, the representation itself is most important, even if it cannot fully represent the subject. The subject can only be represented by an interpretation, introduced in the composition.

Nietzsche, who anticipated modern aesthetics more than any other philosophical writer of the 19th century, referred to the idea of the semiotic origin of art in his essay, "Happy Science" (261): "What is originality? something that does not yet have a name, that cannot be called, even though it is right in front of everybody's eyes. This is how human beings usually are: only a name makes a thing apparent at all. Original people are generally the ones who give the names." Bruni's conceptual compositions divide into two distinctive cases: The 'growing' and the 'being' types of composition. "Cardinals" is a 'growing' style composition in which the picture is filled from one corner, as from a spring. (According to this definition, all perspective compositions may be termed 'growing'.) The picture signed with "RomAmoR" is a 'being' composition, for the distribution of the colors, shapes and objects coexists stratigraphically.

Aside from these compositional questions that nowadays form an important part of informational aesthetics, there is another subject not specifically expressed in these lithograhs. It concerns the reality, theme, and mode of the aesthetic. It is apparent that an artistically-created aesthetic reality cannot, in fact, imply a continuity, because it is characterized and created by selection and coordination. To the contrary, it can only be perceived as a manifold 'discontinuum.' Nature may be understood as a continuous sequence of contained causality. The nature of art represents an open system with gaps, frames, borders, empty spaces, jumps and coincidences. It is a system of created meaning both chosen and combined, of objects with one condition: they have to be compatible and coherent so that the 'discontinuum' does not fall apart, for it is only held together through the coordination of the inherent critic, the painter.

Here, I close my description and discussion of three lithographs in Bruno Bruni's already extensive work. It seems to me that today the analysis of the theoretic mind involved in artistic work is more important than the mere hermeneutic explanation. I have attempted to prove this by a stringent analysis in my essay about Bruno Bruni's lithographs.

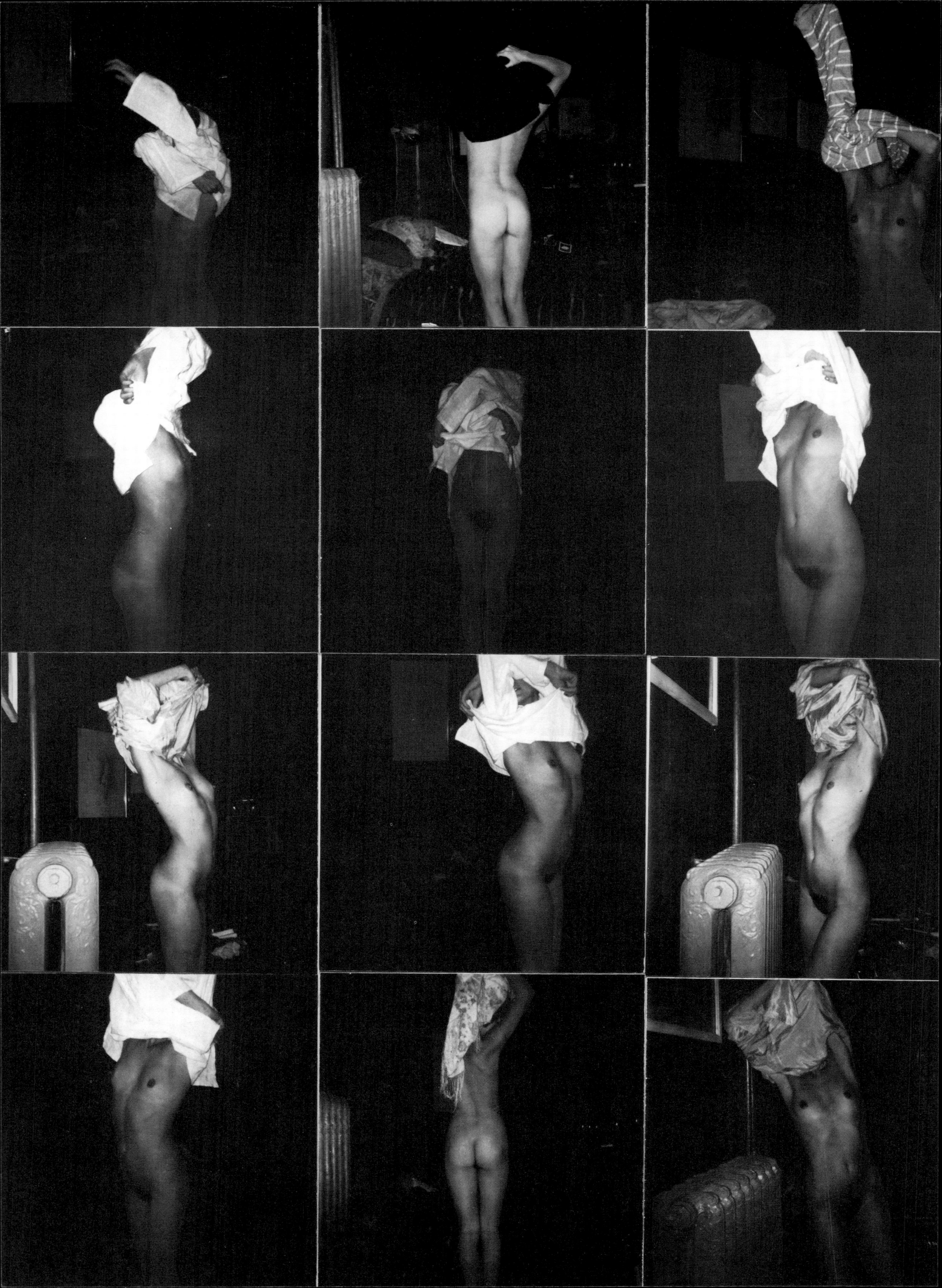

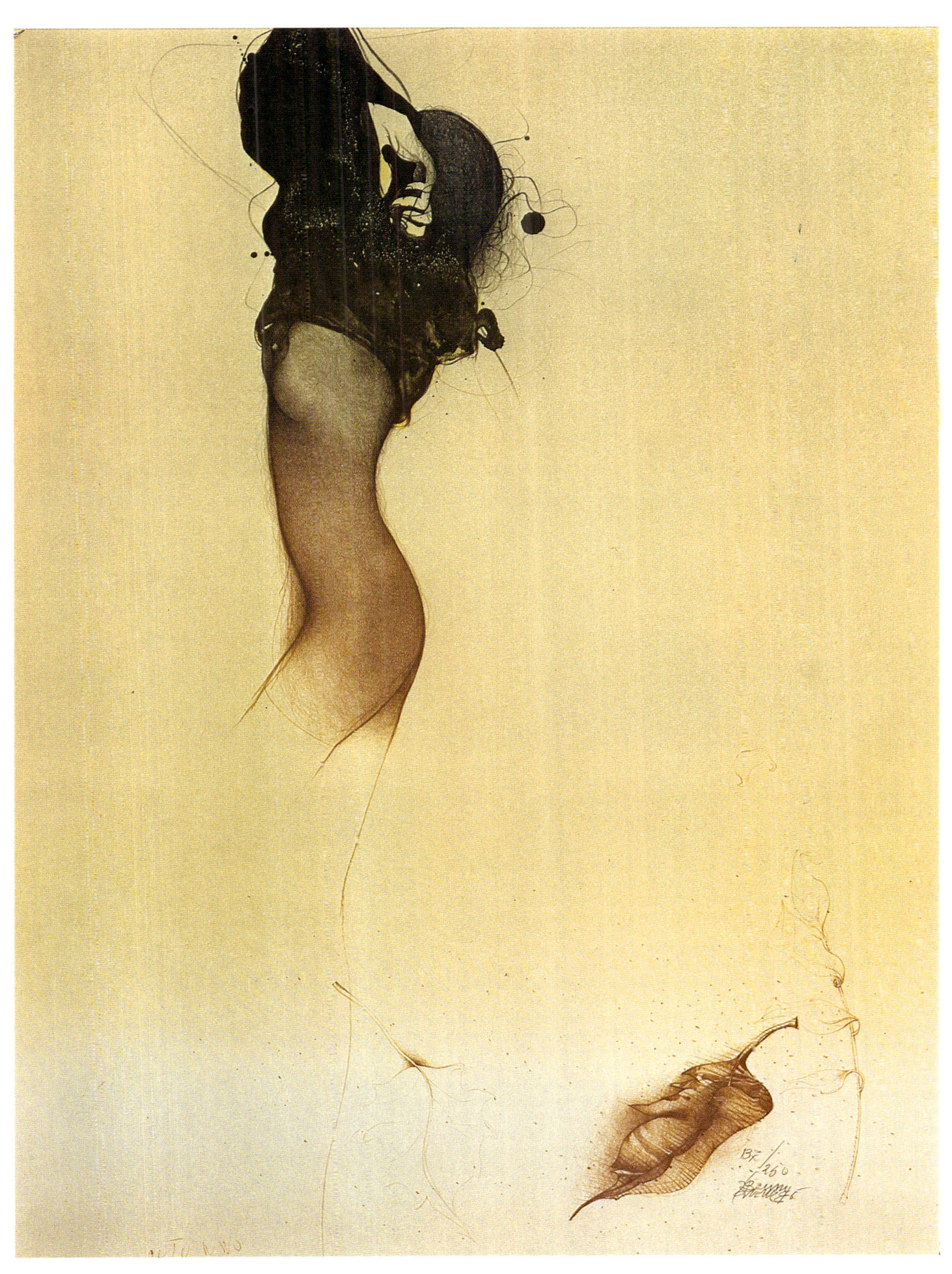

"Autunno" 1976
lithograph in three colours, 76x56 cm

◁ Working photos

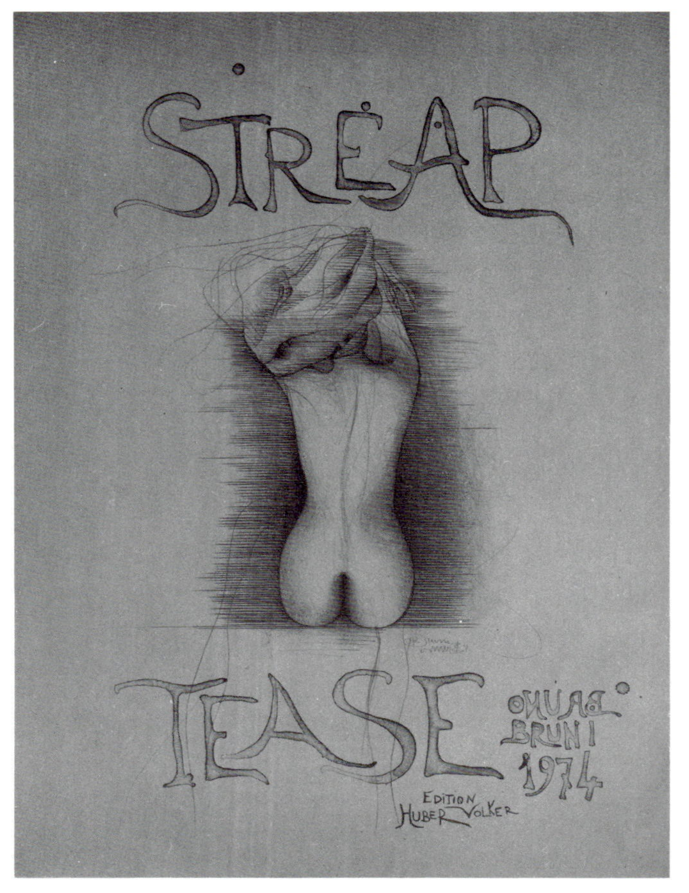

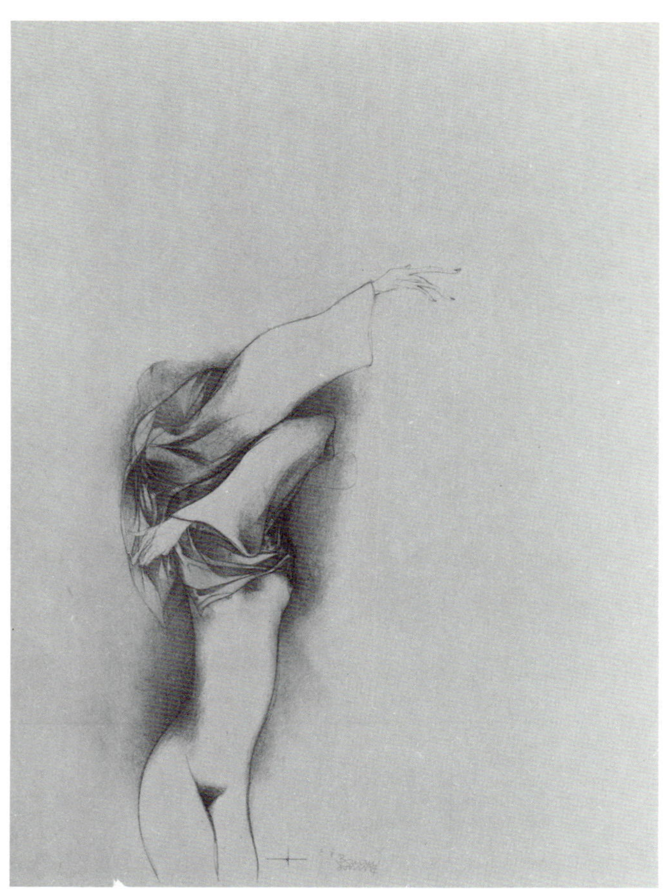

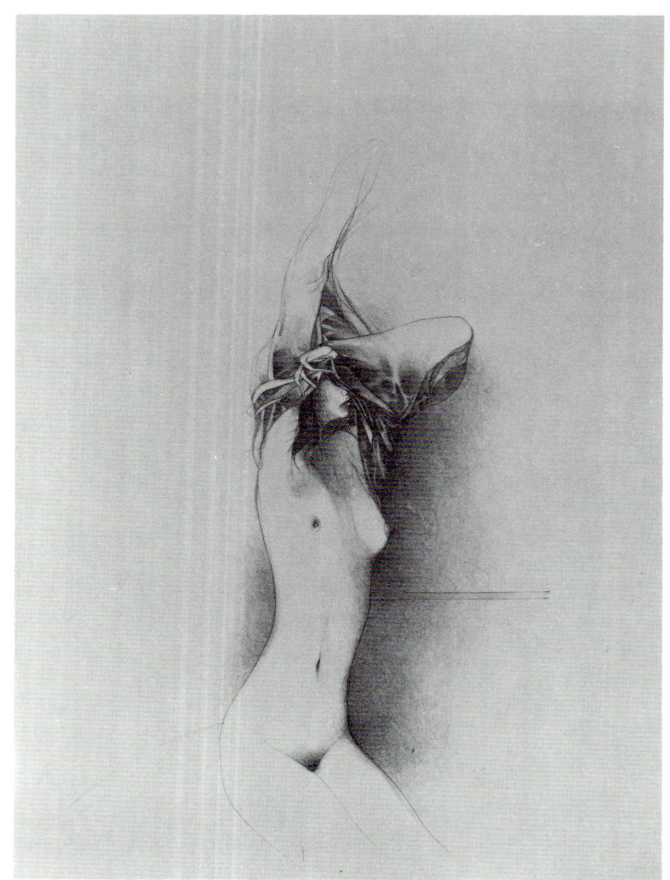

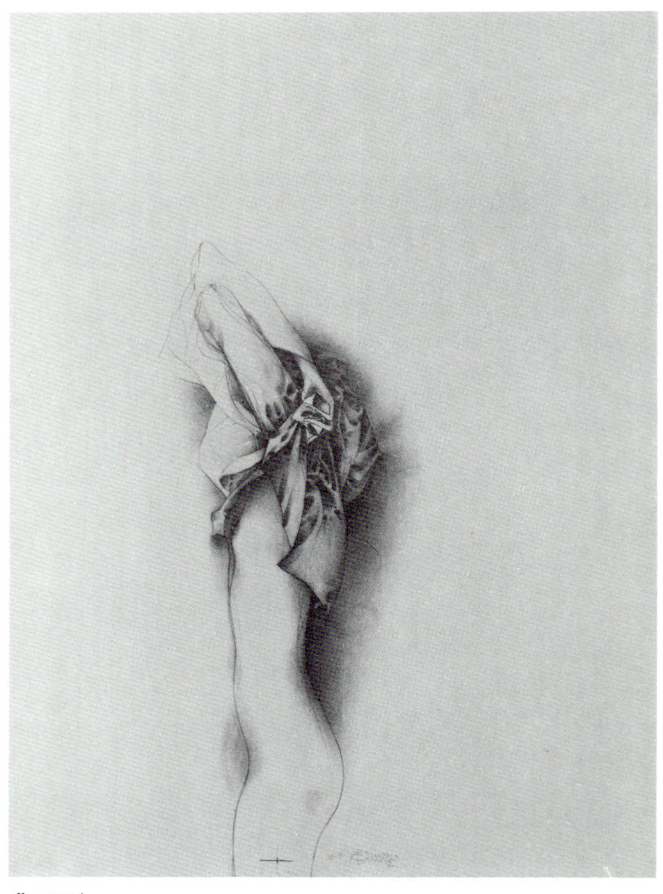

"Streap-Tease" 1974

portfolio with four coloured lithographs and one title page

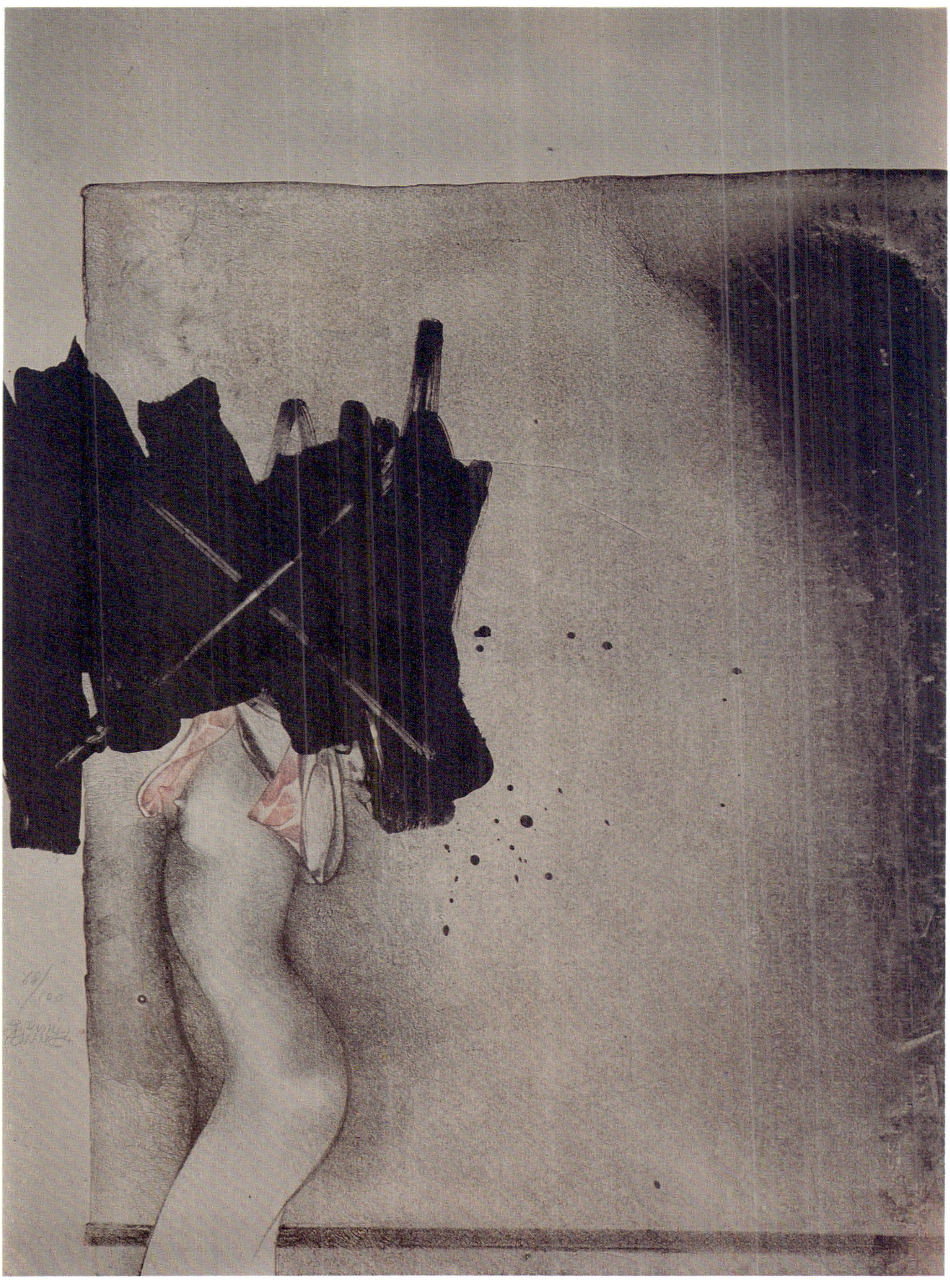

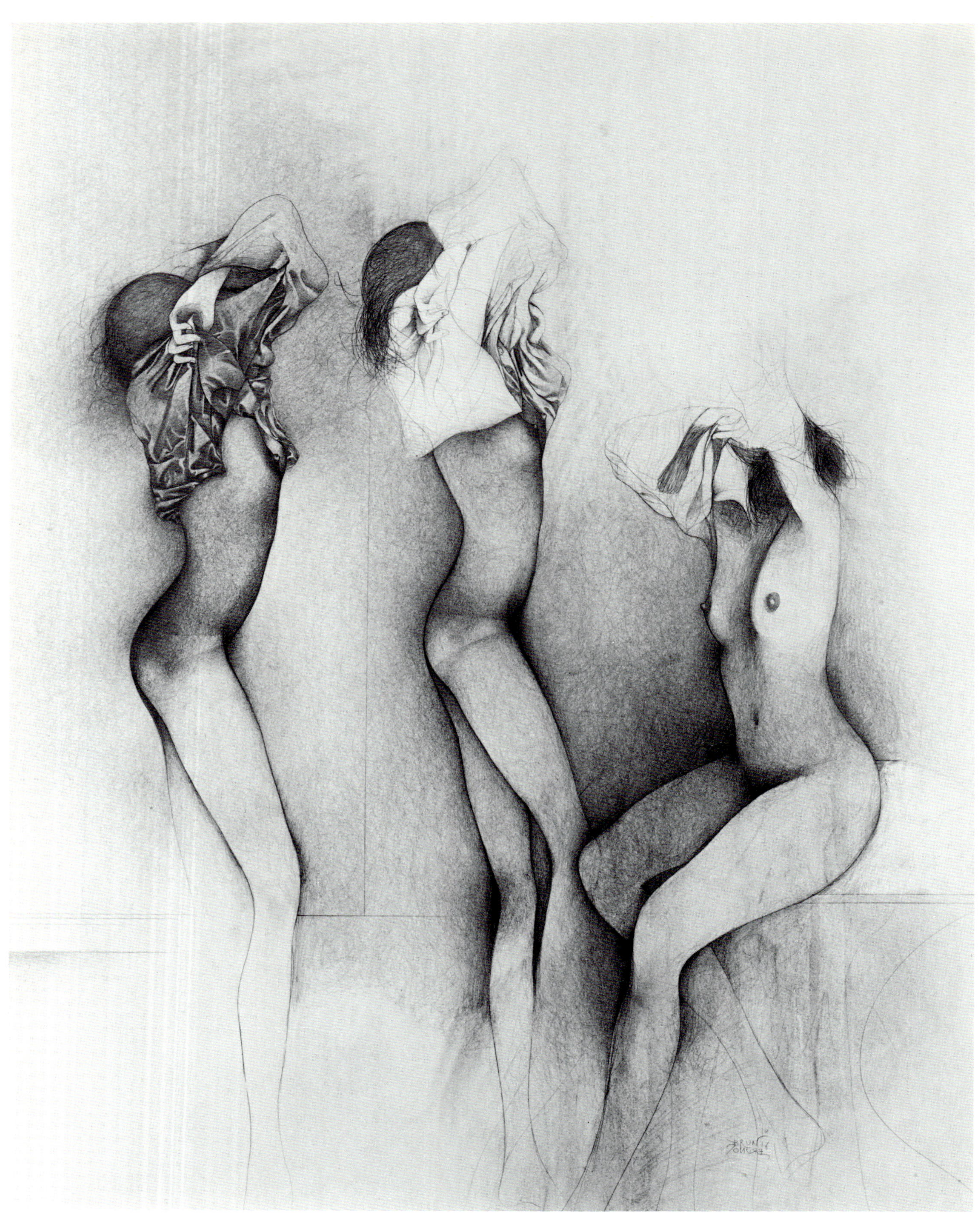

"Drei Figuren" 1976, *pencil drawing, 98x79 cm*

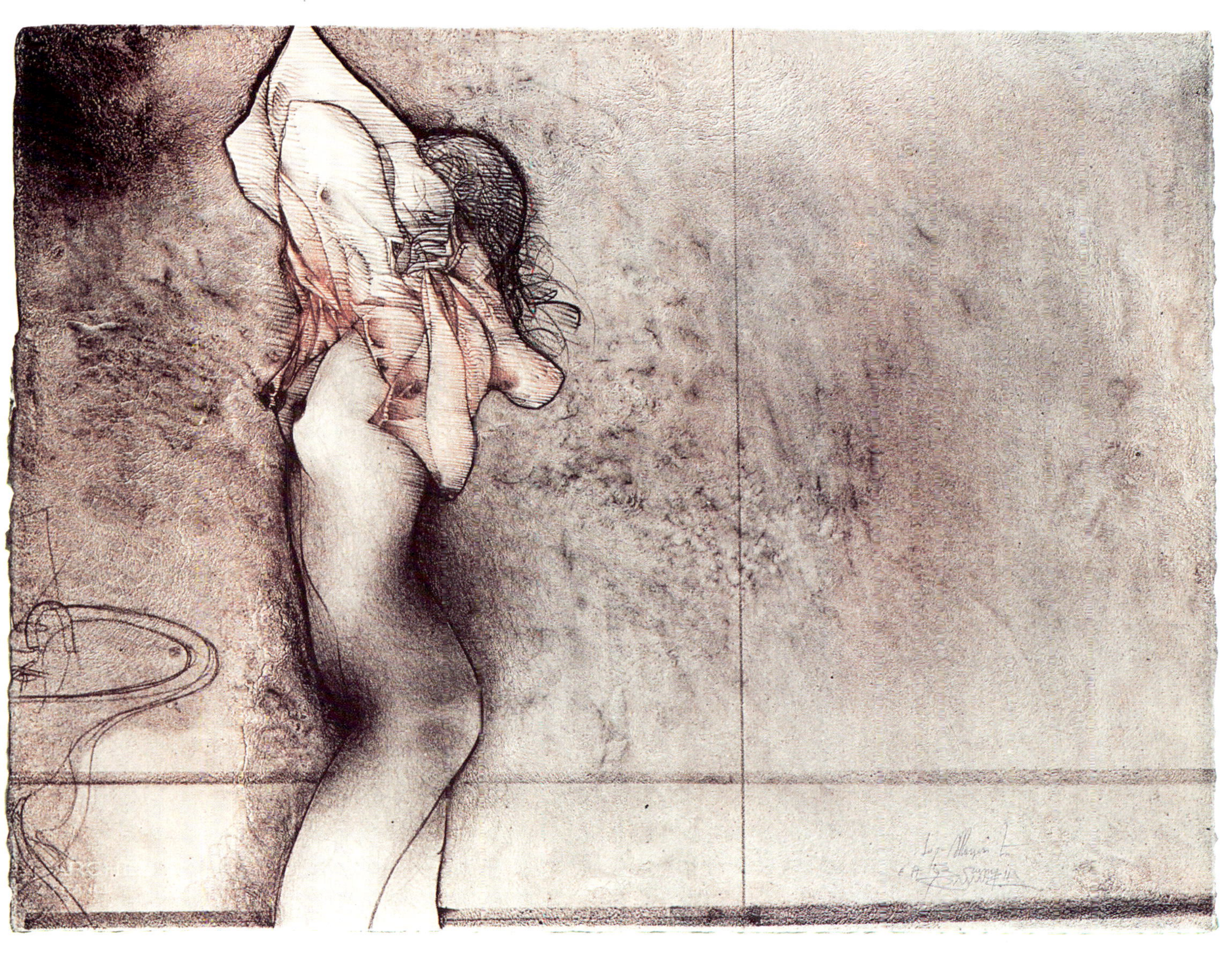

"Nella Stanza" 1974
lithograph in three colours, 51x65.5 cm

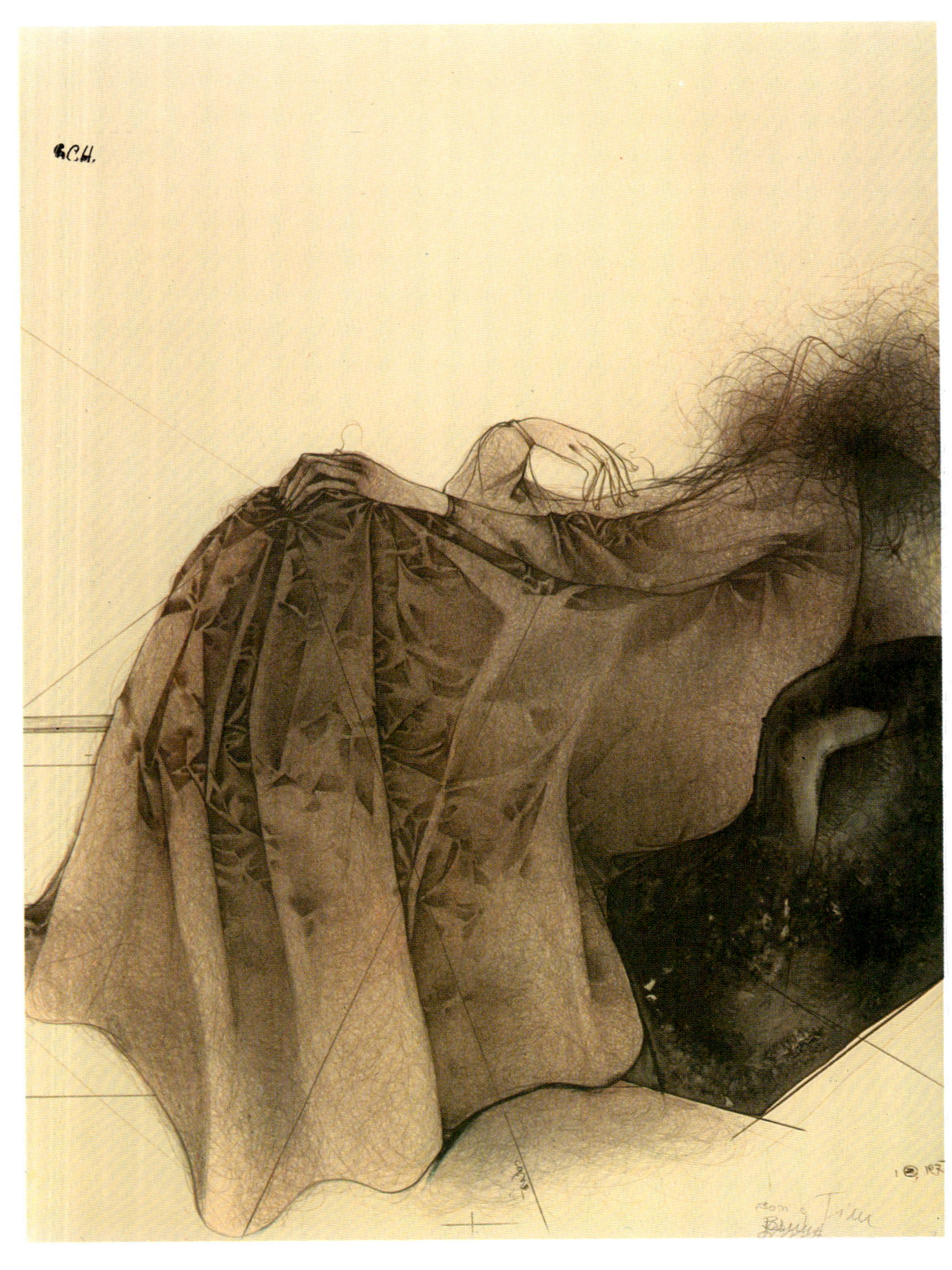

"Nachbarin! Euer Fläschchen!" 1975
lithograph in four colours, 76x56 cm

"Donna che ride" 1975, *gouache, 109x80 cm* ▷

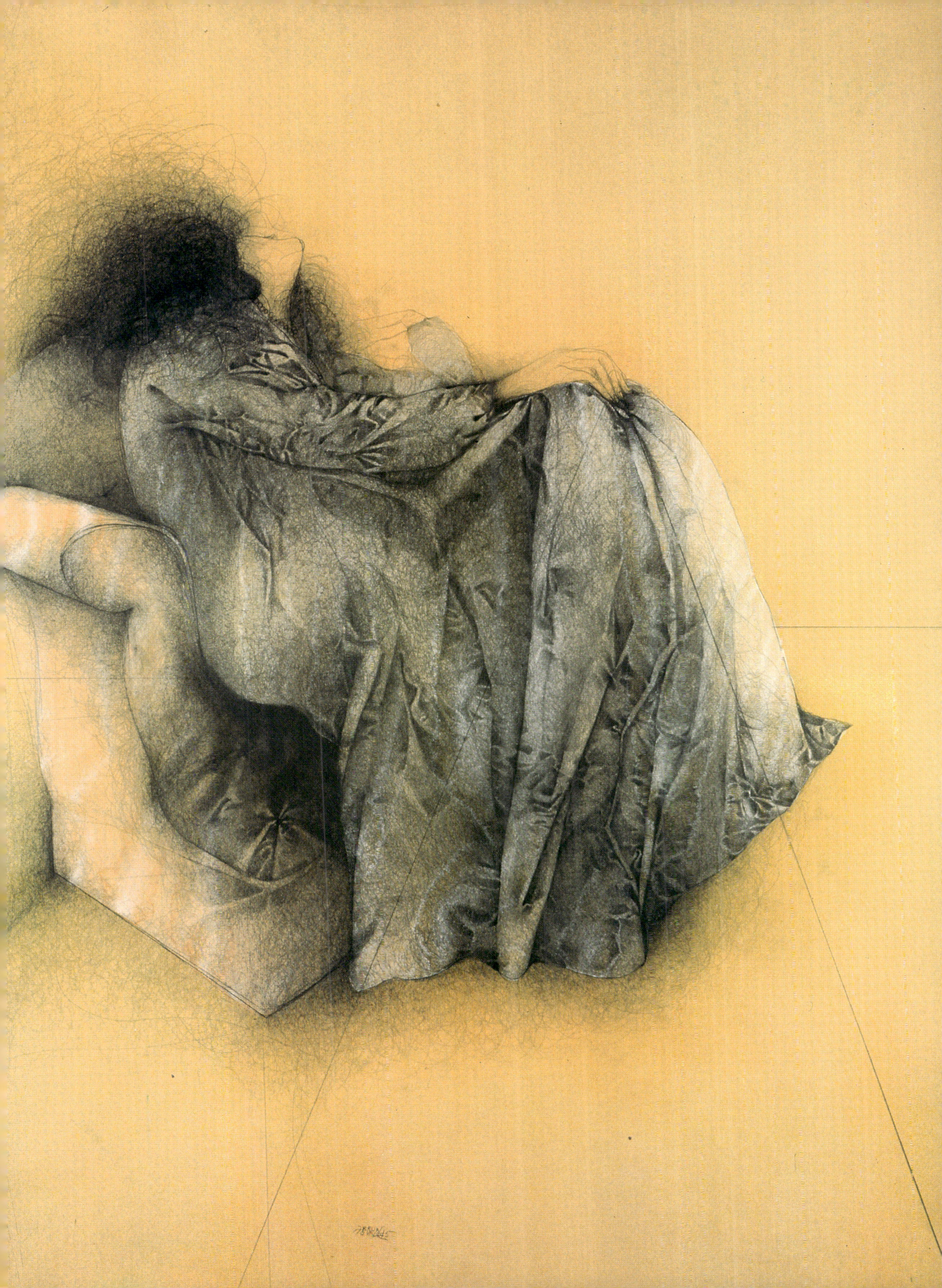

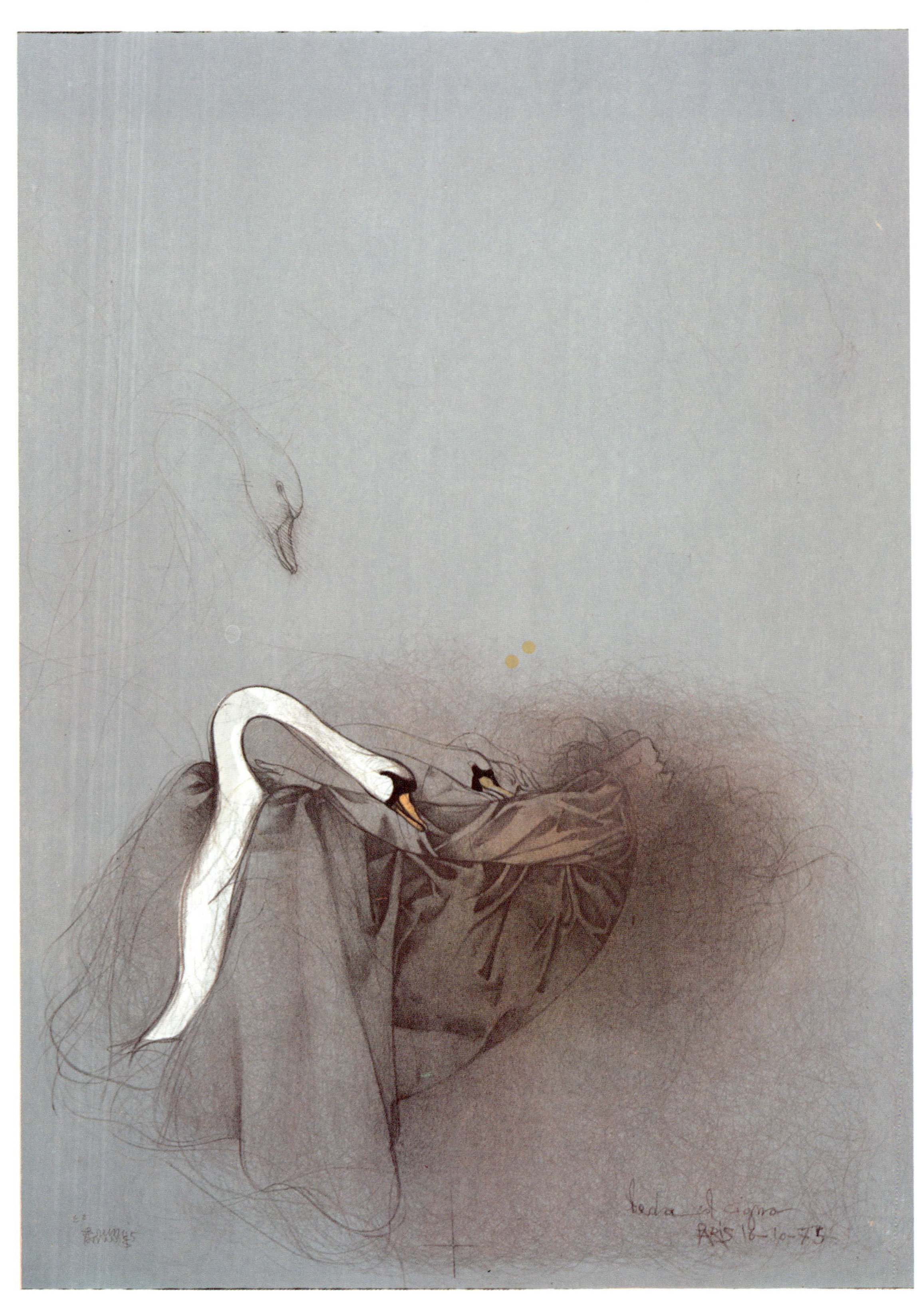

"Leda col cigno" 1975
lithograph in four colours, 76x56 cm

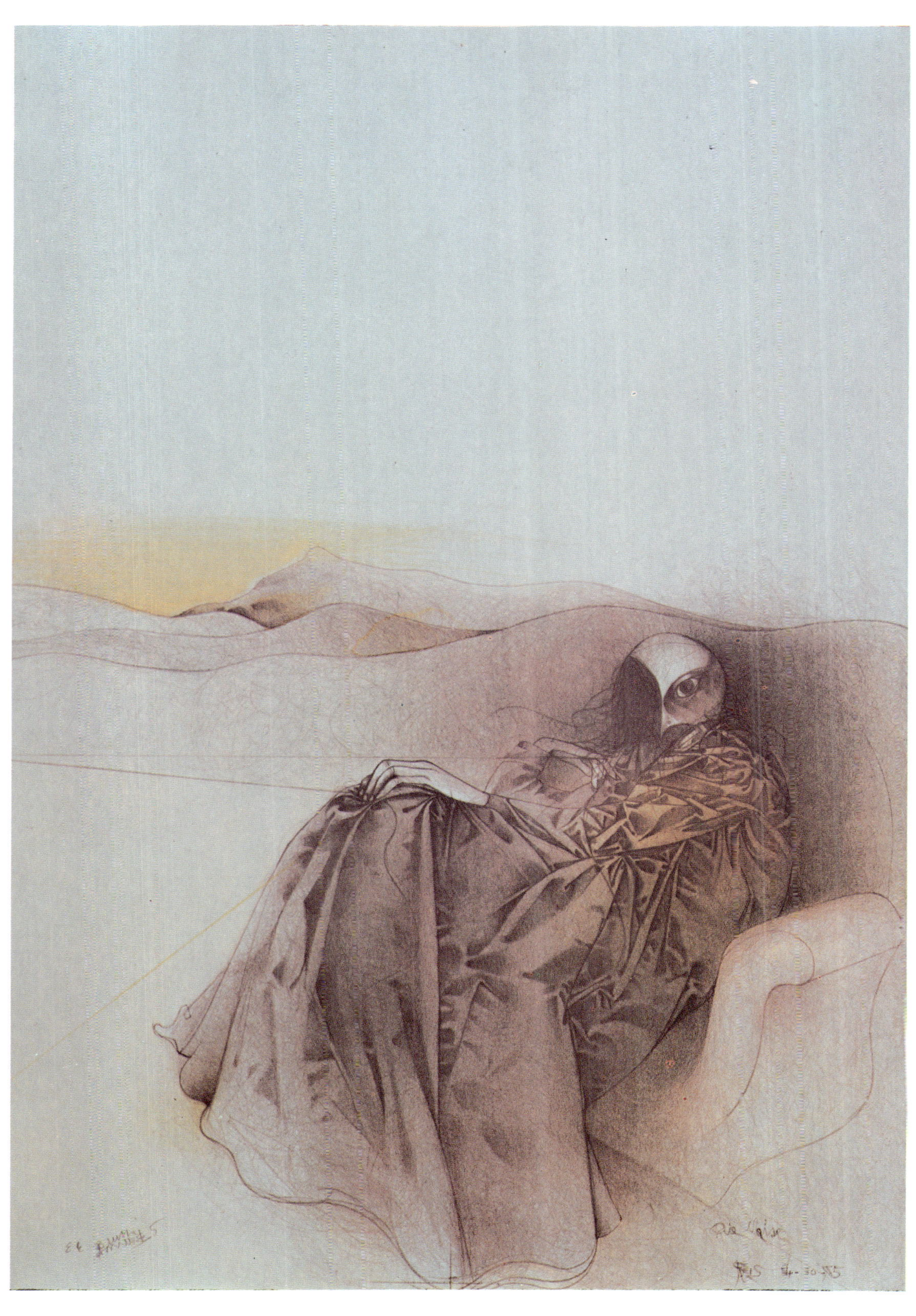

"Die Weise" 1975
lithograph in four colours, 76x56 cm

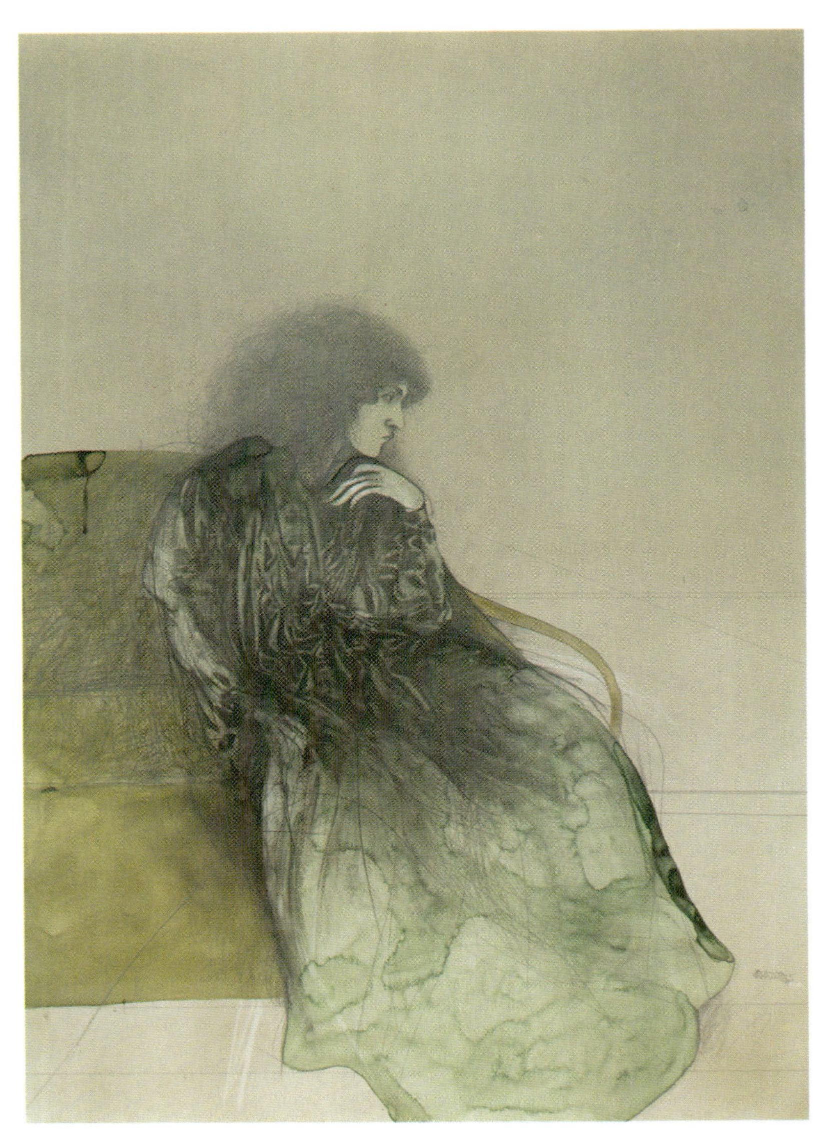

"A Rossetti" 1975, *gouache, 95x70 cm*

Dieter Hoffmann

The "Déjàvu" of the lying Woman

Looking at Bruno Bruni's compositions of reclining women, we see, simultaneously, paintings of women from several centuries. The earliest may be Giorgione's "Venus" (Dresden), a painting of absolute calm, beauty and mystery.

Titian adapted Giorgione's "Venus" by adding the little figure of Cupid holding a bird in his hand. Later, in Titian's "Venus of Urbino," we see a more informal interpretation of Venus, with greater emphasis on her accessories and coquettish expressions. The jewelry on her naked skin and the little dog form a striking contrast to the two elaborately dressed women in the background. Looking at one of the women who is kneeling and busy arranging a trunk, it is unclear whether she is looking for clothes for her mistress or hiding a reward of love.

Giorgione's painting is one of idealized reality, made striking by the unexpected nudity of the reclining figure. While Giorgione's "Venus" may think she is not publically on display, she lies in the shelter of an interior setting that appears to us to be quite public. Suggested here are some of those qualities that, centuries later, were so shocking in Manet's famous painting, "Déjeuner sur l'herbe": the possibility of discovery. The artist arouses our curiosity further by transferring us into that background space, thereby exposing the nude to glances from all sides. The exciting contrast of nudity and civilized surroundings was surpassed in the nineteenth century by Manet who exaggerated the tension by introducing solemn feasting guests, dressed black.

This same subject has been even more provocatively explored in the twentieth century by Paul Delvaux who arranged his nudes in a series of ghost-like streetcar depots and railway stations. At the turn of the century, Henri Rousseau dreamed of his primitive nude 'Jadwiga' on a red velvet couch

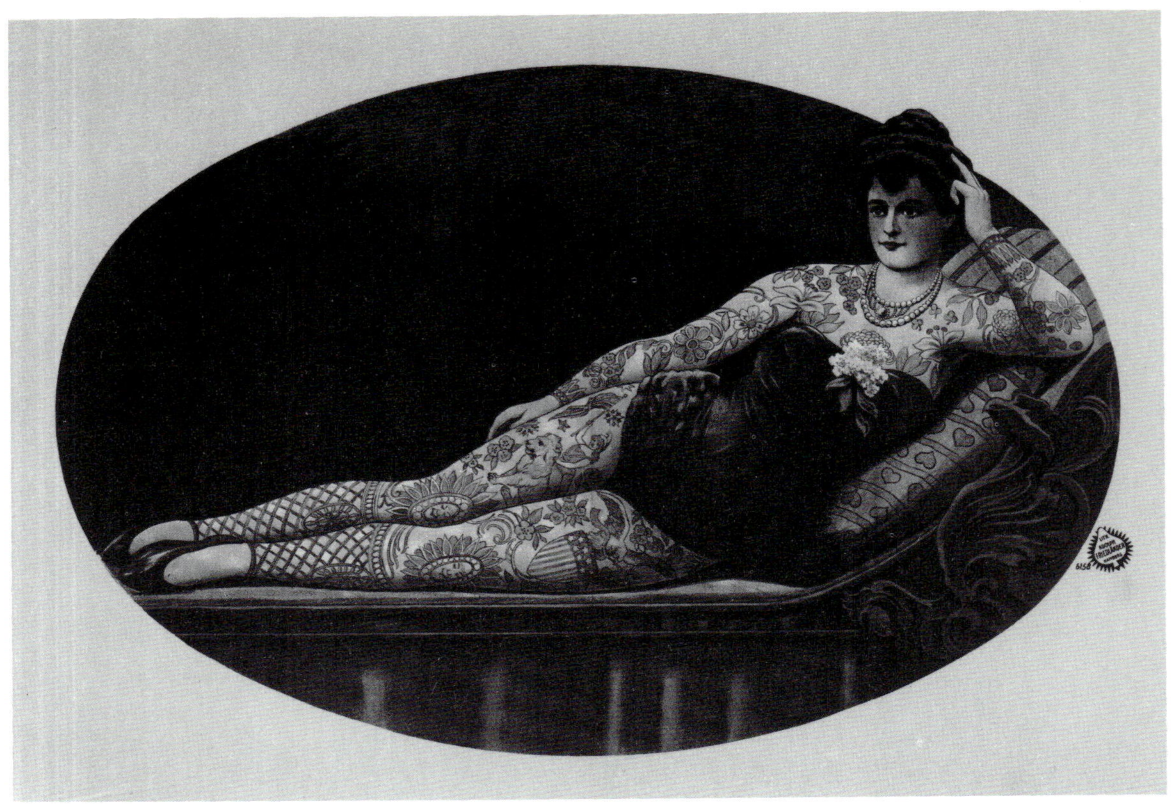

8

in the midst of a jungle setting. David's "Madame Récamier" appears as frozen in her Triclinium position as in a dead language; Rousseau, thawed her somewhat by placing her in a rare jungle of the senses. A similar theme is found in 19th century circus posters which often featured a woman as 'lion tamer' reclining in the salon, tent or show-booth and surrounded by roaring lions. Another circus performer, tattooed, reclines in an oval – the picture itself becomes the eye of the spectator.

The most extraordinary aspect of Giorgione's painting is the fluid harmony of the figure in a landscape setting that echoes the undulating motion of nature. Interestingly, three centuries later, the French surrealist, Paul Eluard, wrote a beautiful poem, comparing the landscape to a woman and a woman to the landscape.

The Venus paintings of later centuries are not as silent as Giorgione's and Delvaux'; their gestures are more flamboyant. Consider Goya's naked and dressed Maja and Beckmann's reclining woman, who suggests the sensuality of orgasm. But we can find no indication in these paintings of the liberation of the human soul or ability to coexist. To the contrary, "Odalisque" by Ingres shows the frozen figure of a prostitute whose fan suggests the dominant attitude of a peacock: the fan interrupts the lines around her vagina in a striking way, like a painful coitus interuptus. In Maerten van Heemskerck's painting "Venus and Cupid" (1545), Venus appears as a hermaphrodite. Unlike the cold and calculating Odalisque of Jean-Dominique Ingres or Canova's

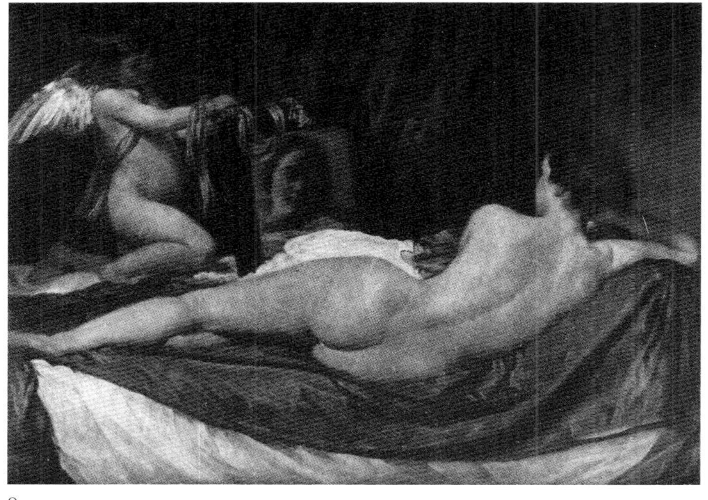

9

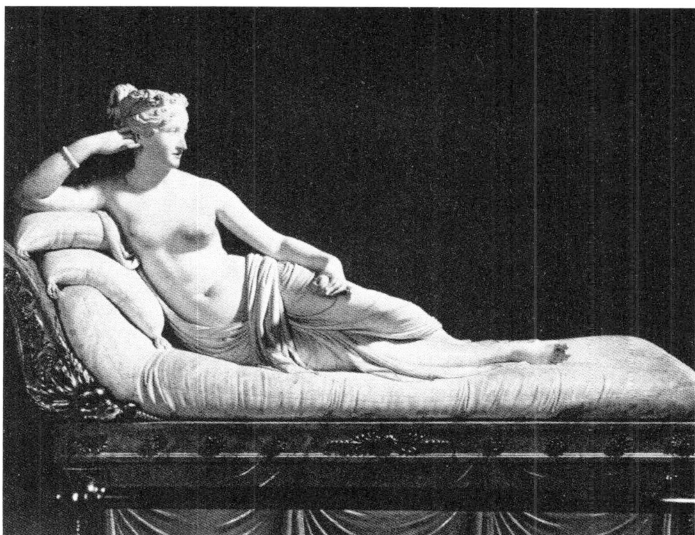

10

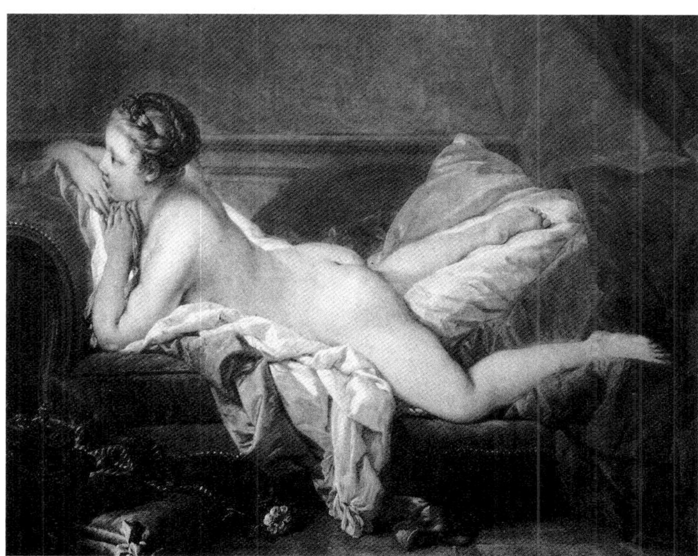

11

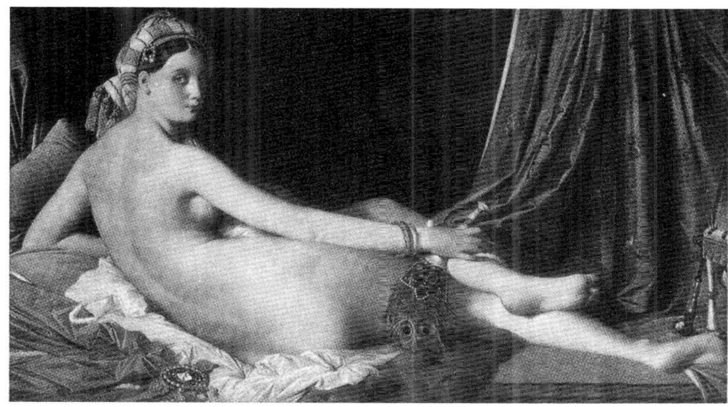

12

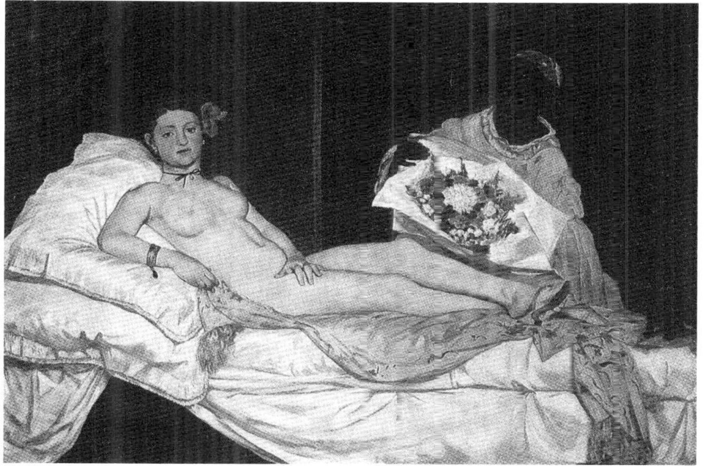

13

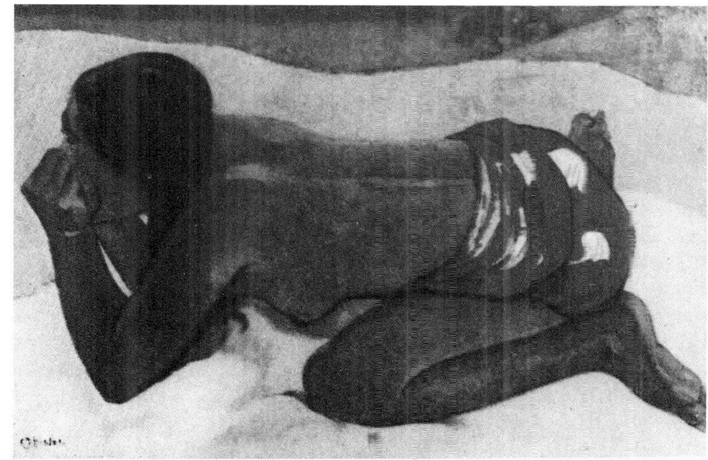

14

8 Anonymus 1913 “Tattooed Woman” circus poster
9 Diego Velasquez “Venus in Front of a Mirror”
10 Antonio Canova, “Paolina Borghese”
11 François Boucher “Resting Girl”
12 Dominique Ingres, “Odalisque”
13 Edouard Manet “Olympia”
14 Paul Gauguin “Otahi”

snow-white marble sculpture of Paolina Bonaparte in the Palazzo Borghese, Rome, van Heemskerck's merely suggests a cold disposition. Picasso learned from Ingres when he wanted to cool off. Bruno Bruni also adapted images from Ingres' paintings; he also paraphrases Boucher i. e. the painting of the fifteen-year-old mistress of Louis XV incitingly riding her pillow. This 'Resting Girl' of Rokoko, Louise O'Murphy is also masturbating. (No wonder she prefers a soft pillow to the embrace of a weak king).

In contrast to Boucher's women, Paul Gaugin's figure of "Otahi" squats lasciviously on a South Sea beach. Gaugin's art had a great impact on the Expressionists. In succession the Dresdner artist Schmidt-Kirstein variates this theme sublimely.

The Klimt women of the turn-of-the-century present entirely new images – shivering and nervous, the absolute clitoral-orgastic type. But while the Klimt women prefer 'amour solitaire,' their solitude is somewhat reduced by the implied presence of the 'voyeur,' the art lover, the artificial friend.

One famous woodcut by Albrecht Dürer that illustrates the 16th century theory of proportions shows how the artist studies the nude model in order to fix her features on paper: on the left side of the composition we see the woman, on the right side the painter who, using his pencil instead of his penis, executes a work of art instead of intercourse. The two figures are separated by a wall that allows us to judge the precision of the perspective drawing. Here, artistic and scientific curiosity become interrelated.

Vélasquez accomplished an extraordinary example of 'Voyeurism' in his noble yet detached painting, "Venus in Front of a Mirror," which pictures a woman viewed from the back, looking into a mirror held by a putto and which reveals only a part of her face. Curiously, we cannot see her vagina, even though it should be visible judging from the angle in which the mirror is held.

Dutch Baroque painting is more natural and earthy than the Spanish Baroque. For instance, Rembrandt's "Danäe" is showered by a gold rain – a mythological allusion that refers to the clitoral orgasm. This strong painting is followed by "Female Nude in Bed" (1895) by Lovis Corinth, Reinhold Ewald's "Lying Woman in a Green Bathing Suit" (1930), as well as by Maillol's sculpture, "The Wave." Even Titian's early painting of "Danäe" is full of movement – the gold rain is the incarnation of Jupiter who was a potent sexual symbol. The voluptuous nymph in the painting, "Nymph and Shepend Woman" does not hesitate to touch herself between the legs, while the shepherd, nearby, holds onto his flute. "Venus and the Organ Player" is an unusual painting. Here, Ottavio Farnese plays the organ outdoor with his back turned to his bored lover who plays with her dog. He has his art and she, the animal, but they do not have each other. The alienation of this couple is emphasized by the background park landscape which repeats the rhythmic parade of organ pipes in the series of trees that line the park. In our century,

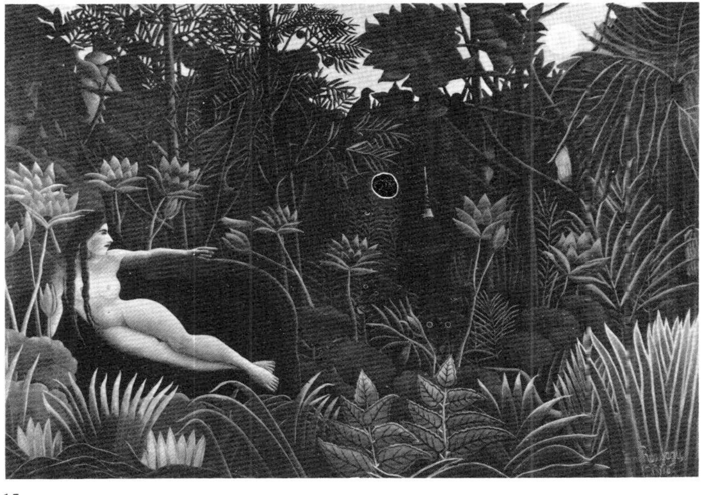

15

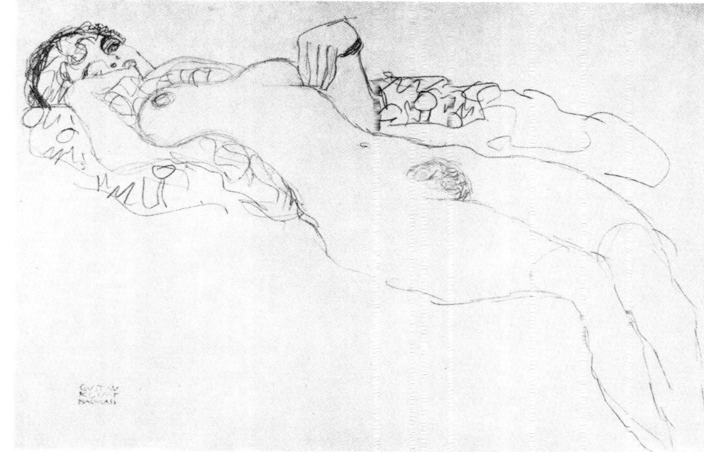

18

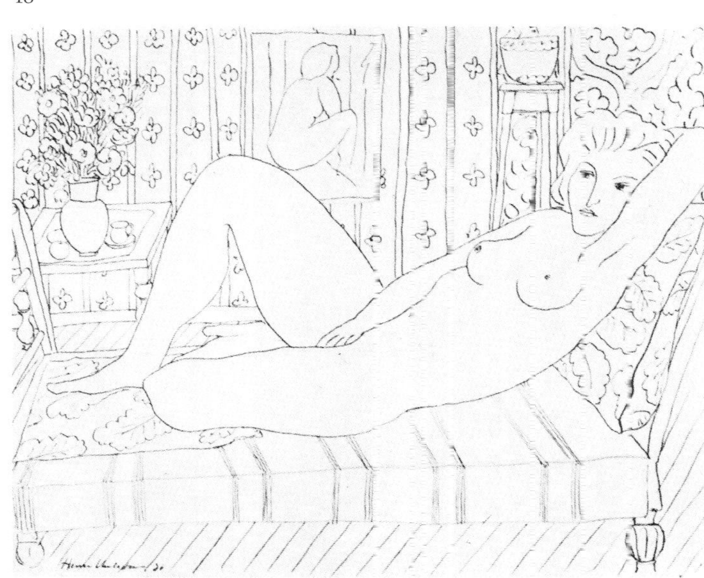

19

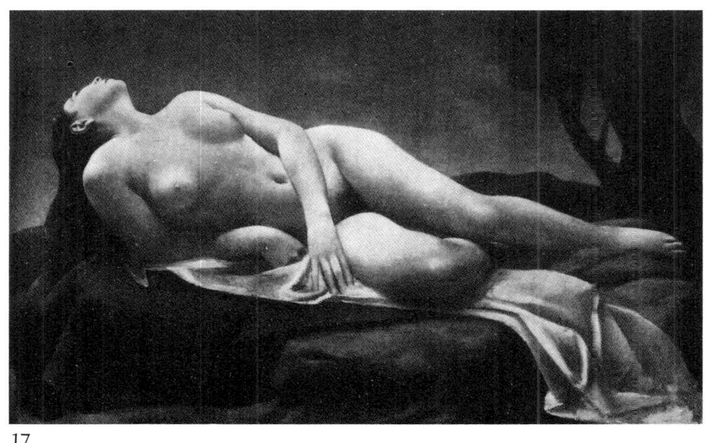

16

17

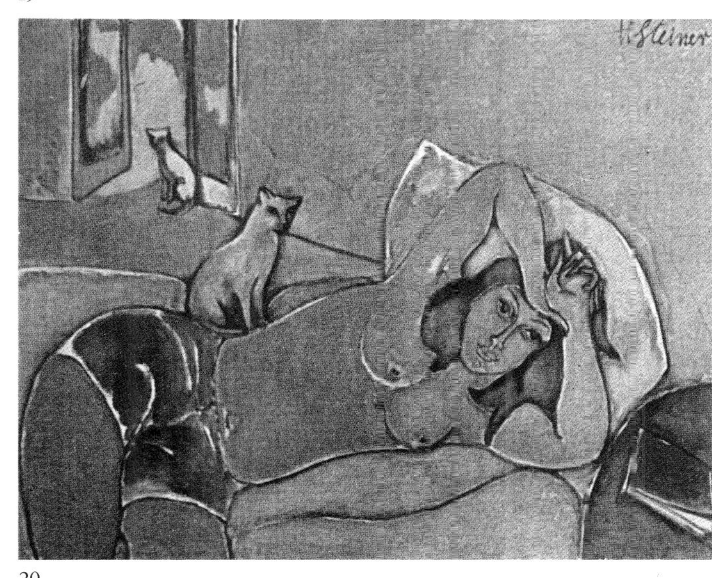

20

15 Henri Rousseau "Jadwiga"
16 Amadeo Modigliani "Nude on a White Pillow"
17 Ubaldo Oppi "Study to Jephtas Daughter"
18 Gustav Klimt "Reclining Nude to the Left"
19 Henri Matisse "Reclining Nude"
20 Heinrich Steiner "Reclining Girl with Cat"

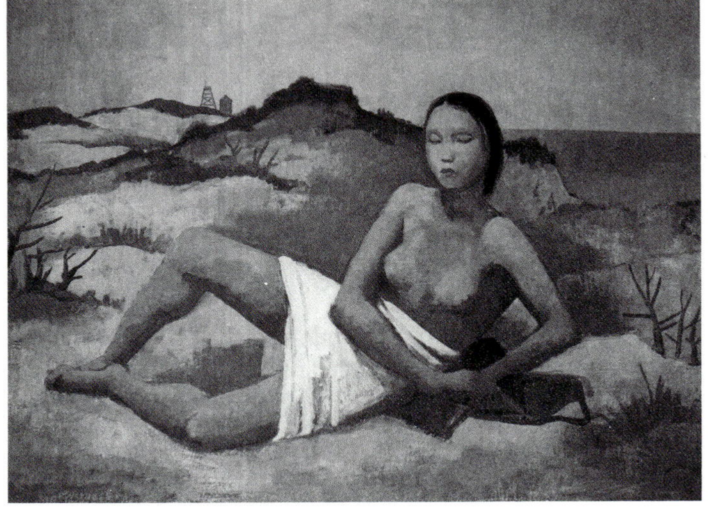

21

22

23

21 Carl Hofer “Girl in the Dunes”
22 Otto Dix “Woman on a Leopard-skin”
23 Paul Delvaux “Iron Age”
24 Max Beckmann “Sleeping Woman”
25 Max Ackermann “With Comb and Mirror”
26 Fernando Botero “Country Concert”

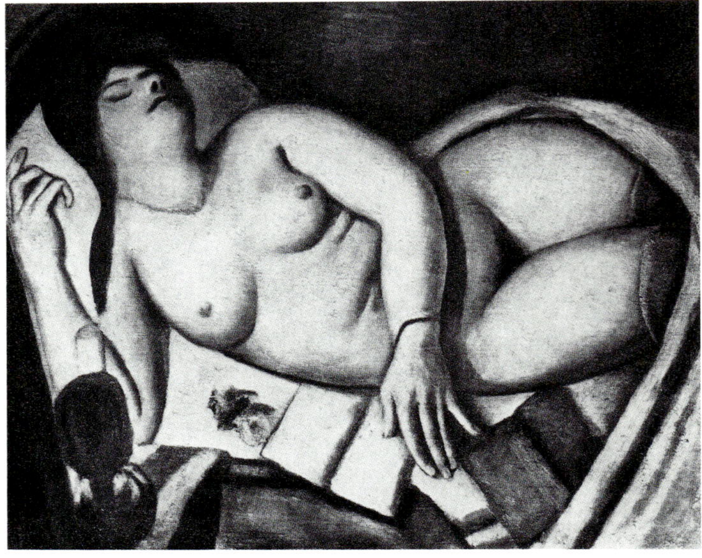

24

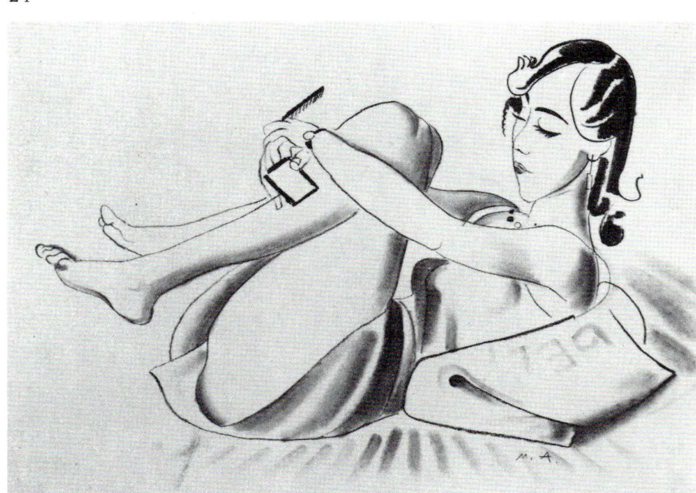

25

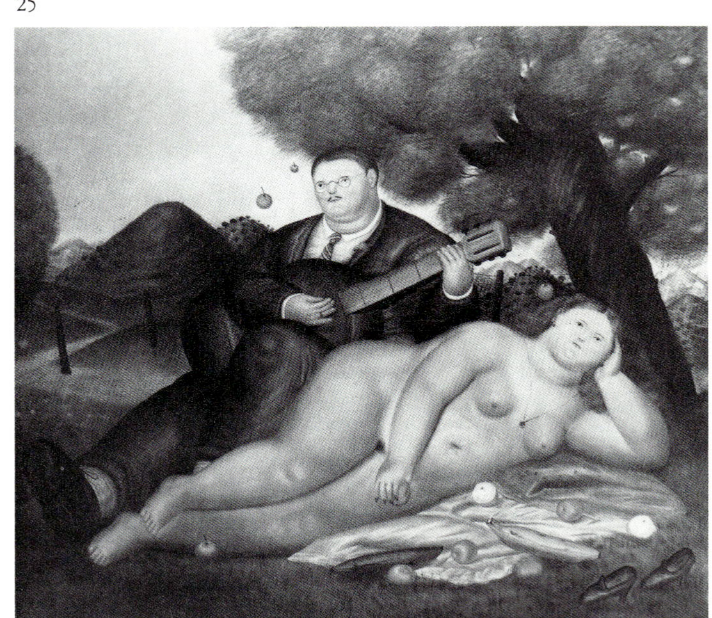

26

did Edvard Munch paint more alienated lovers than did Titian four hundred years before? The colors of the famous Venetian painter burn in desparate glory. Perhaps the sadness of the painting precluded a scandal in Titian's day . . . but then would the Renaissance ever have admitted a scandal?

Today, it is not so difficult to comprehend the indignation caused by Edouard Manet's "Olympia" of 1865. The painting is a paradox of the hypocritical idealized world of the old masters (even though Manet felt quite close to them). While the composer Jacques Offenbach successfully parodied the Olympia theme in his operetta, parody and humor were not accepted in the visual arts. In his painting, Manet shows us a maid (or little whore) named 'Olympia'. (Well, that always happens, lower class people often choose pretentious names.) She herself has a black maid, but then she can afford service. The girl is painted in a provocative manner. While the masturbating nudes of the Renaissance never appeared to be provocative, Olympia is: her hand doesn't play on her lap, it covers it; the window is open, but the box-office is closed. Such a realistic presentation implies a certain loss of humanity. Yet we are still a long way from the sloppy, fat women of Otto Dix who do not look for shelter or beauty, or from the fat figures of Fernando Botero.

Beautiful stylized drawings and paintings of women are seen in the work of many contemporary artists: Matisse, Modigliani, Felice Casorati, Ubaldo Oppi, Carl Hofer, Max Ackermann, Heinrich Steiner, Karolus Lodenkämper and Bruno Bruni. The reclining woman of Steiner wears only 'hot pants', Bruni's wears stockings. By showing these women only partially dressed – Manet's Olympia wears just a necklace and slippers – the artists accentuate certain parts of their anatomy. Of course, none of these beautiful women show any sense of emancipation; they are dolls, objects of desire, not so much for the man but for themselves.

"Liegende" 1977, *lithograph in three colours, 56×76 cm* ▷

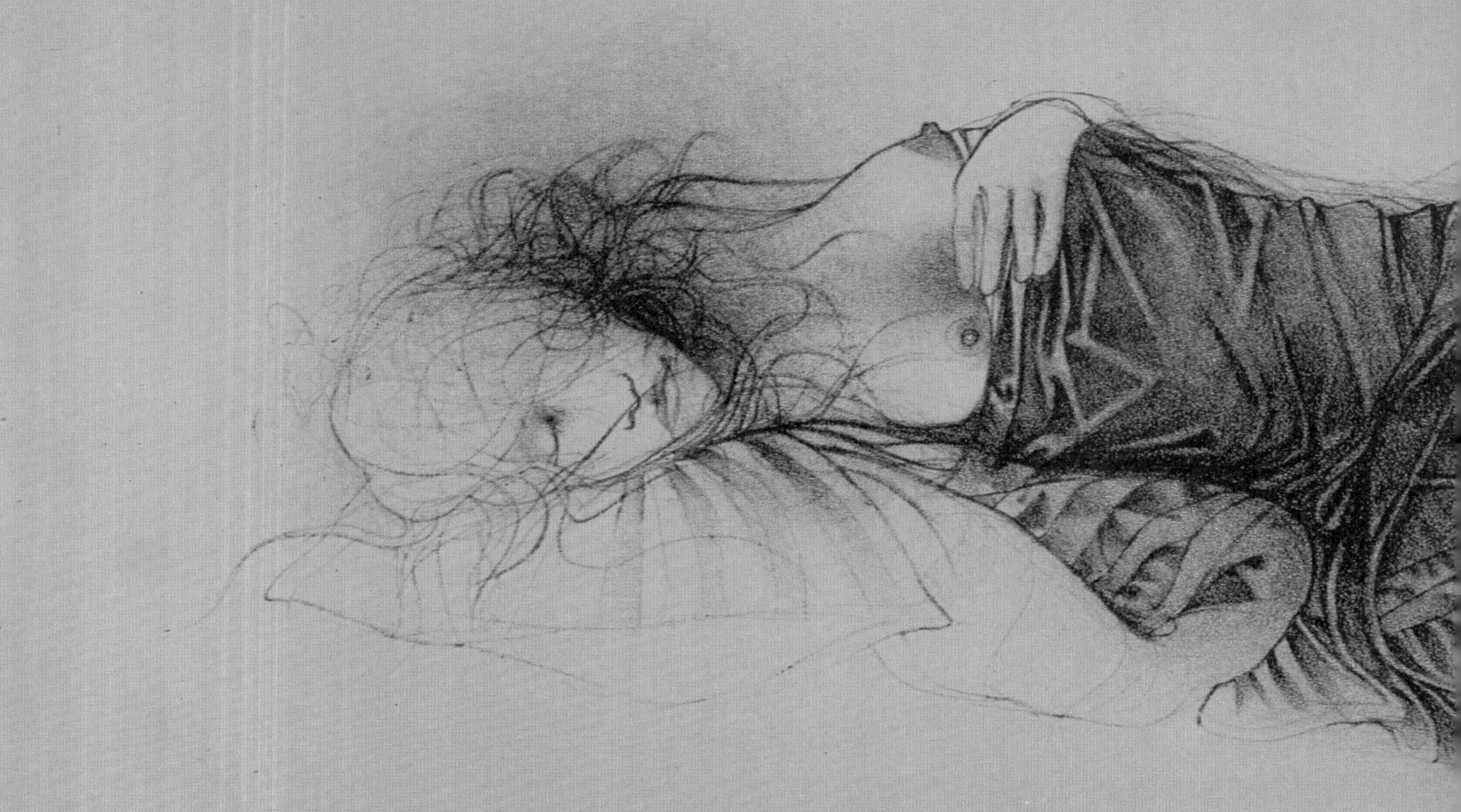

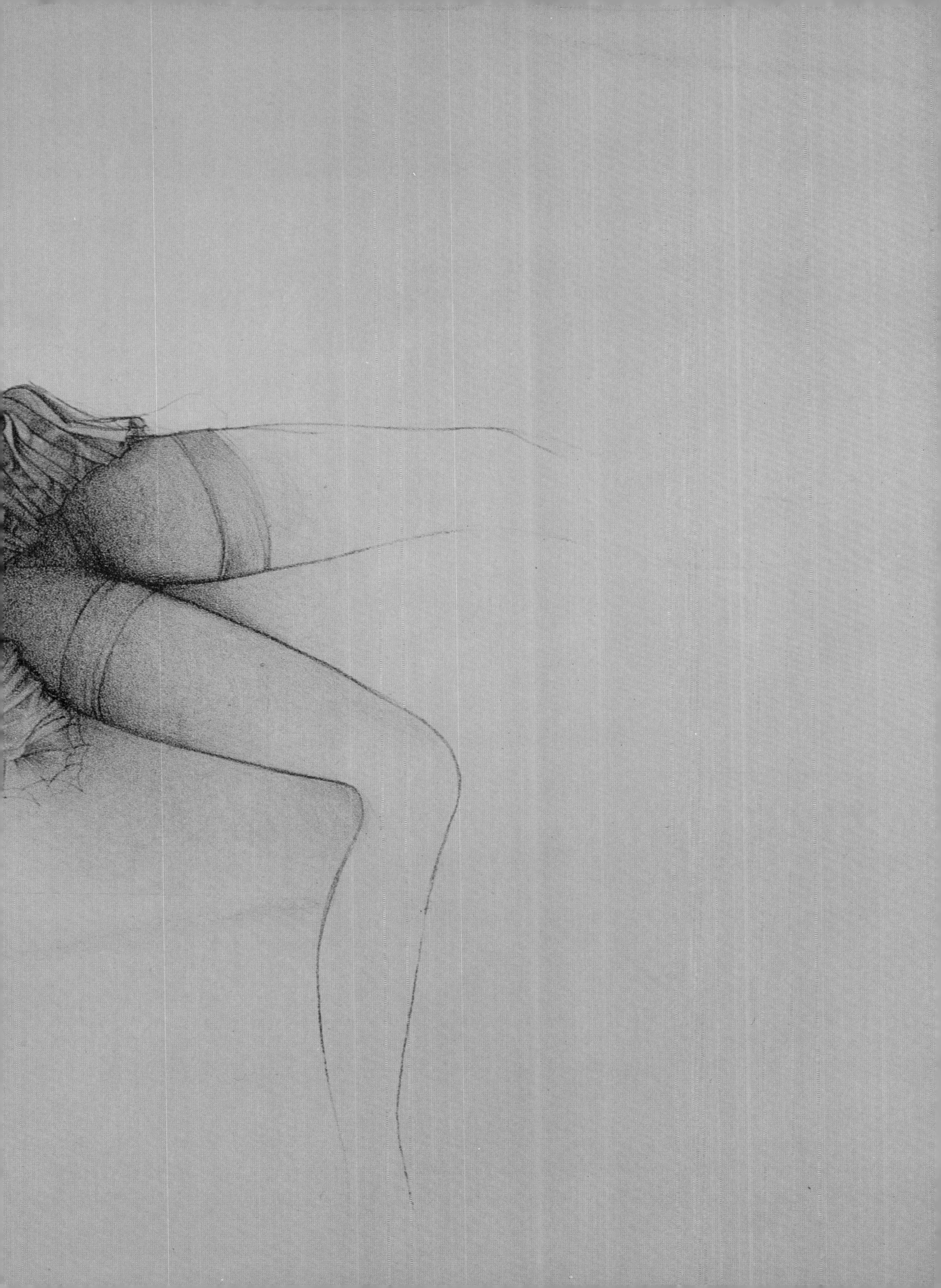

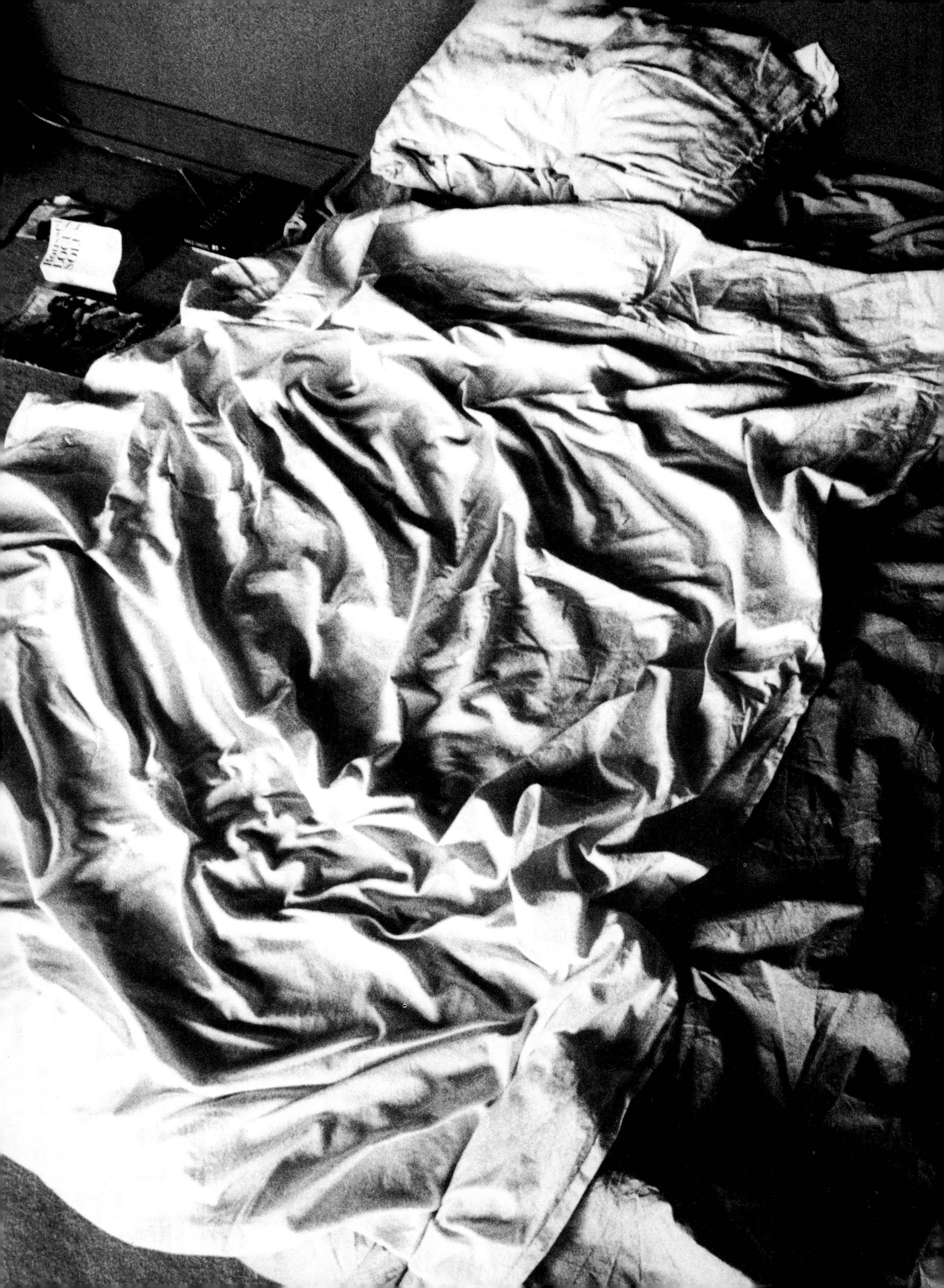

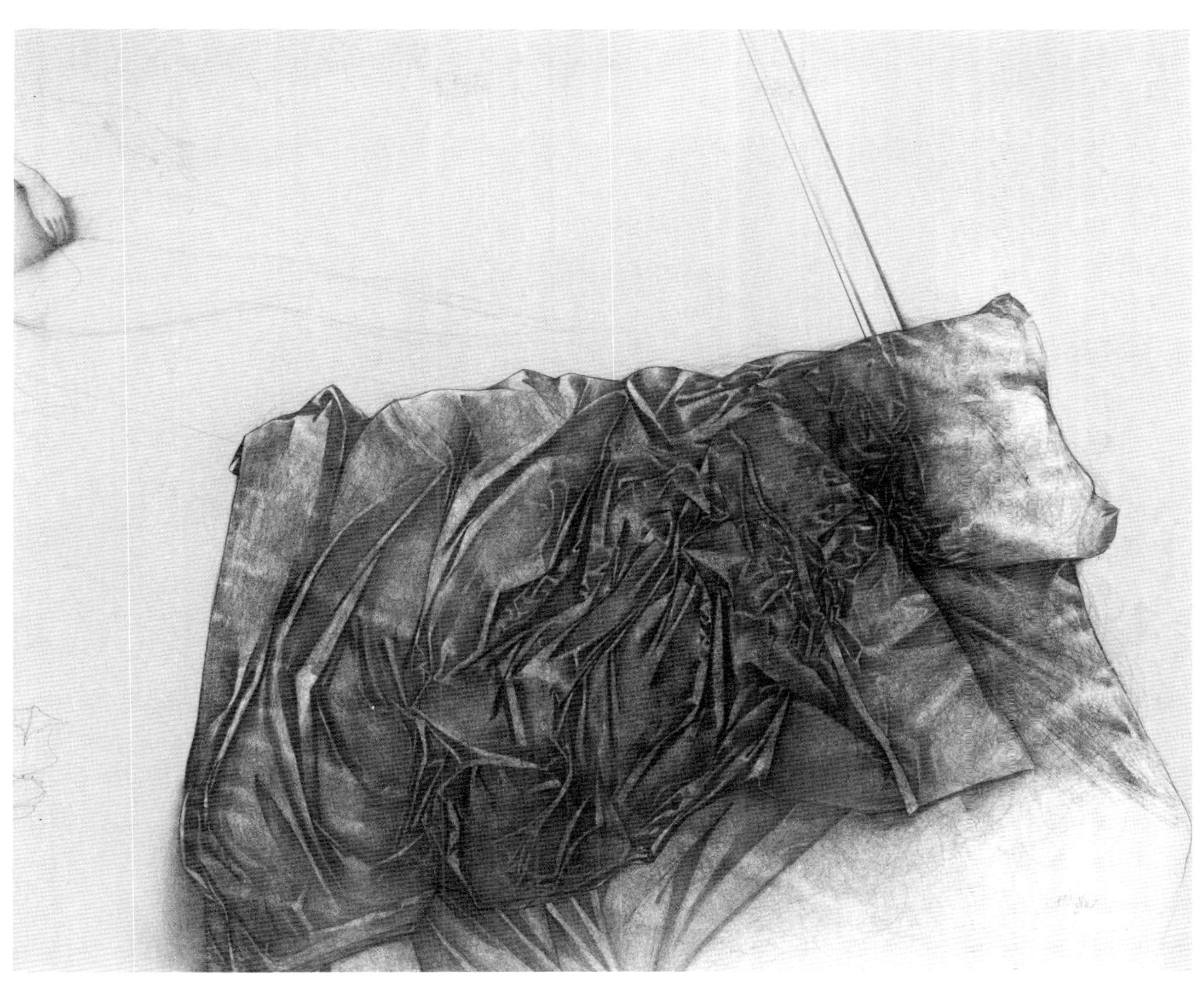

"Bett" 1977, *pencil and crayon, 80x98 cm*
◁ Working photo

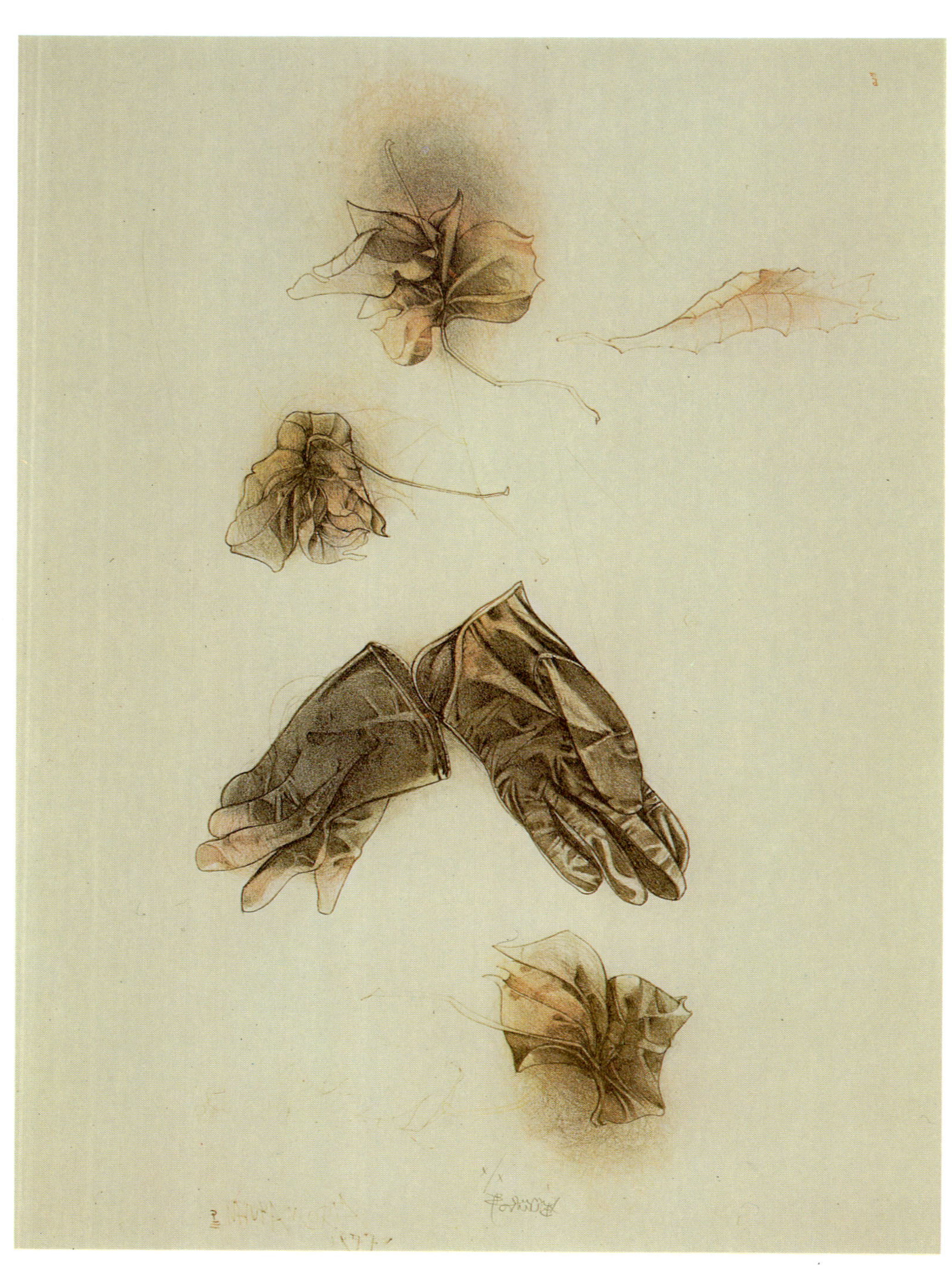

"Natura morta" 1977
lithograph in four colours, 76x56 cm

"Herbstliche Begrüßung" 1977, *lithograph in four colours, 65x50 cm* ▷

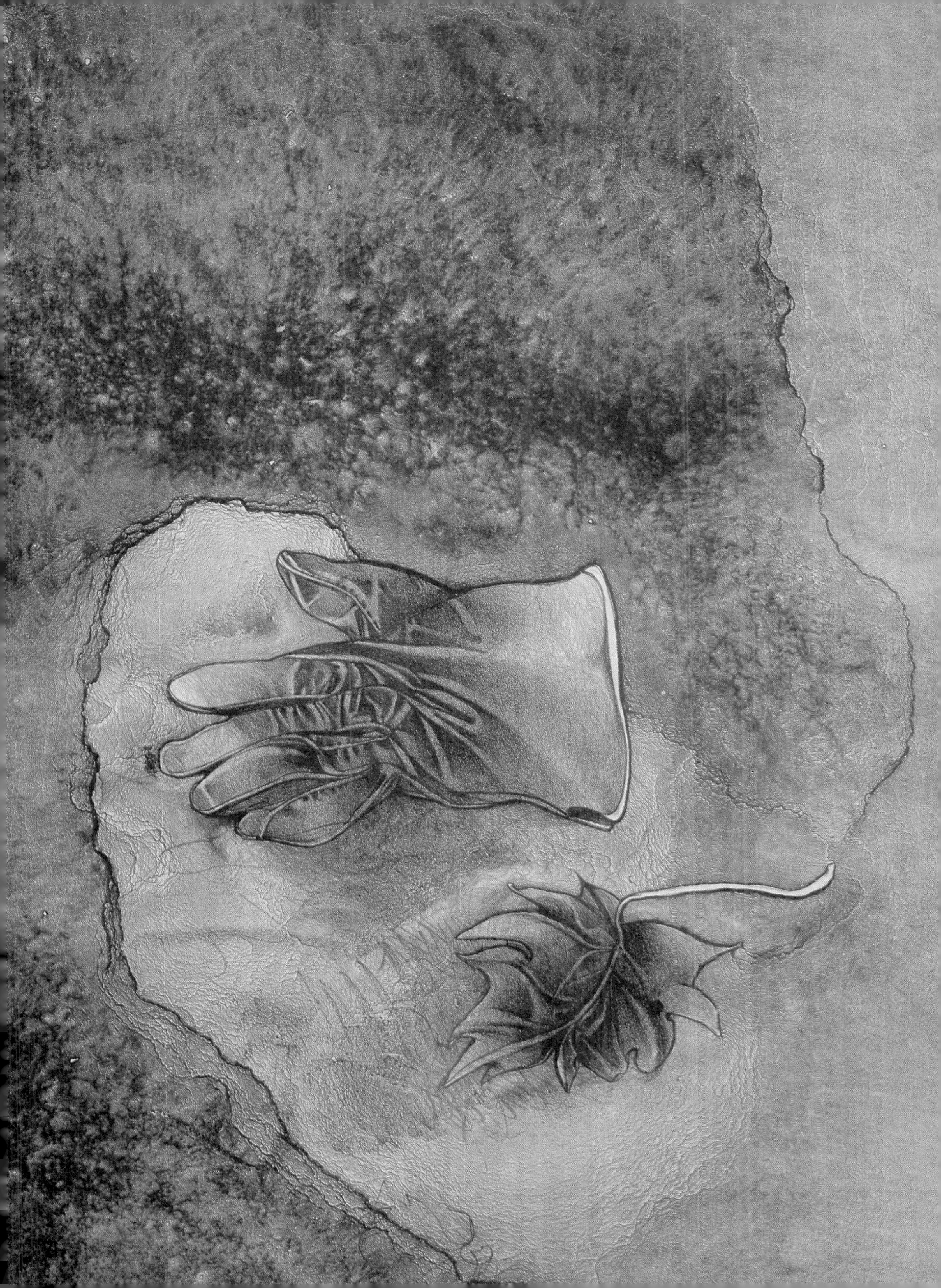

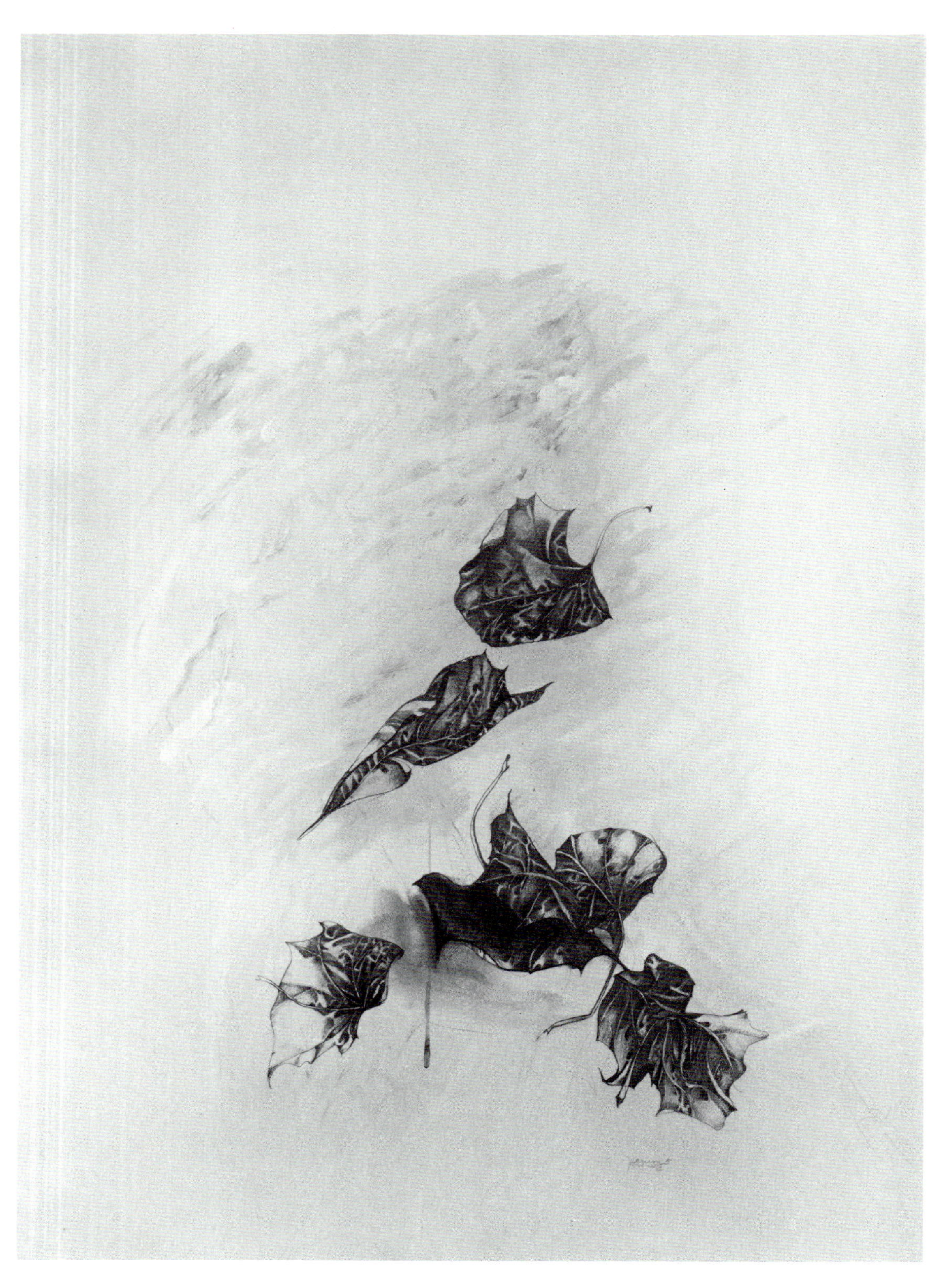

"Foglie" 1975
pencil and gouache, 102x73 cm

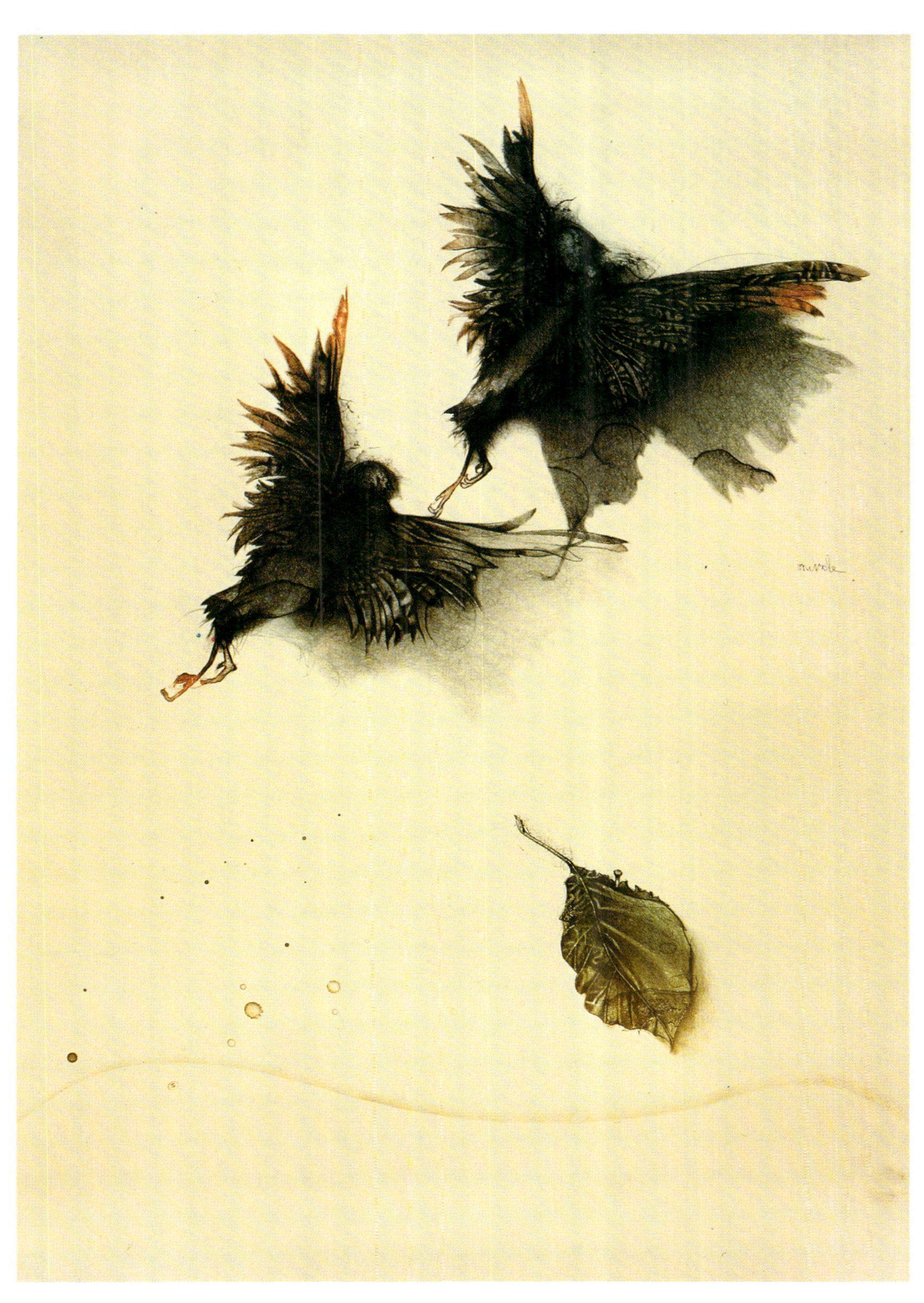

"Il volo" 1977
lithograph in four colours, 100x70 cm

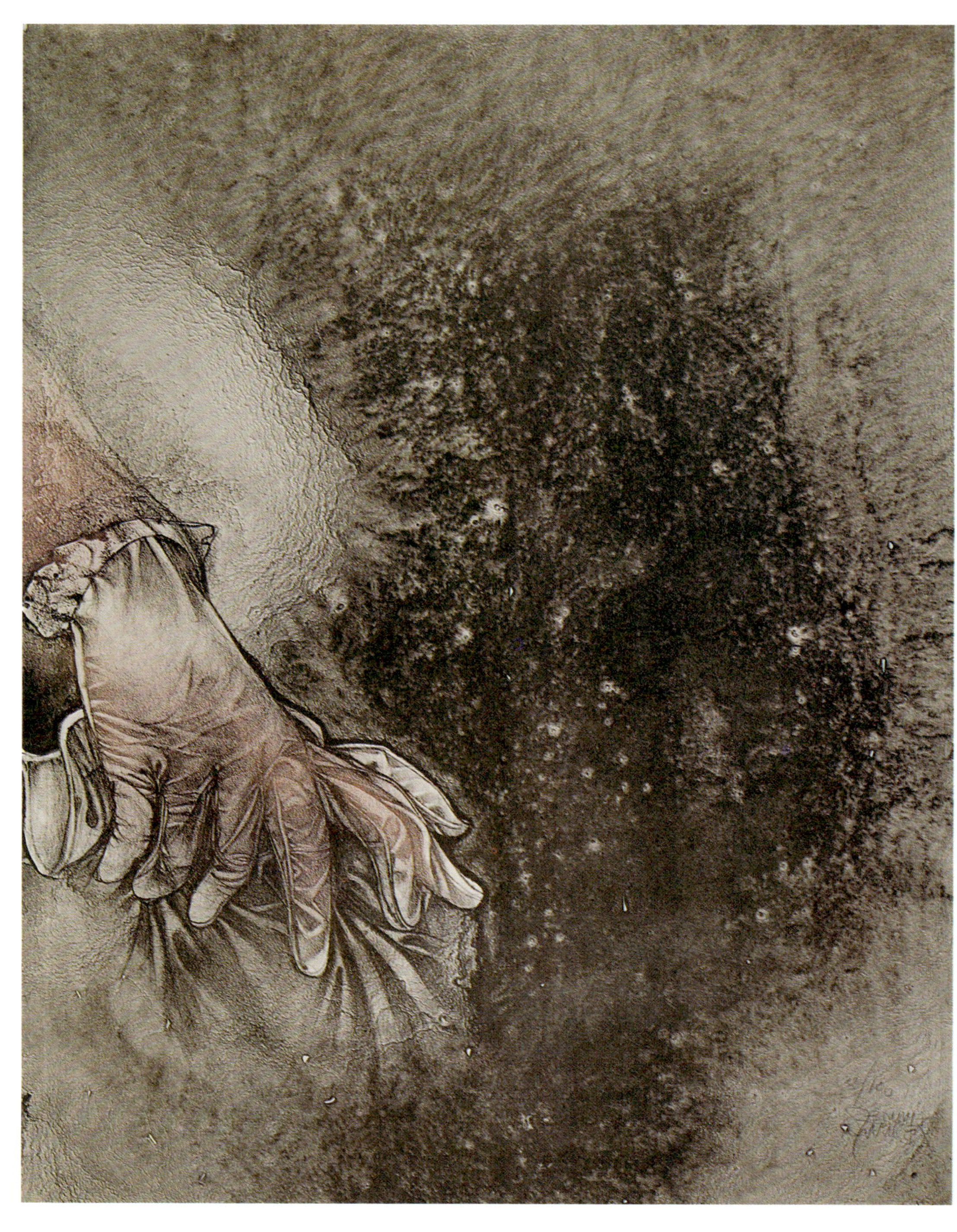

"Nach Tizian" 1977
lithograph in four colours, 65x50 cm

"Stilleben" 1977, *pencil drawing, 105x75 cm* ▷

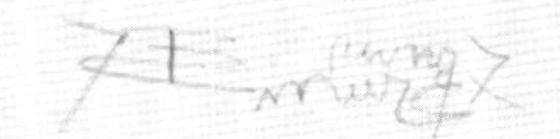

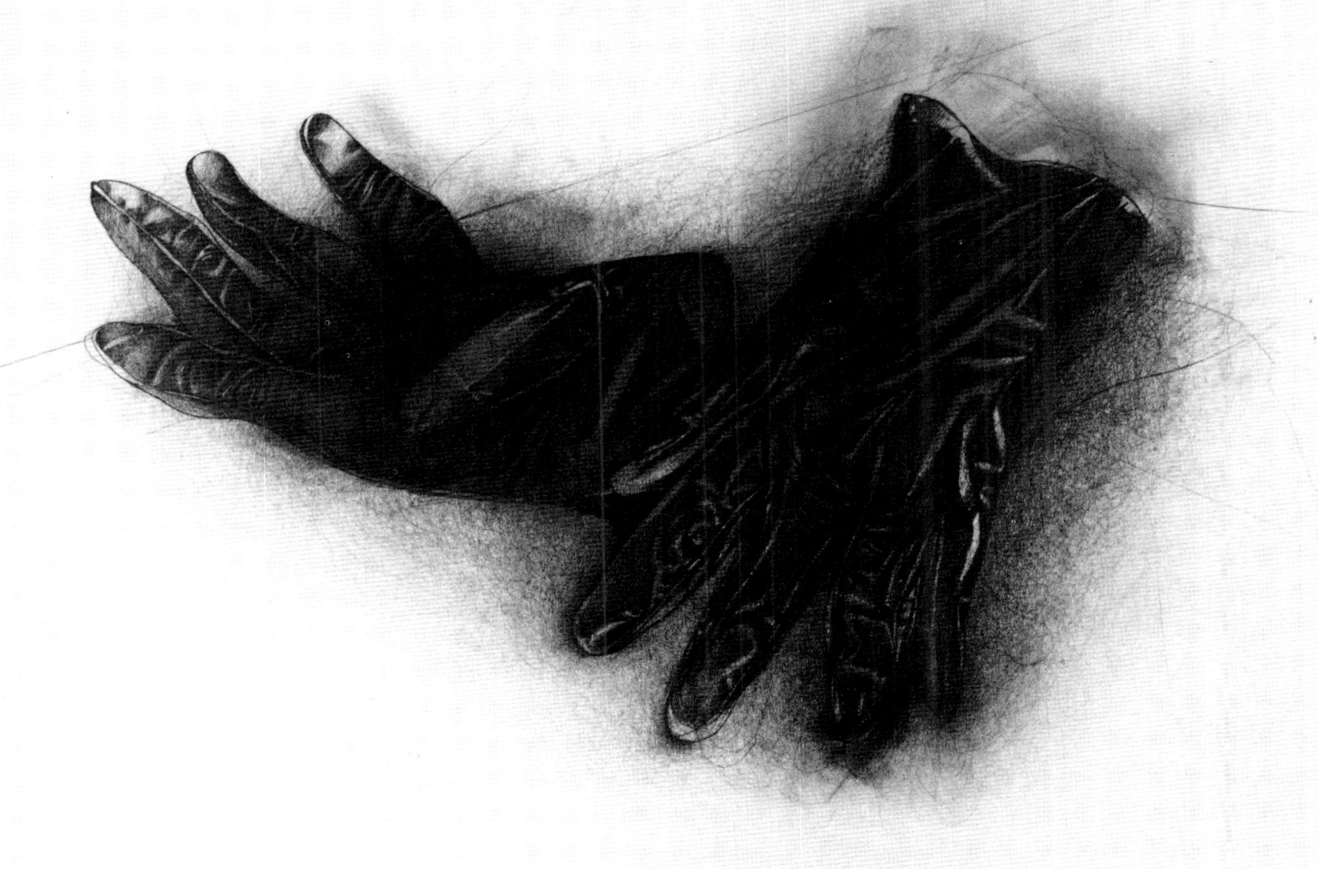

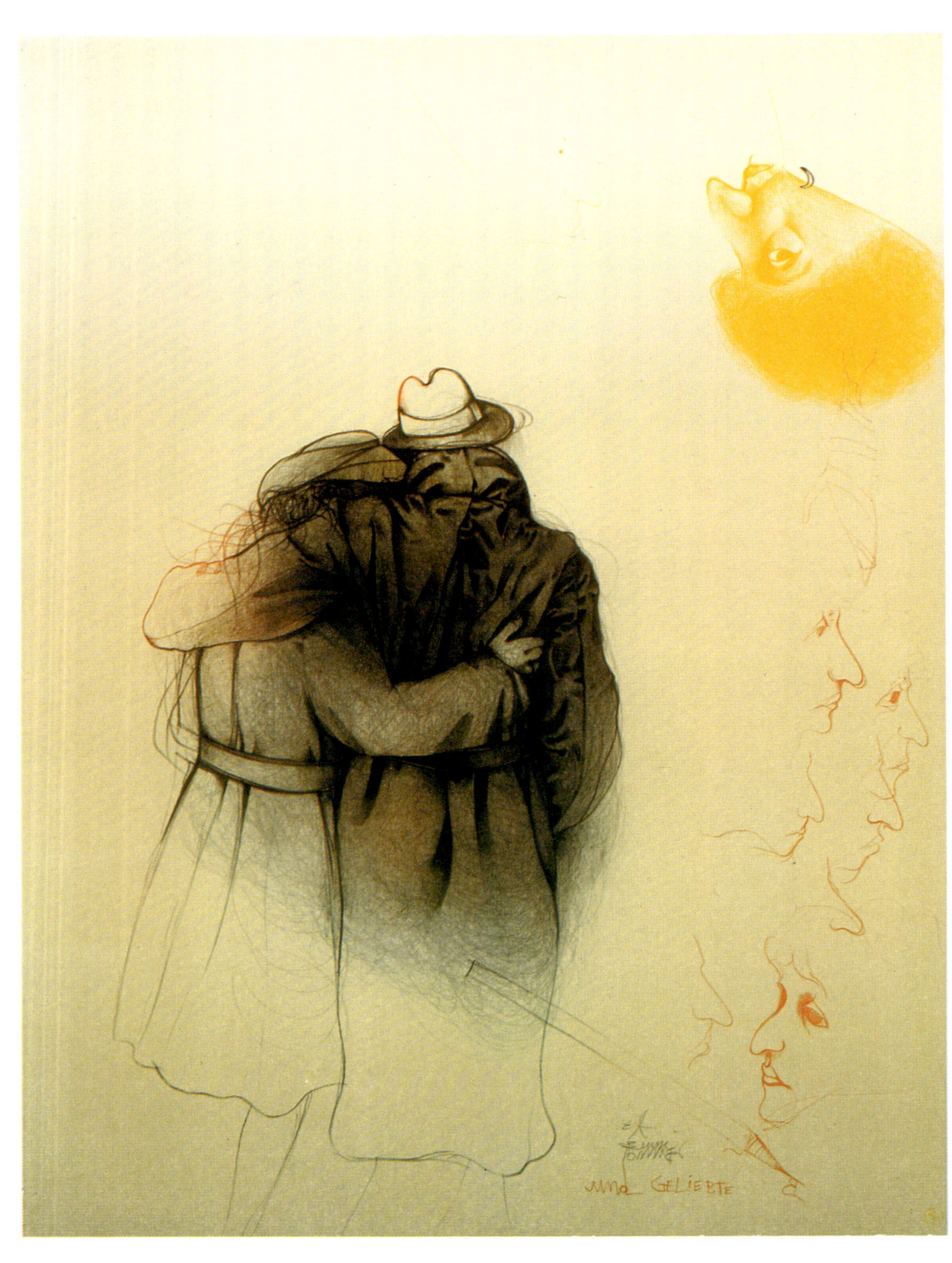

"... und Geliebte" 1976
lithograph in four colours, 65x50 cm

"Paesaggio romantico" 1977, *pencil drawing, 105x75 cm* ▷

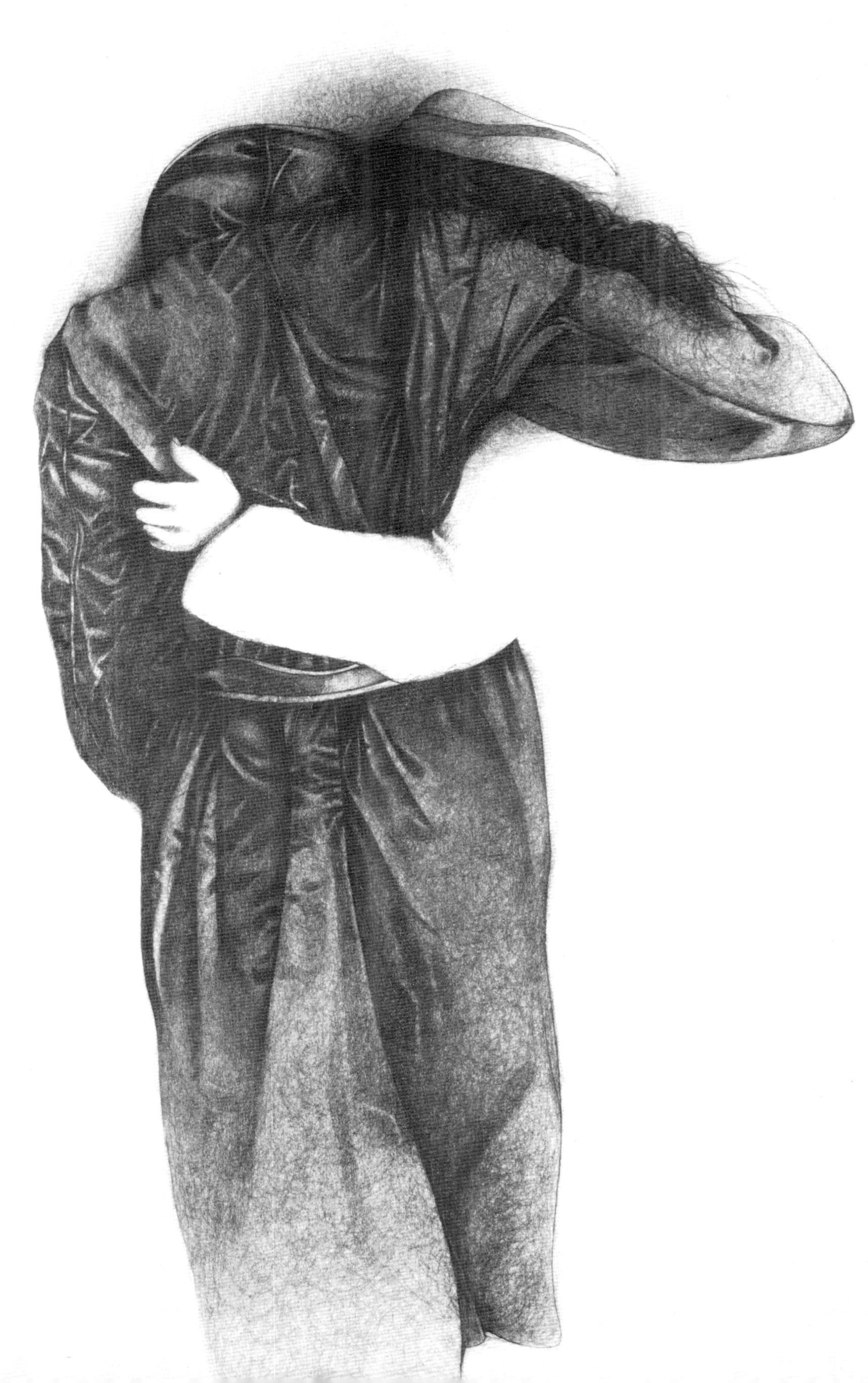

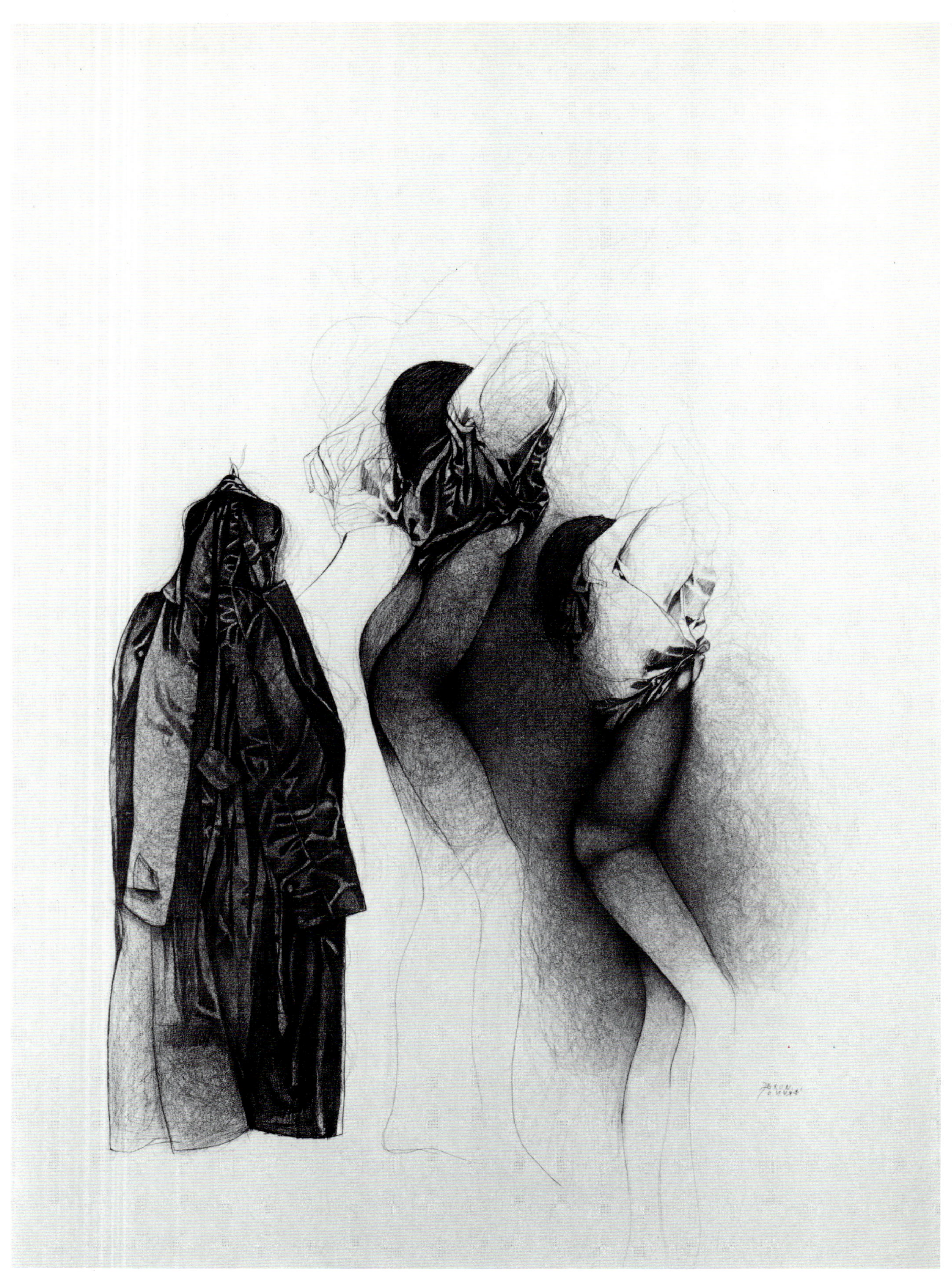

"Without Title" 1976, *pencil drawing, 102x73 cm*

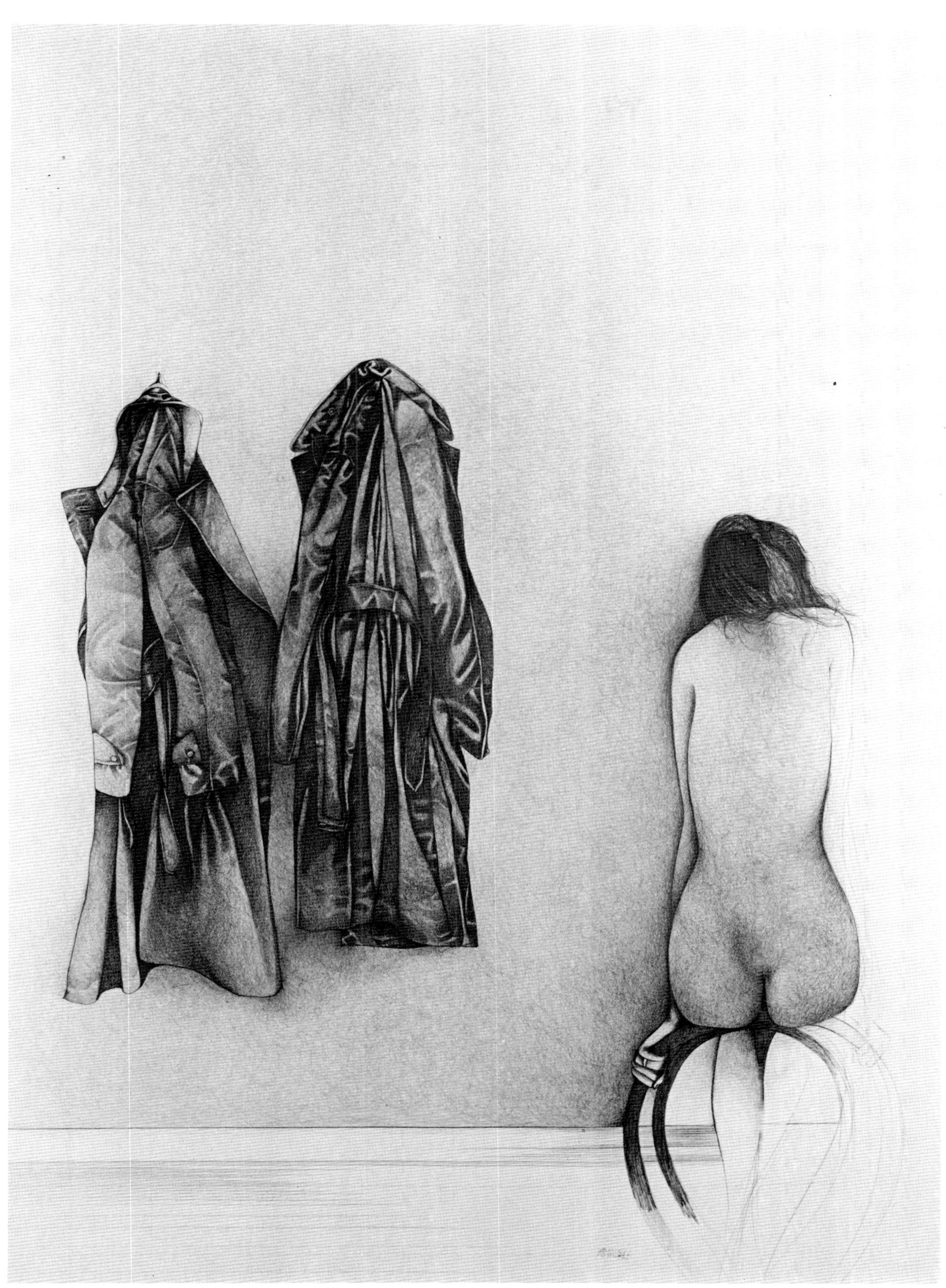

"In the Studio" 1976, *pencil drawing, 96x69 cm*

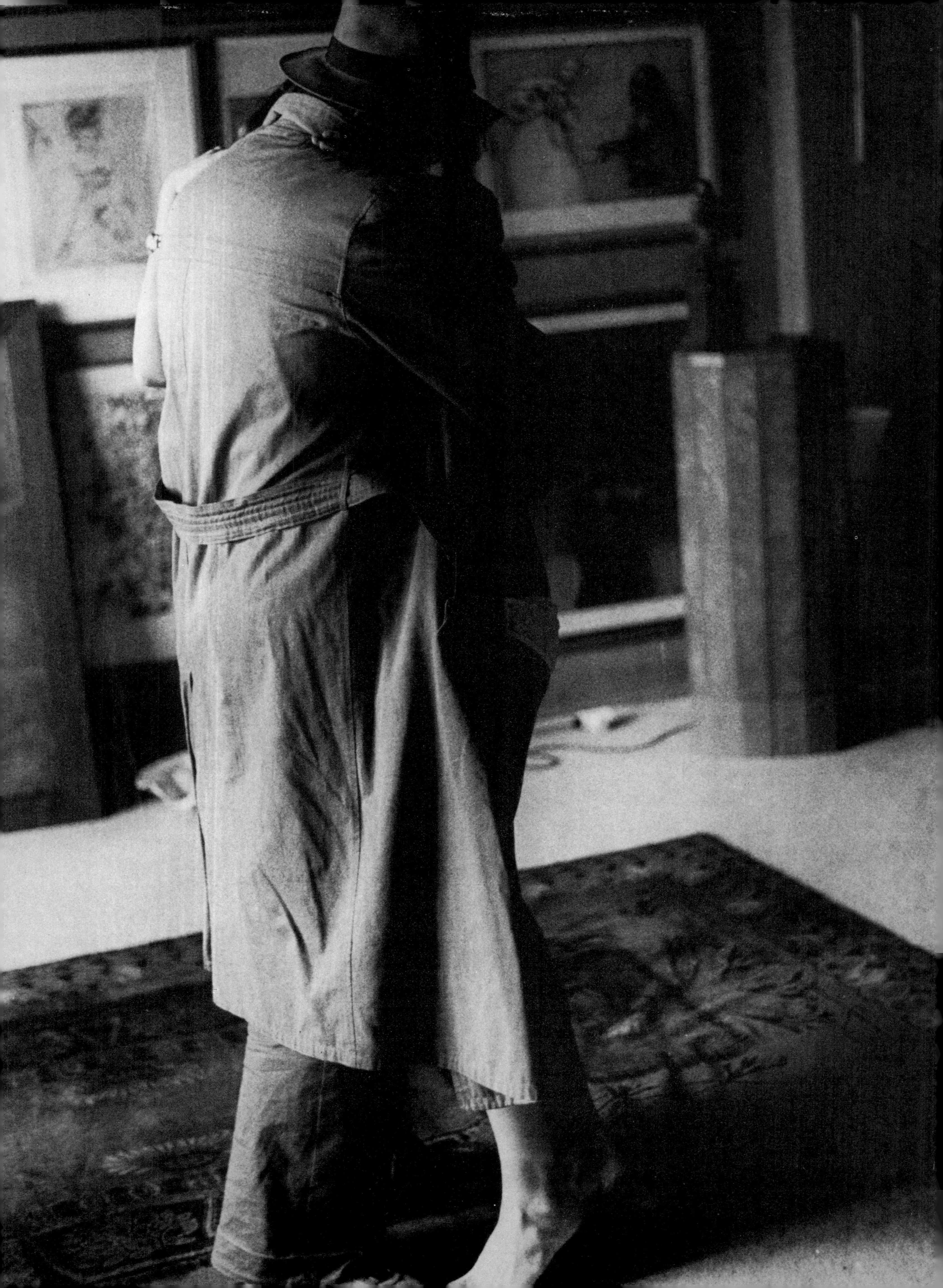

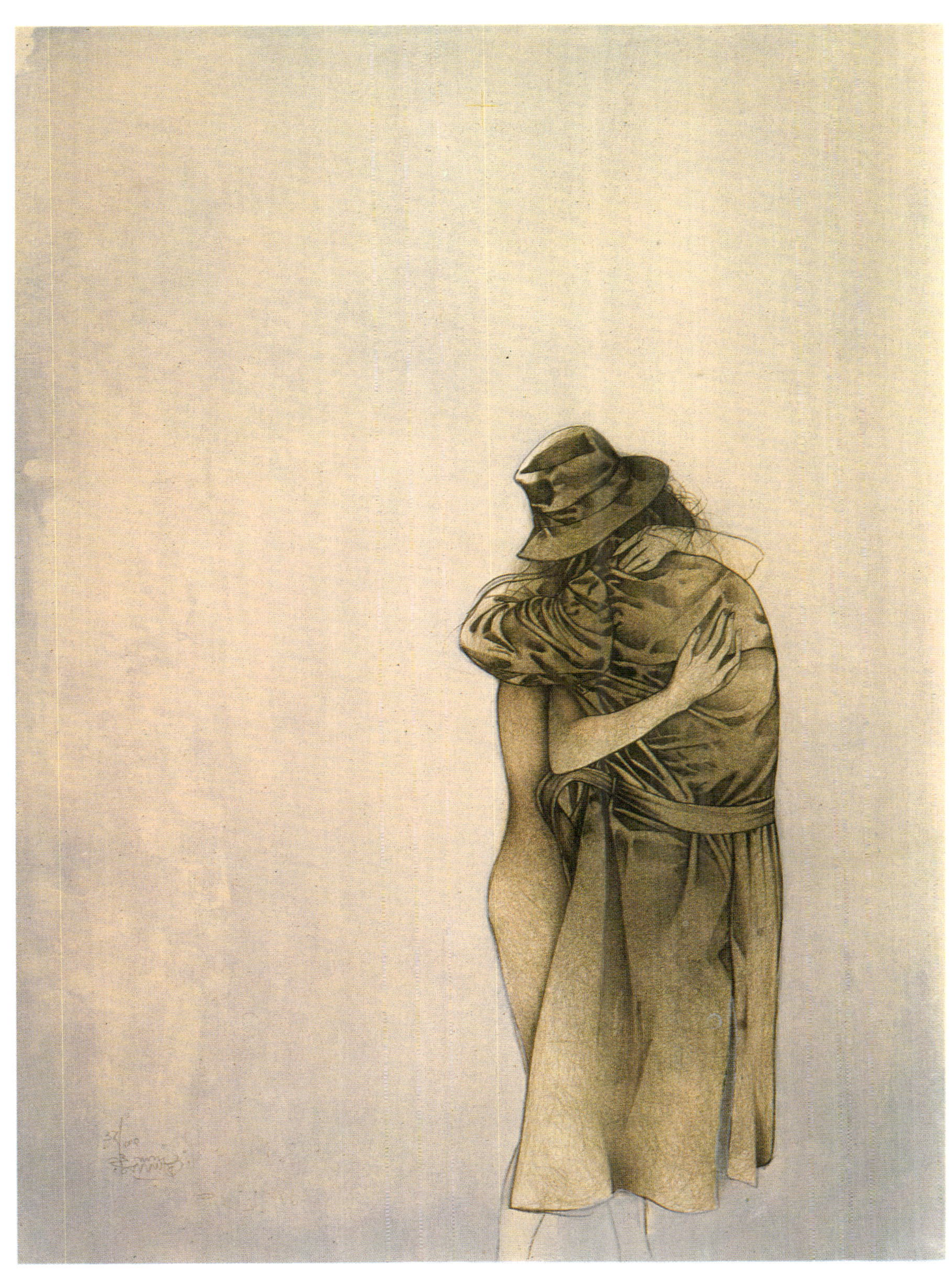

"Zärtlichkeiten" 1976
lithograph in four colours, 76x56 cm, out of series of three lithographs
◁ Working photo

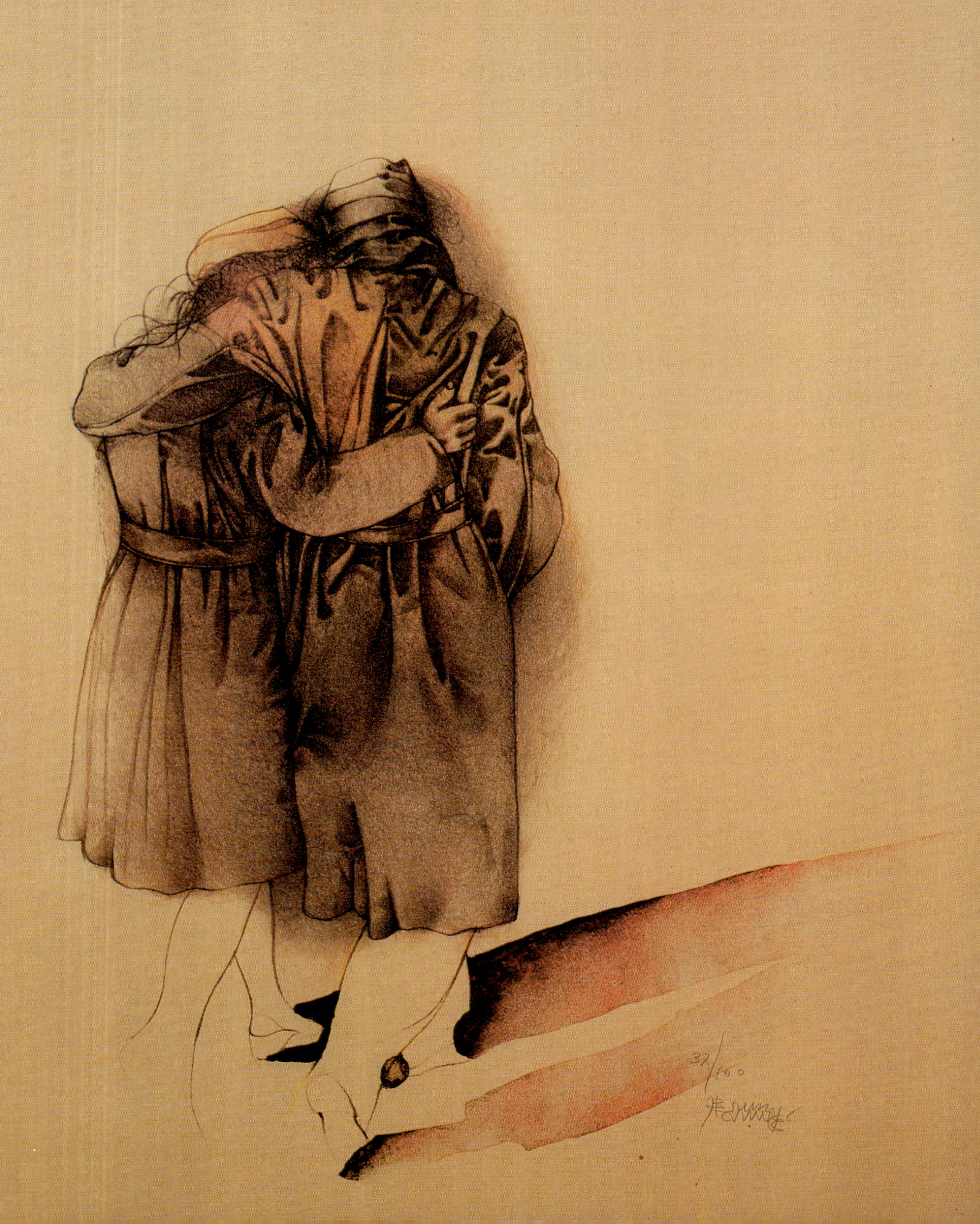

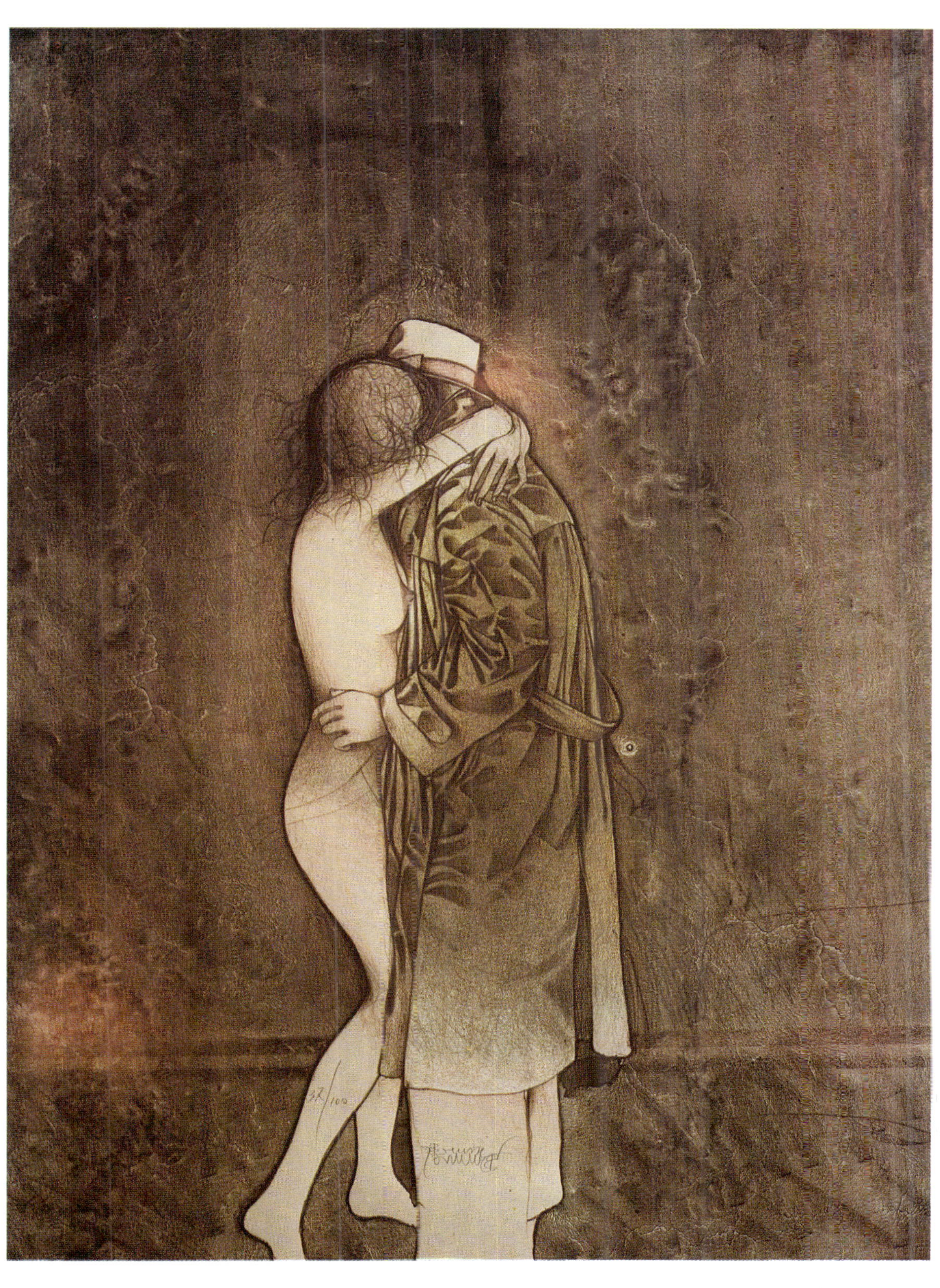

"Zärtlichkeiten" 1976
two lithographs in four colours, 76x56 cm, out of a series of three lithographs

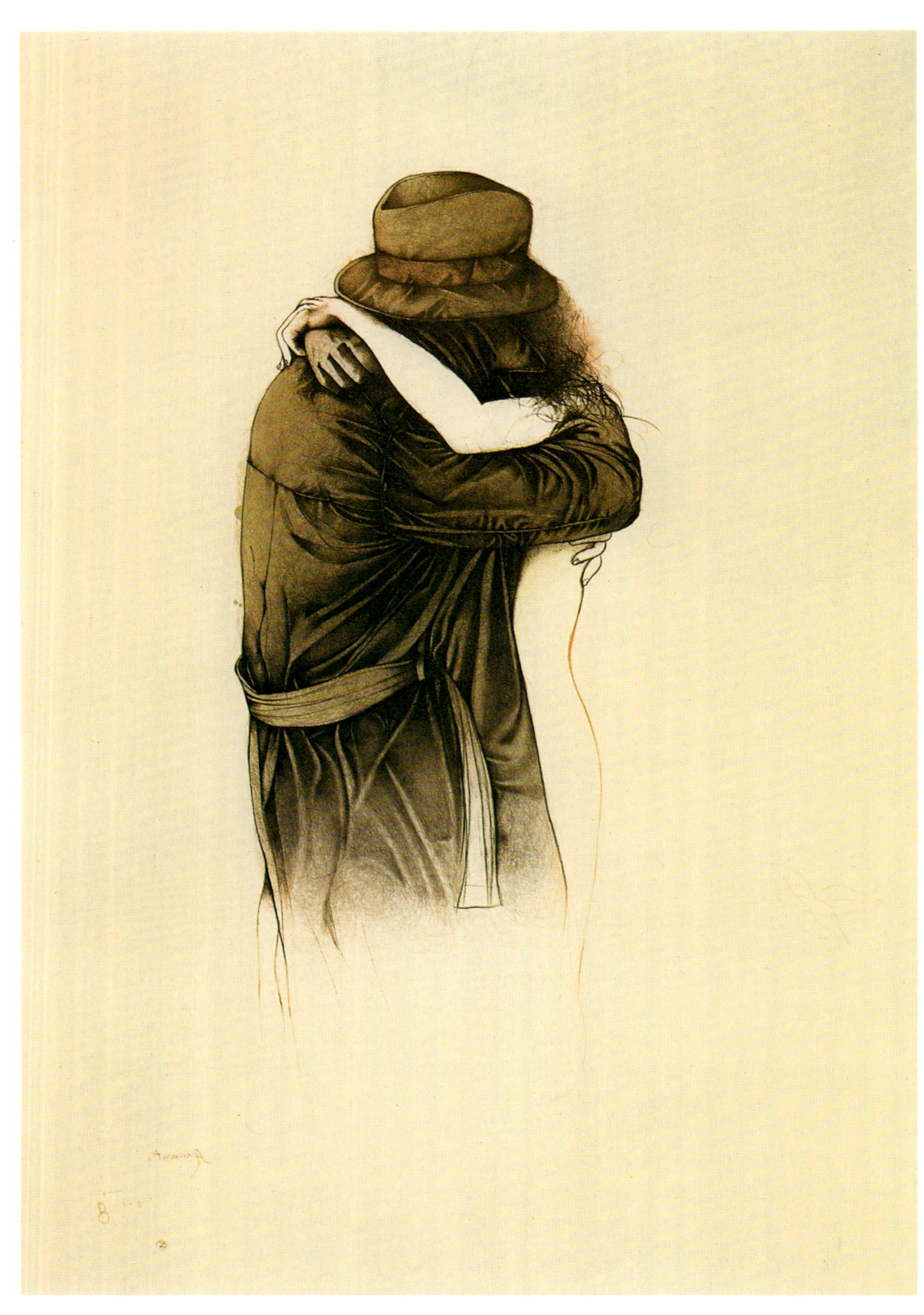

"Amanti" 1978
lithograph in four colours, 100x70 cm

In the printing shop Matthieu, Dielsdorf ▷

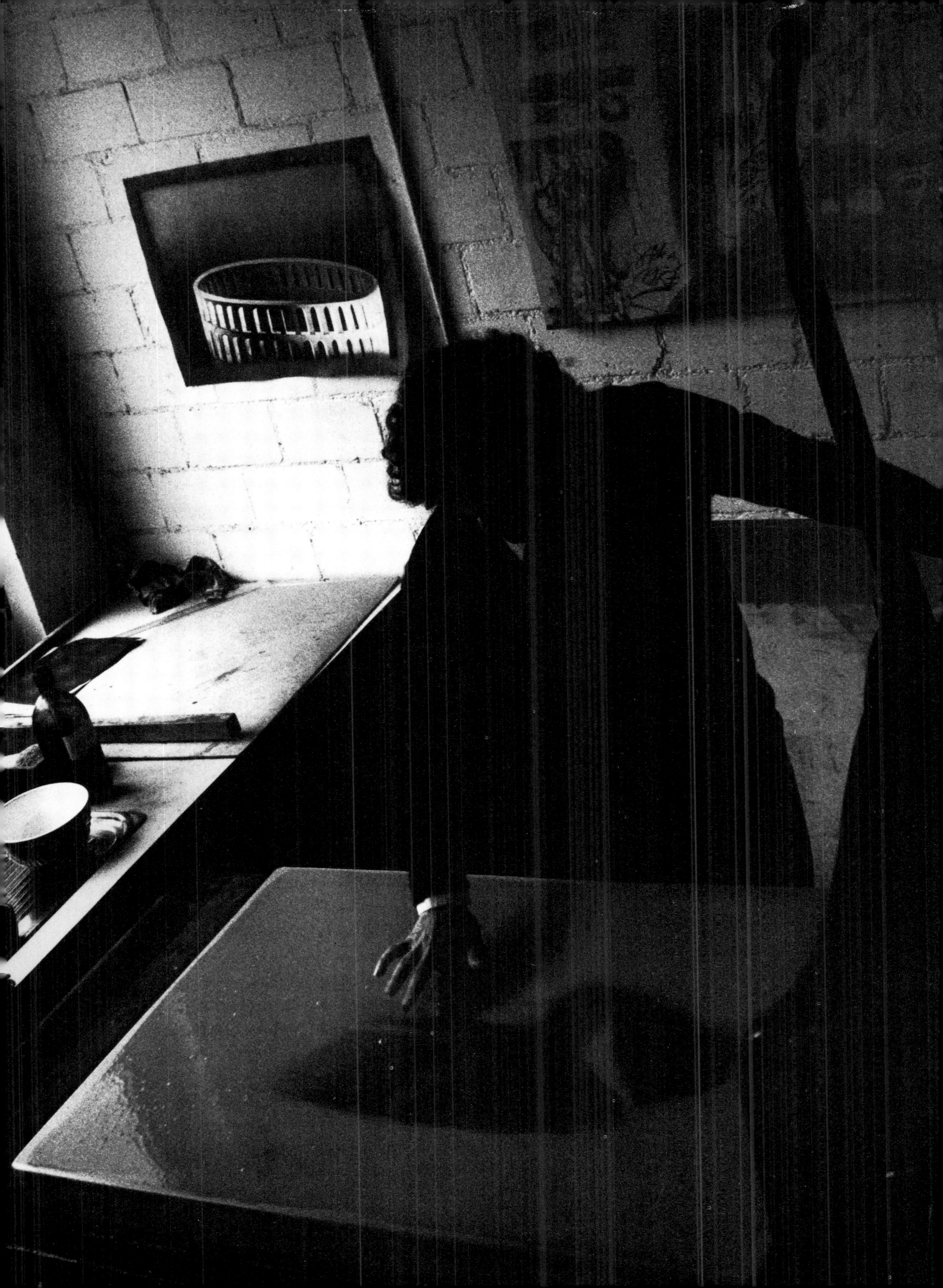

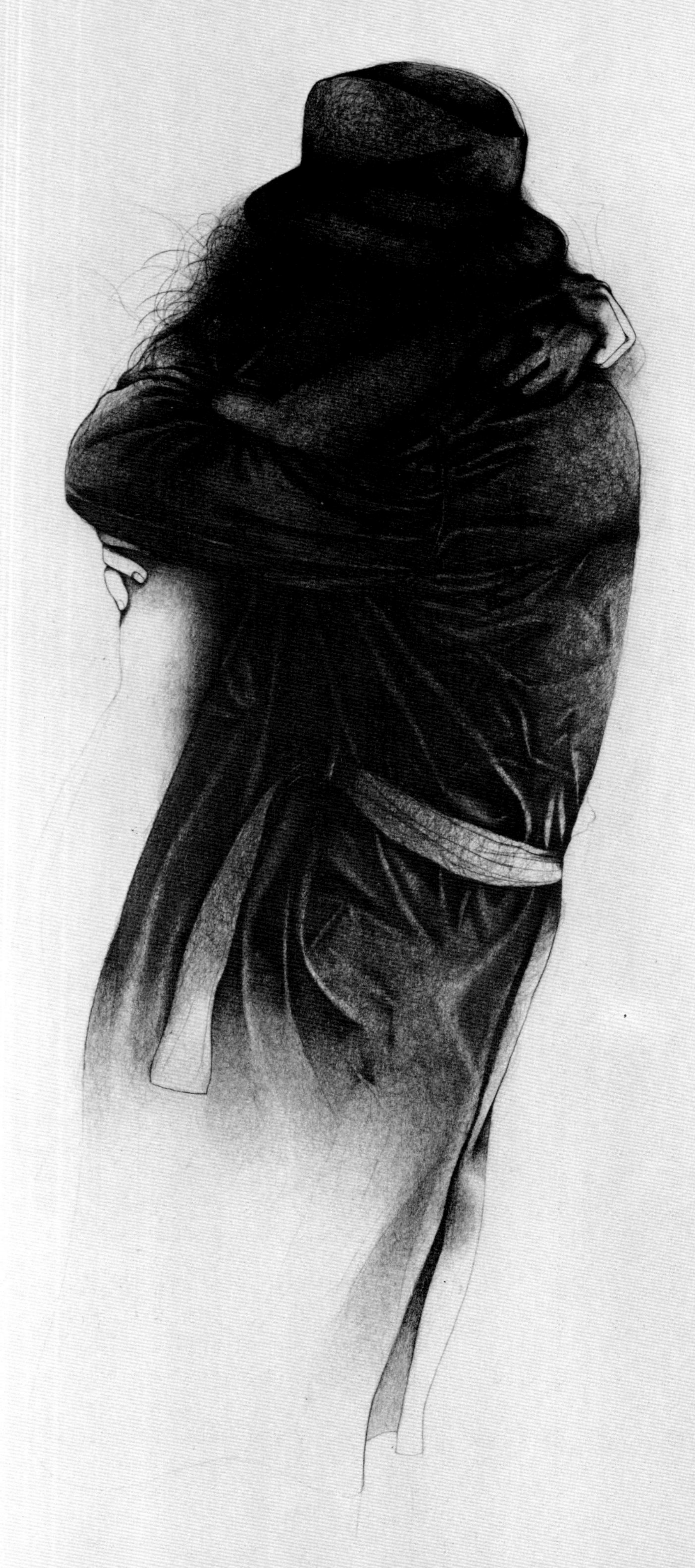

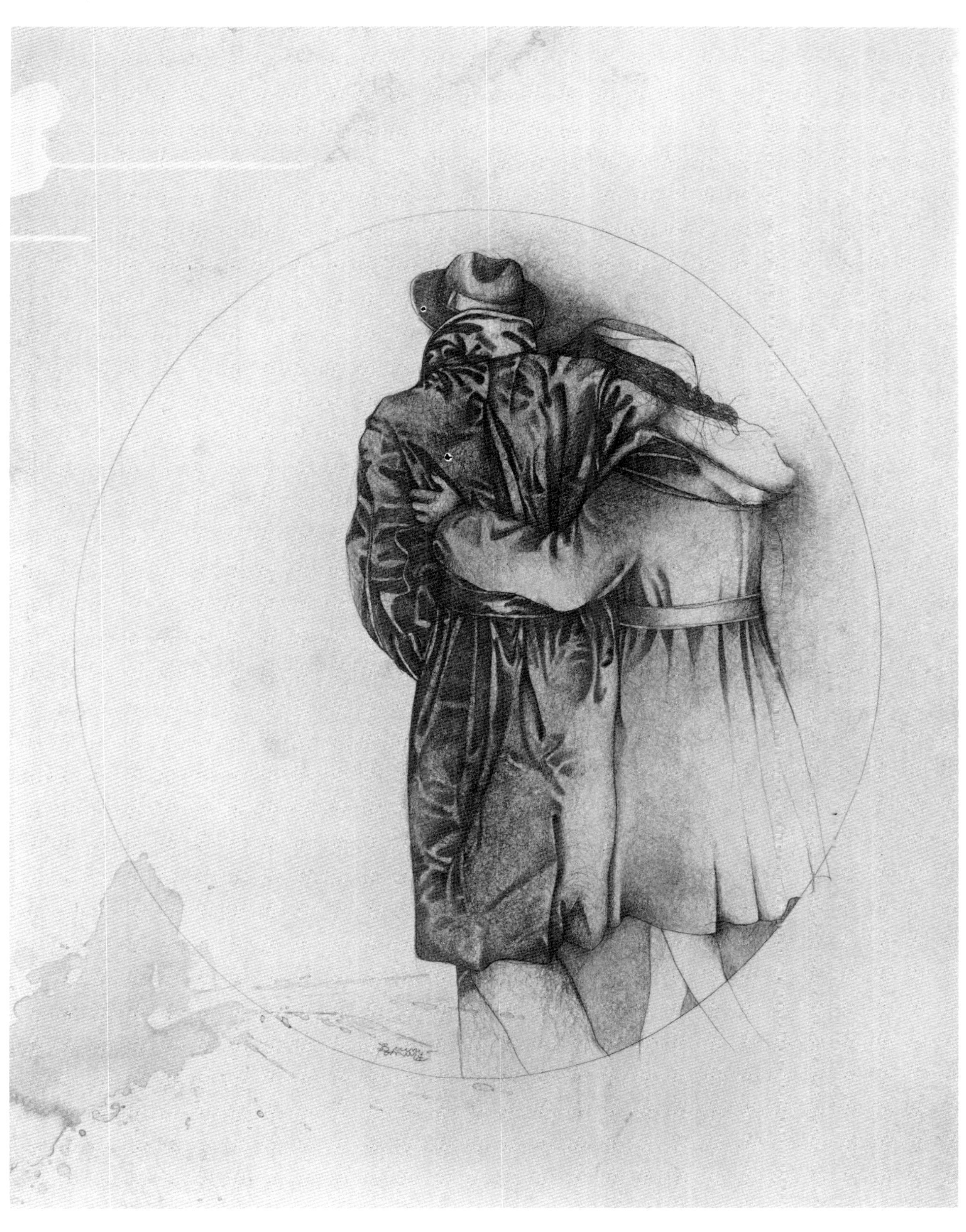

"Passeggiata" 1976, *pencil and gouache, 71x55 cm*
◁ "Umarmung" 1978, *pencil drawing, 102x73 cm*

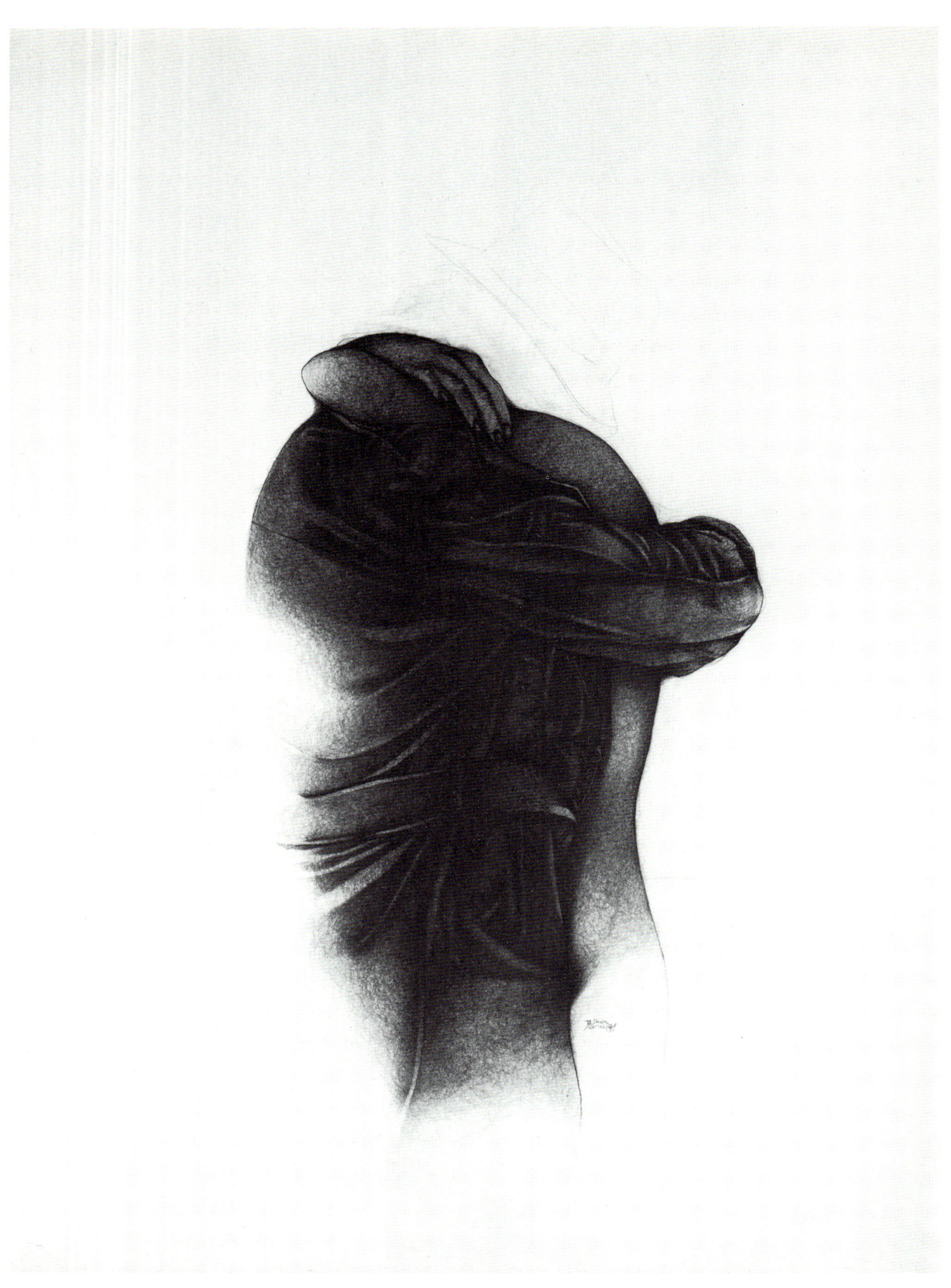

"Der Kuß" 1978, *pencil drawing, 102x73 cm*

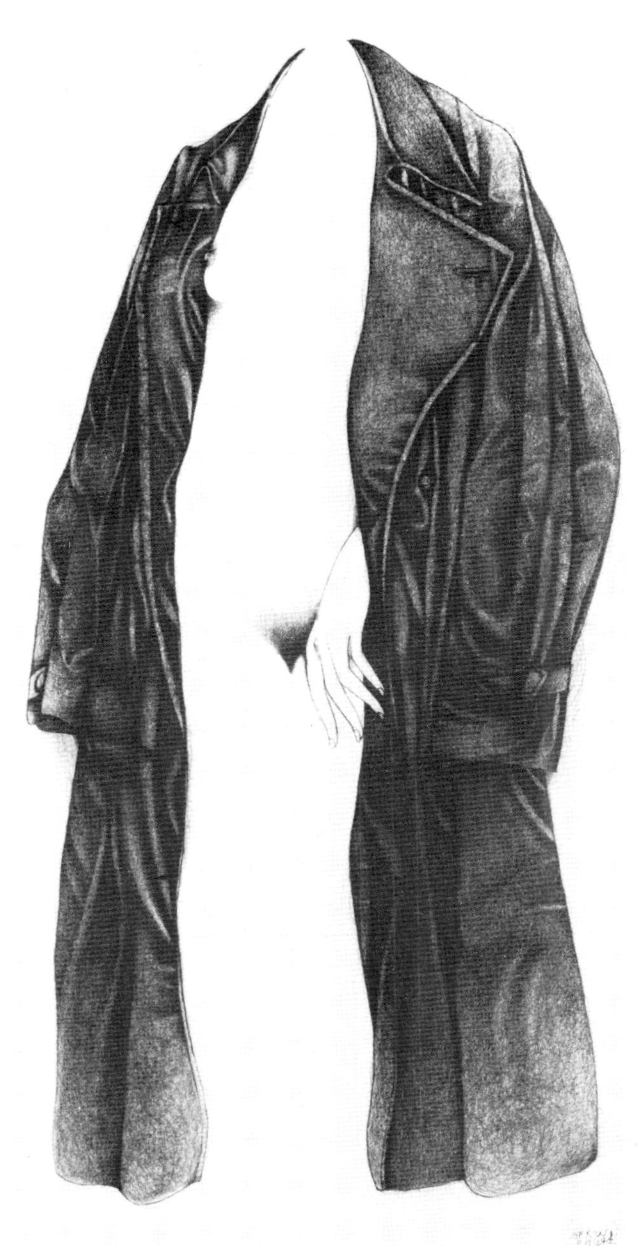

"Cappotto d'oro" 1978, *pencil drawing, 102x73 cm*
"Mäntel" 1976, *pencil drawing, 83x118 cm* ▷

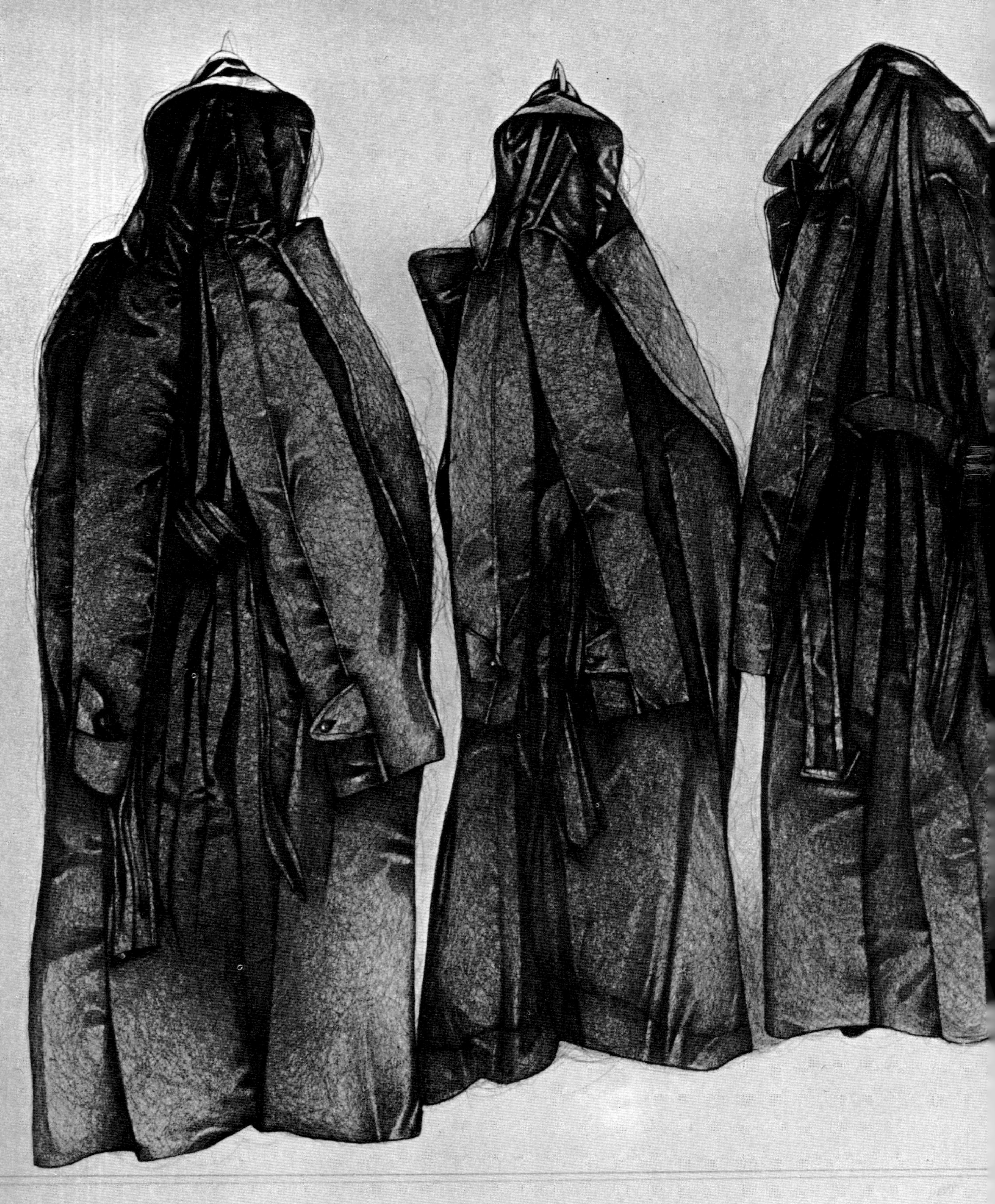

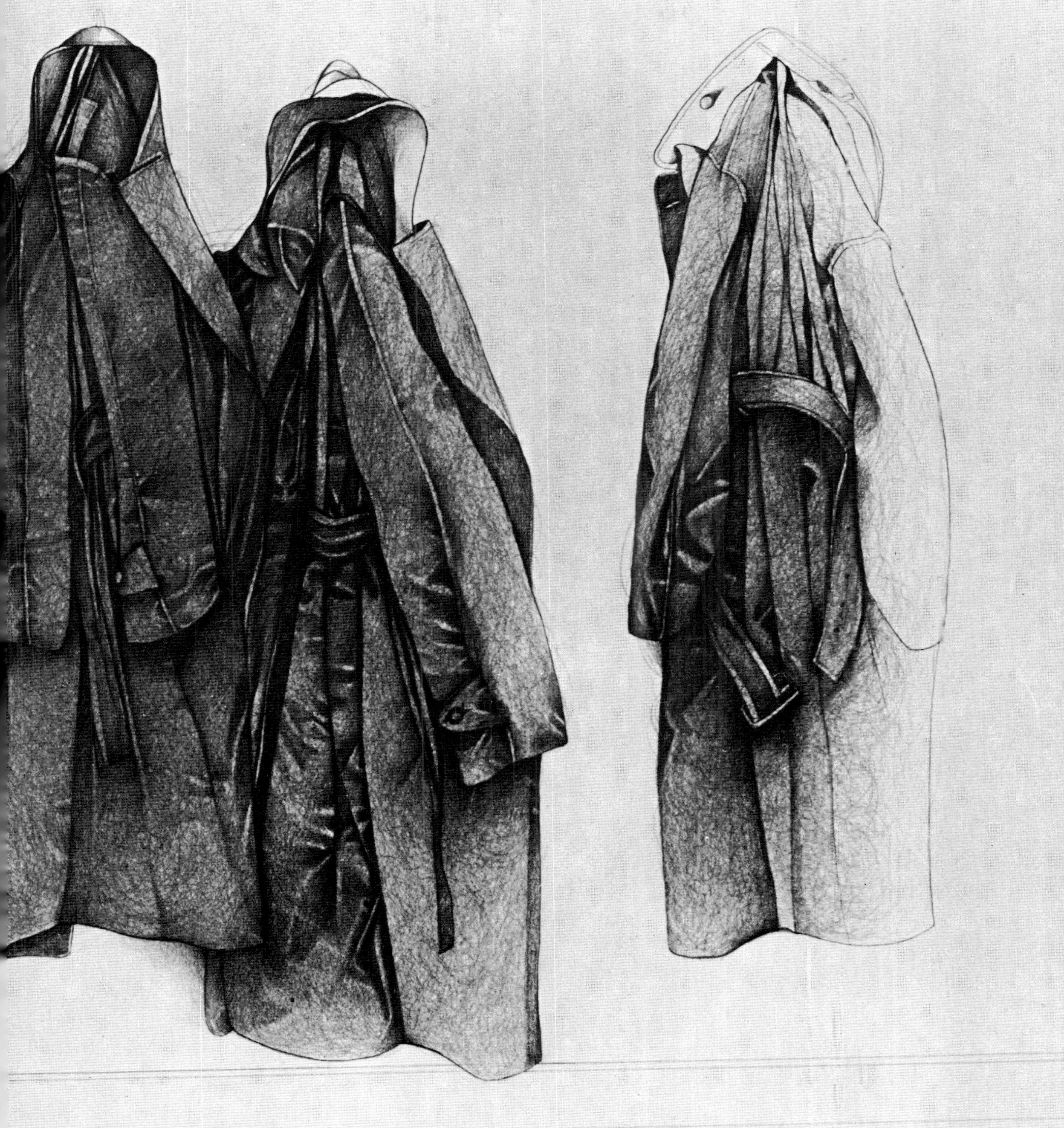

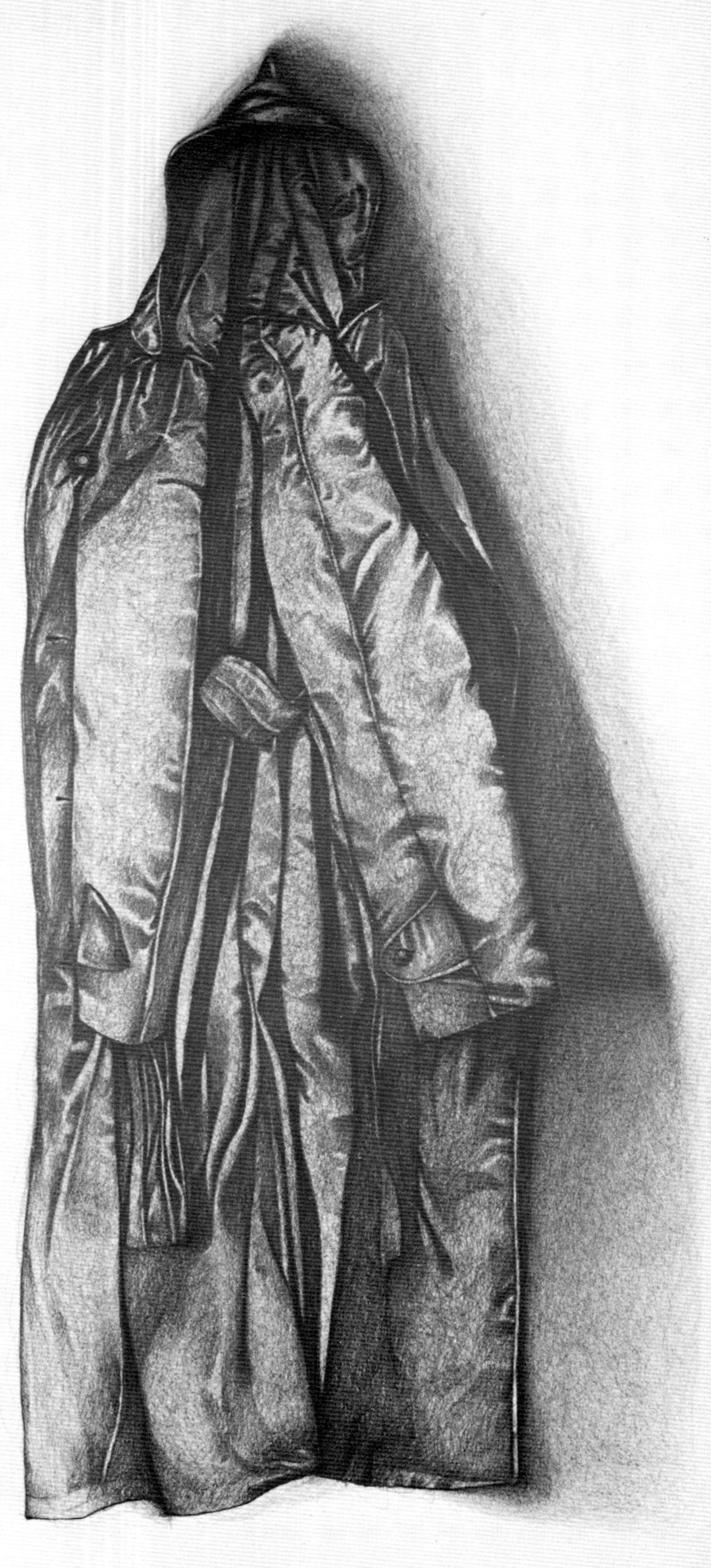

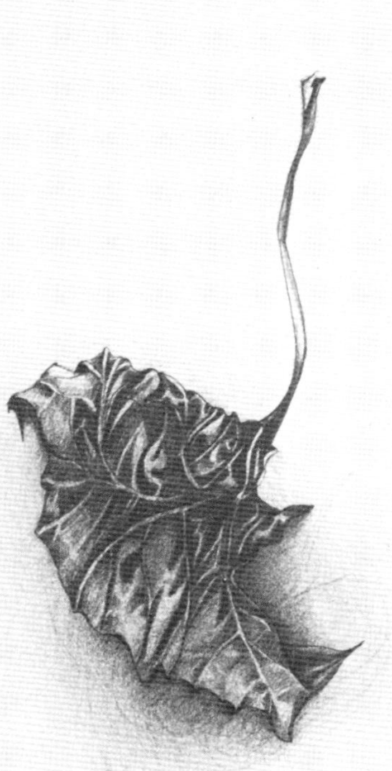

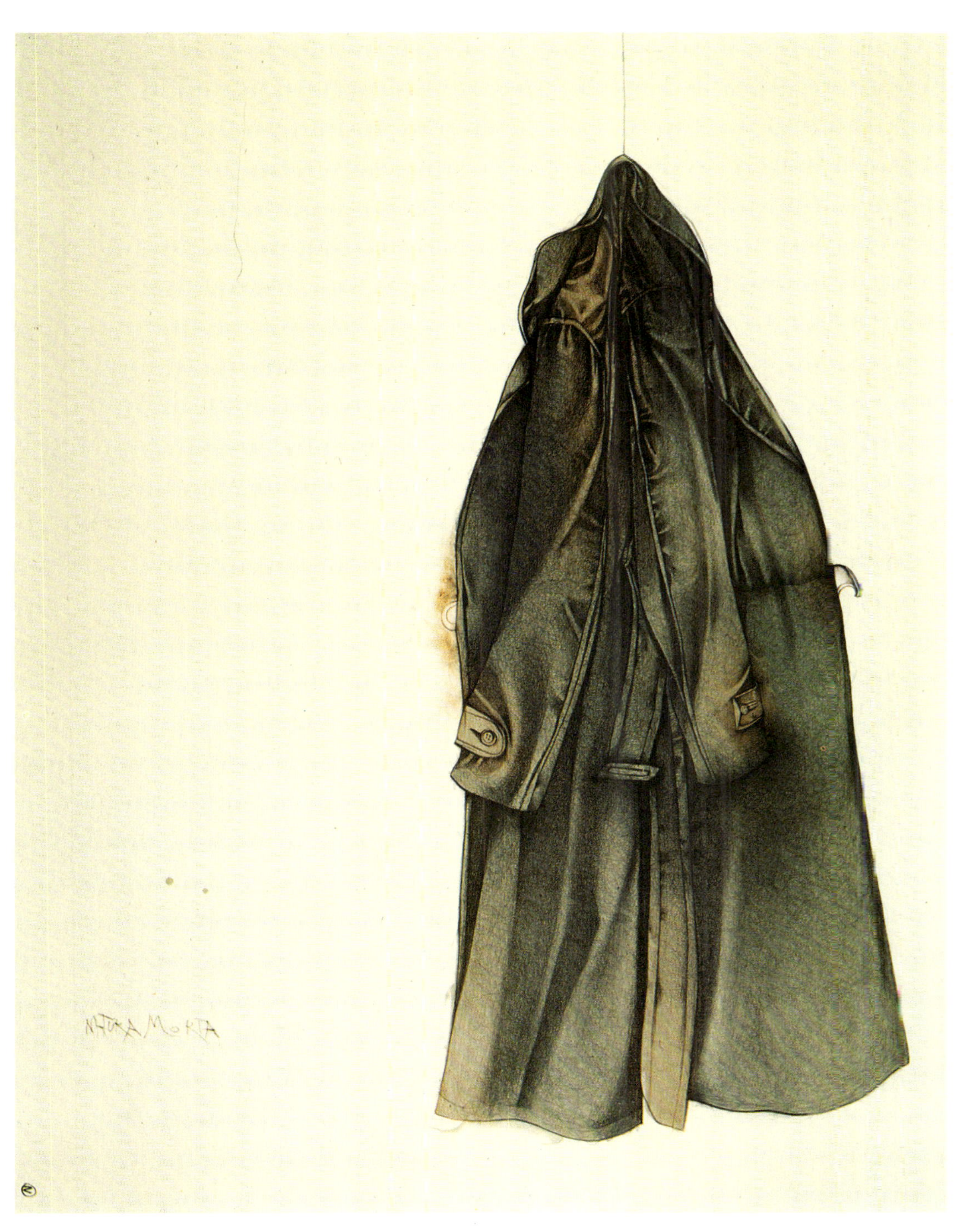

'Il cappotto" 1977
lithograph in four colours, 100x70 cm

◁ "Mantel und Blatt" 1976, *pencil drawing, 87x64.5 cm*

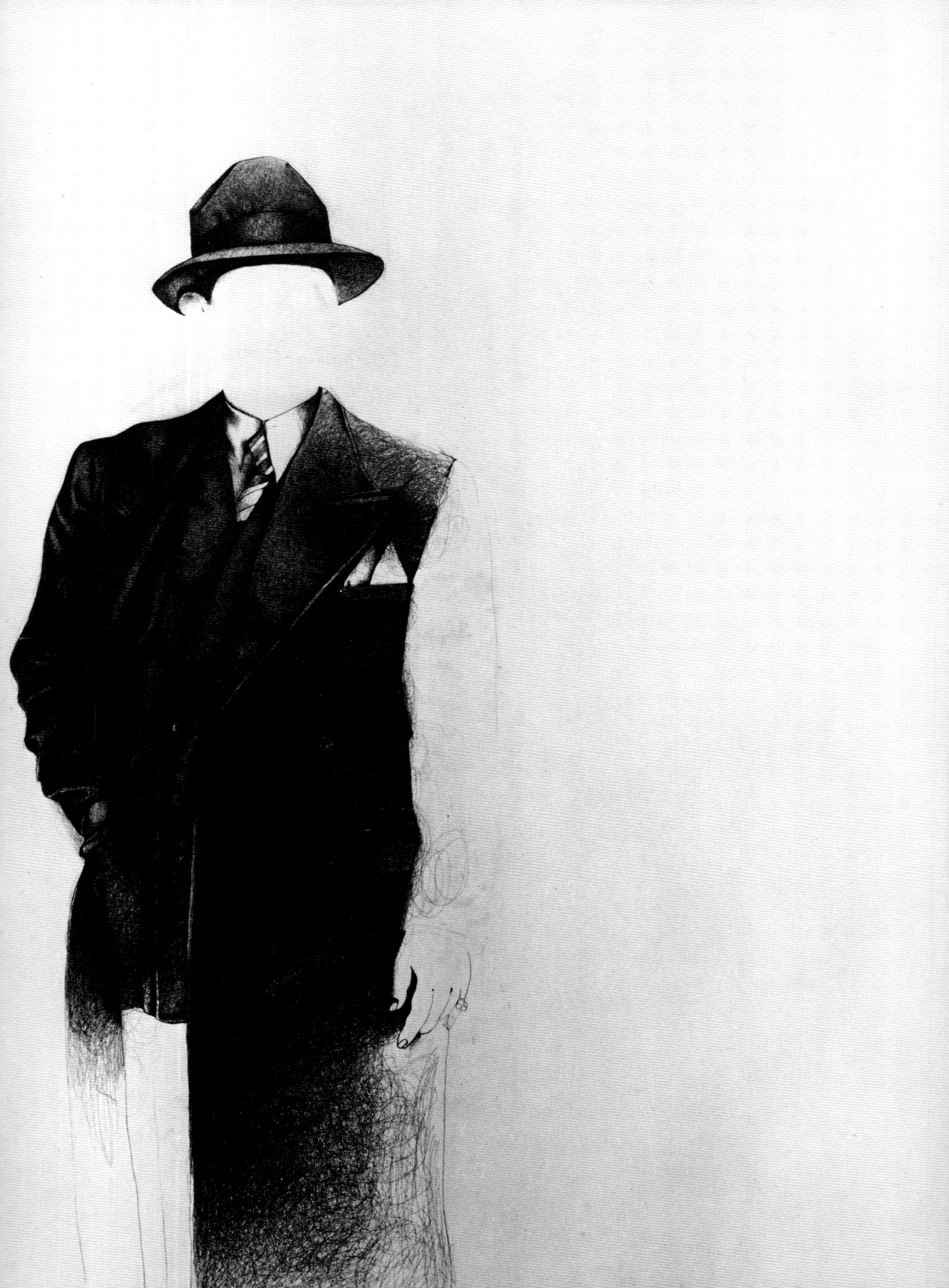

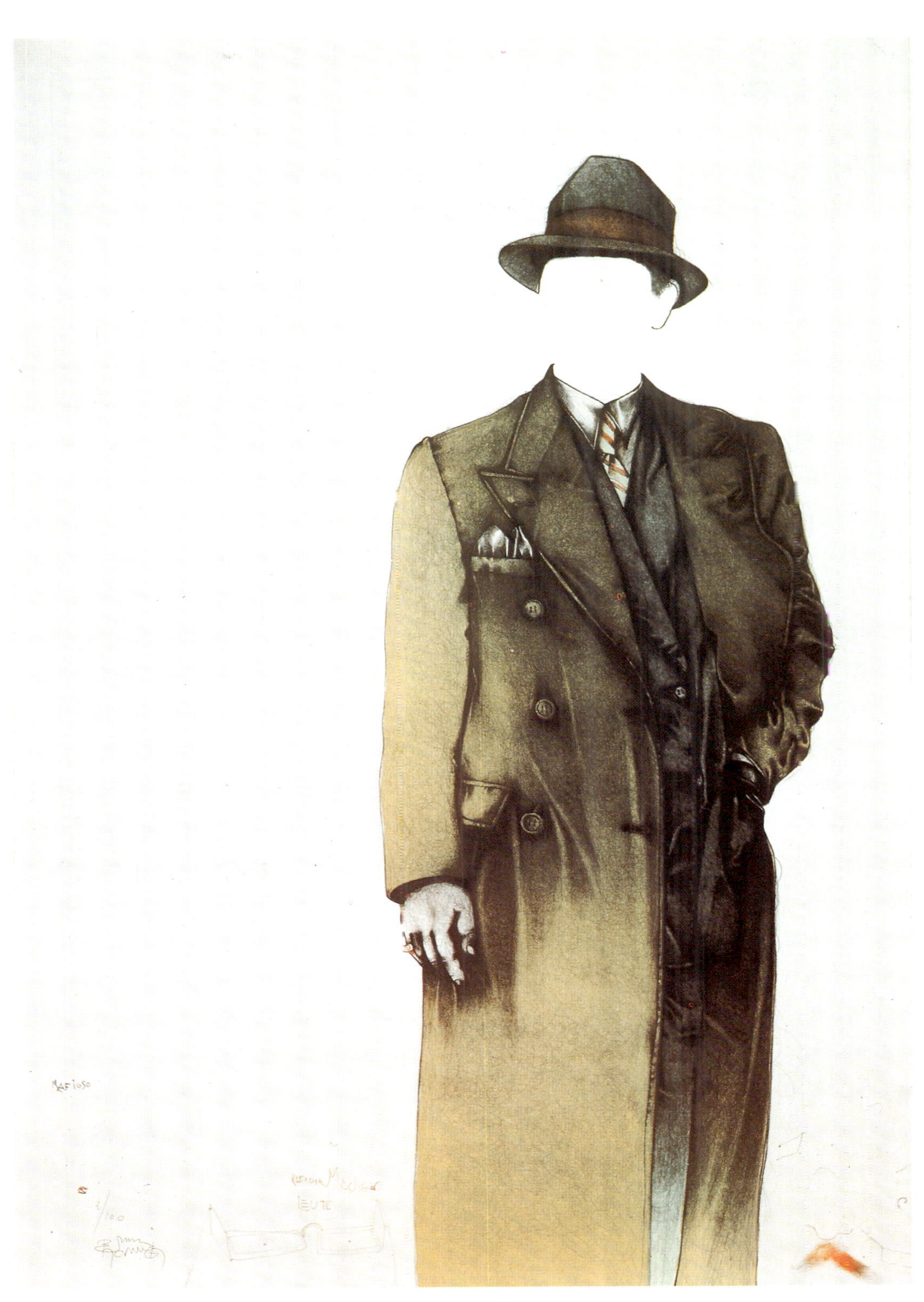

"Kleider machen Leute" 1977
lithograph in five colours, 100x70 cm

◁ "Mafioso" 1977, *pencil drawing, 102x73 cm*

BRONCE SCULPTURES

"Liegende" 1975 ▷
"Sotto la coperta" 1976 ▷▷

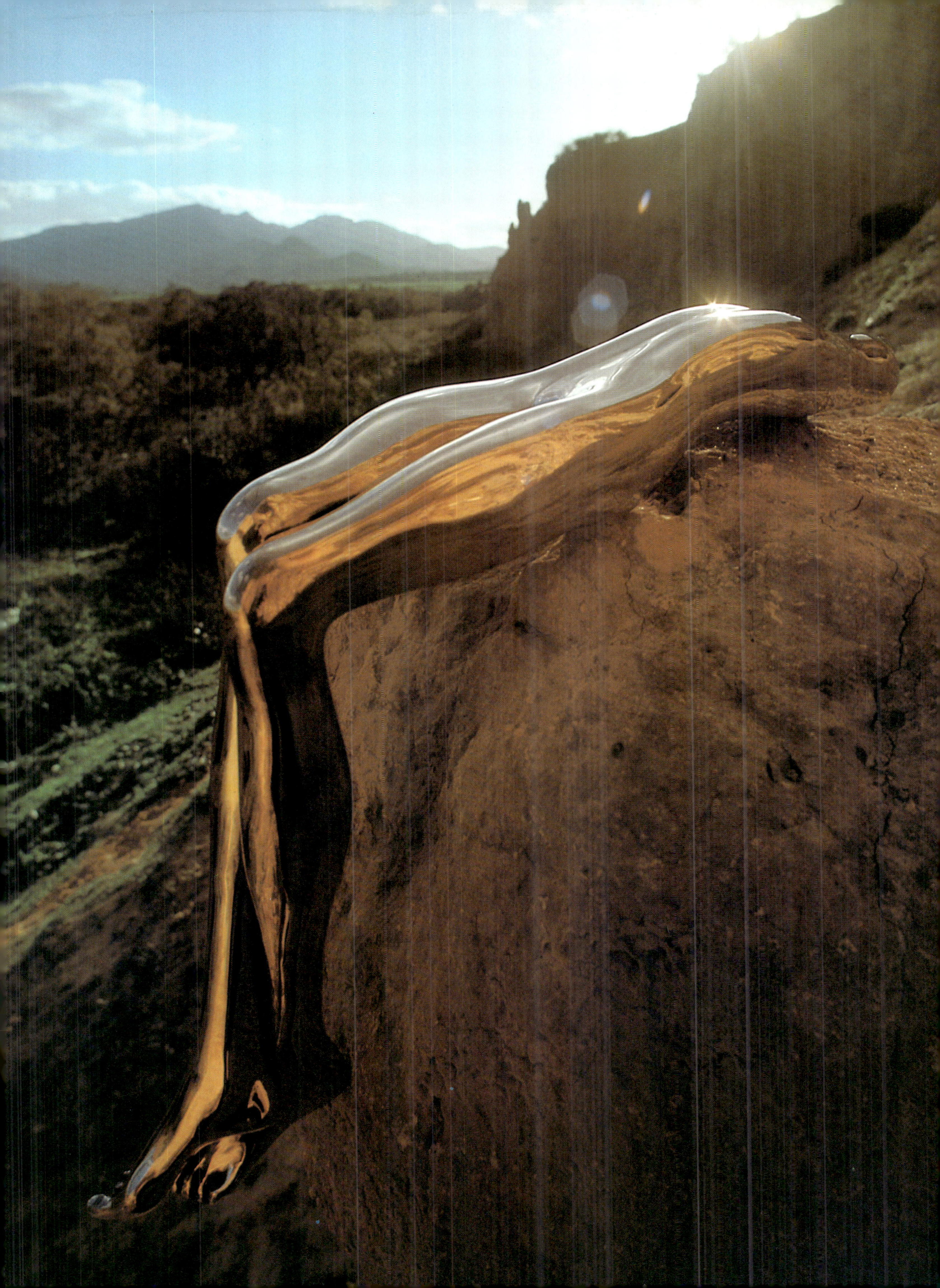

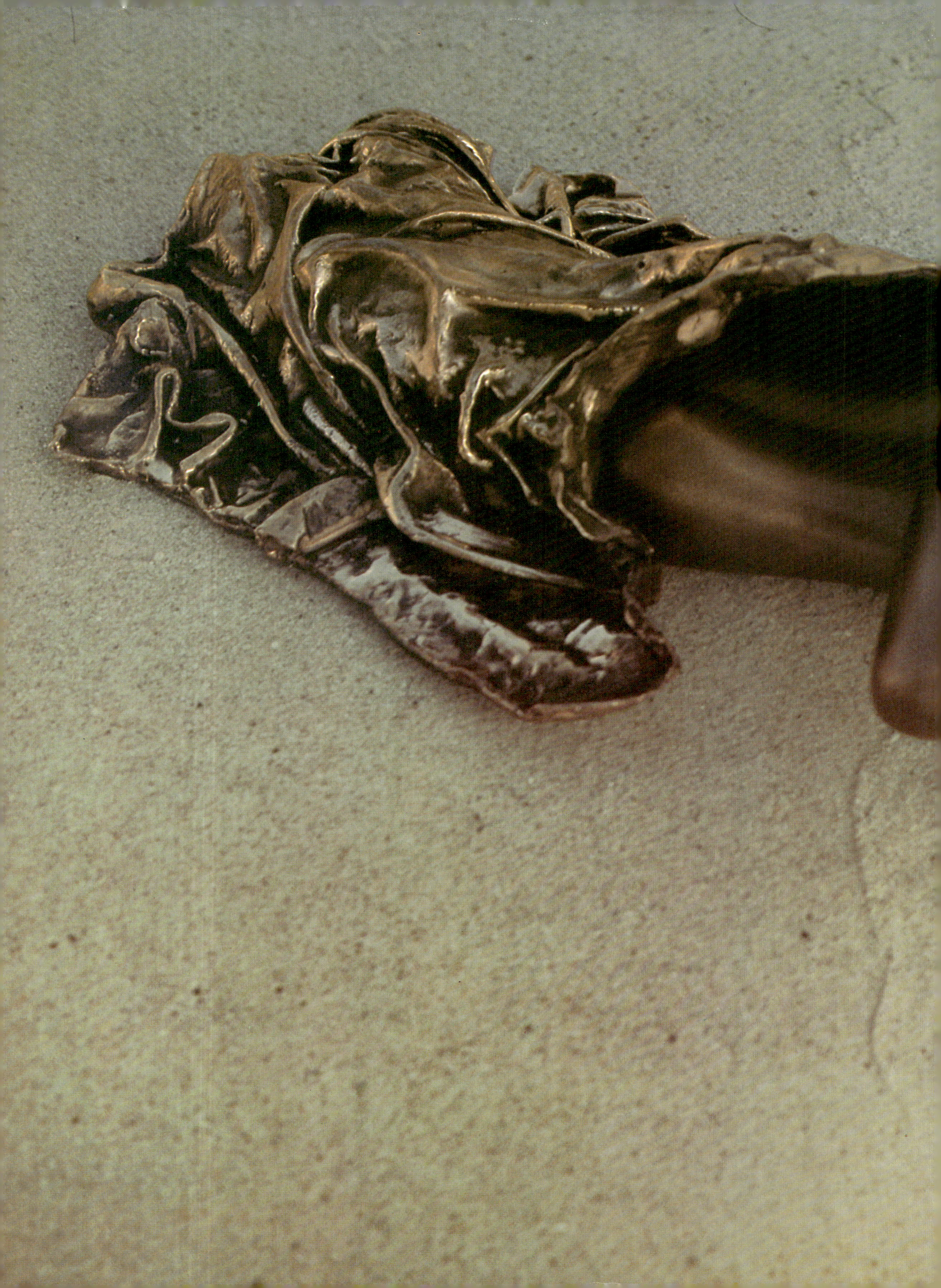

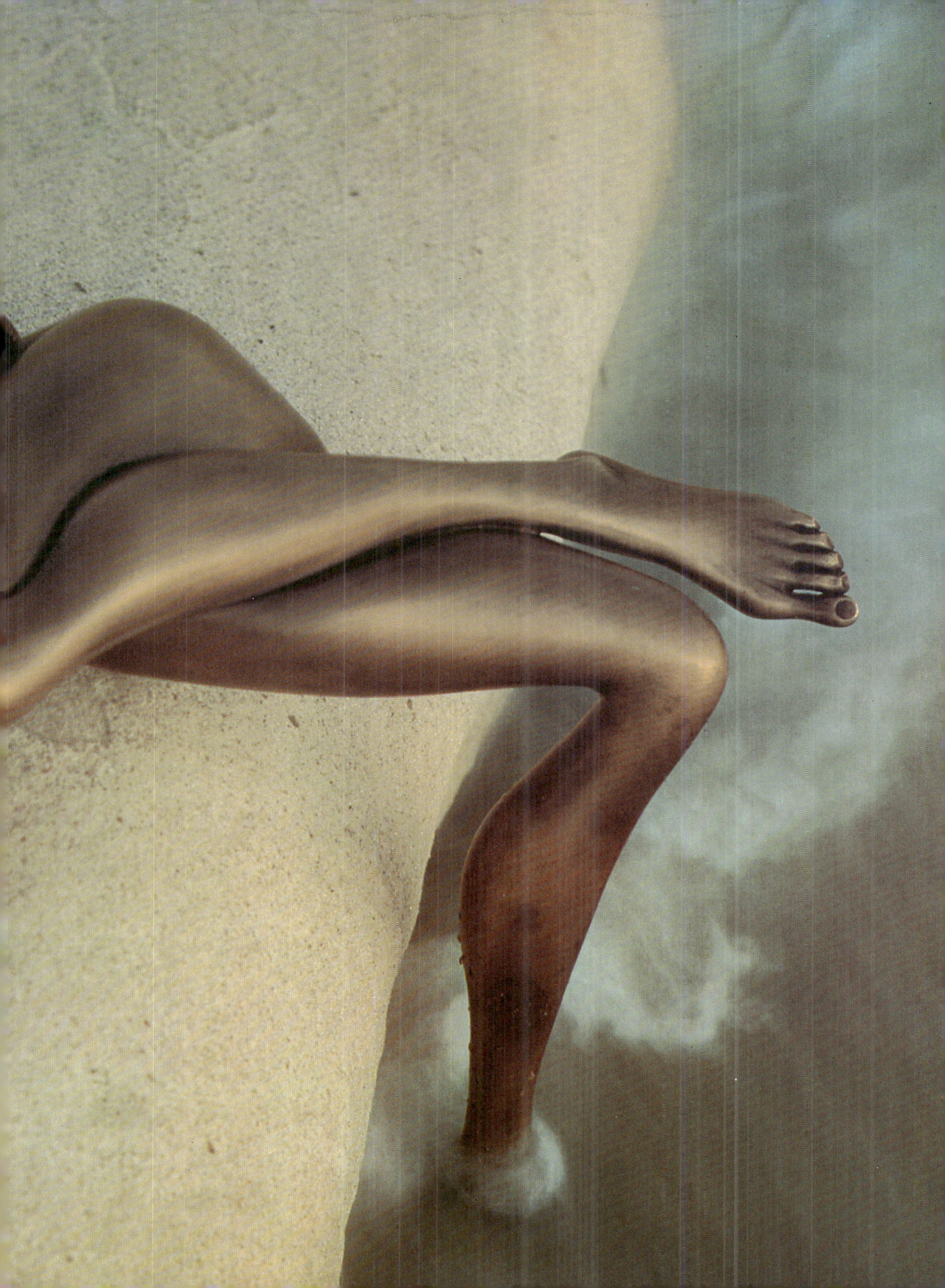

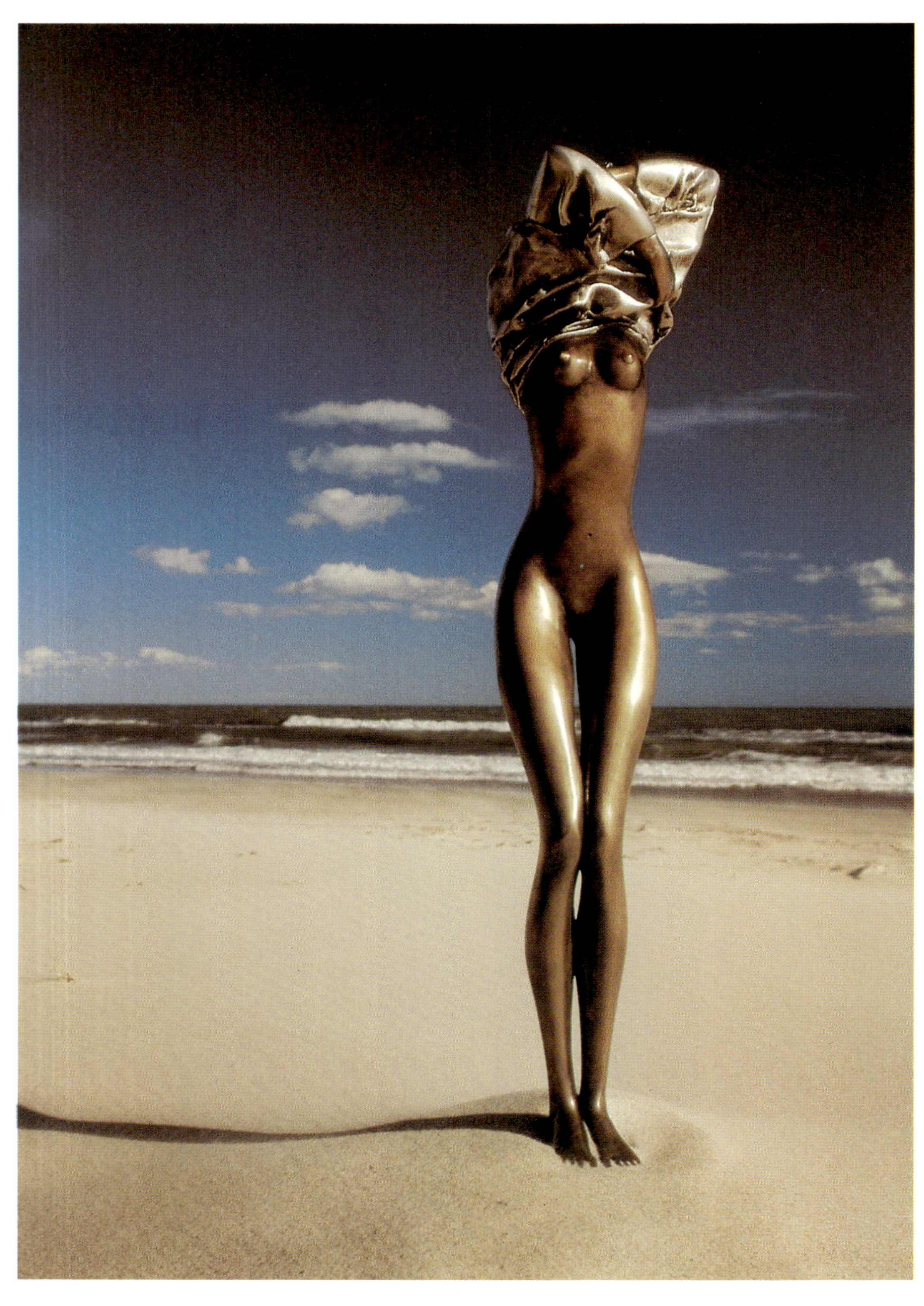

"La venere annoiata" 1976

"Sdraiata" 1976 ▷
"Leda col cigno" 1978 ▷▷

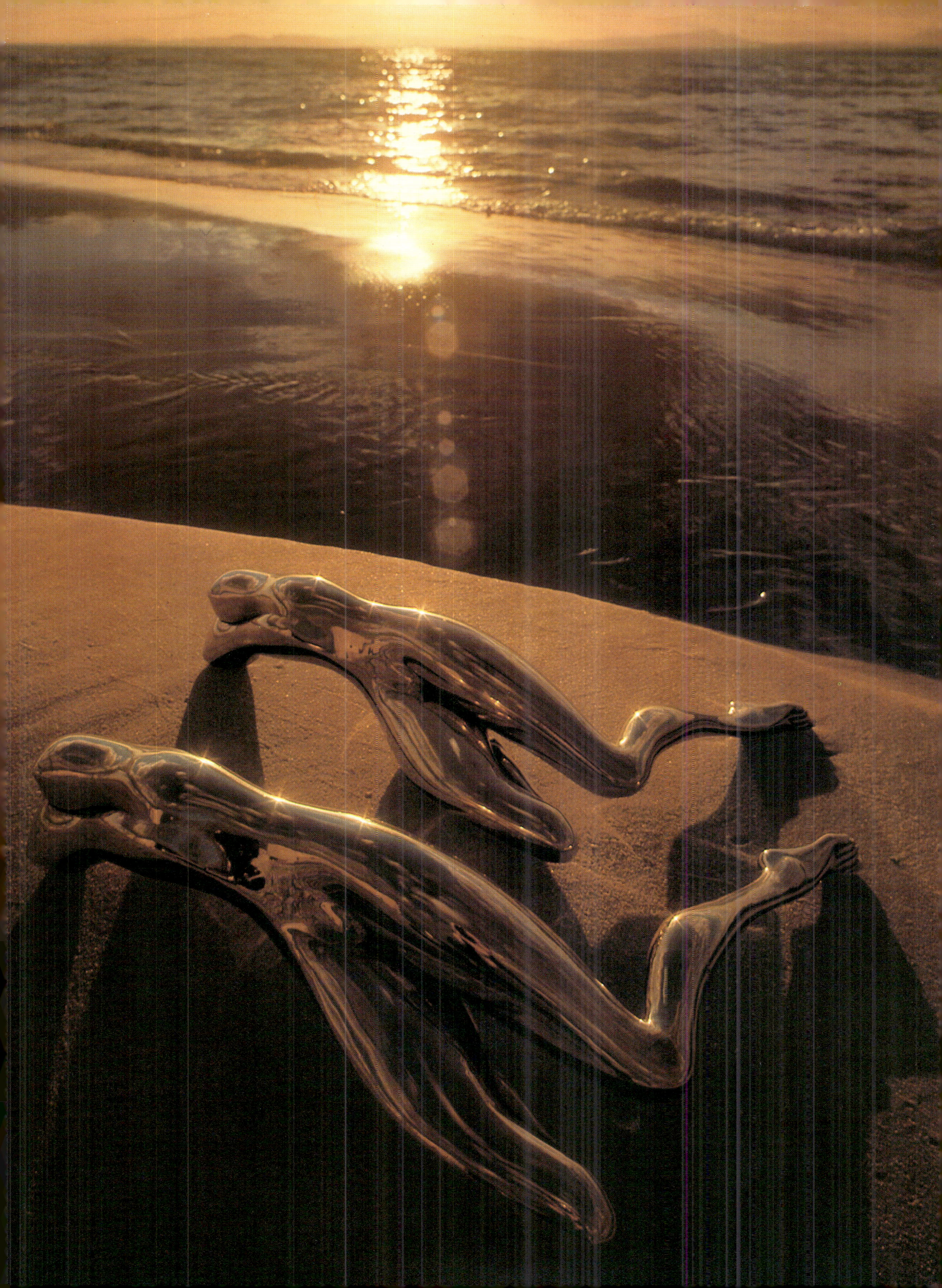

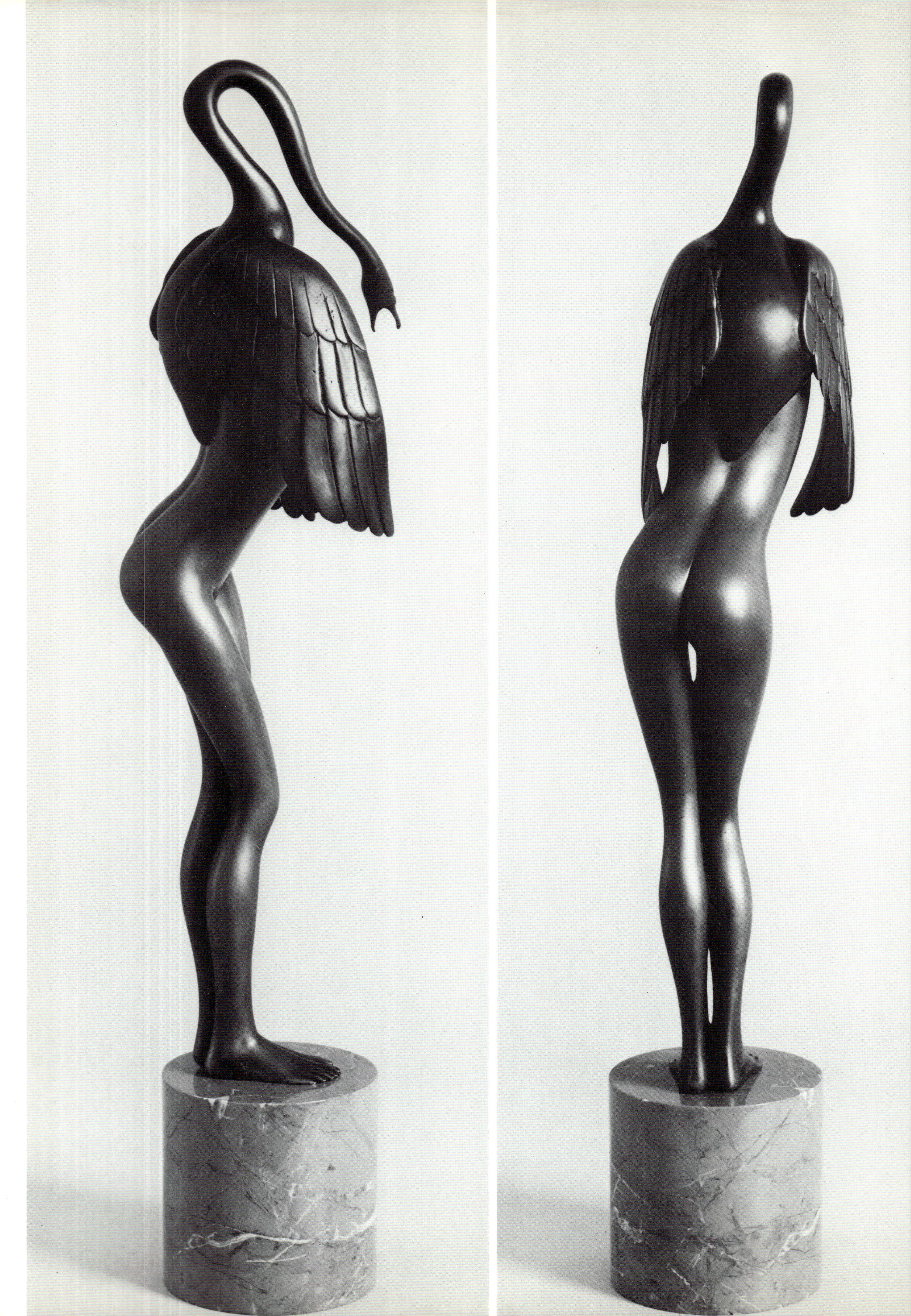

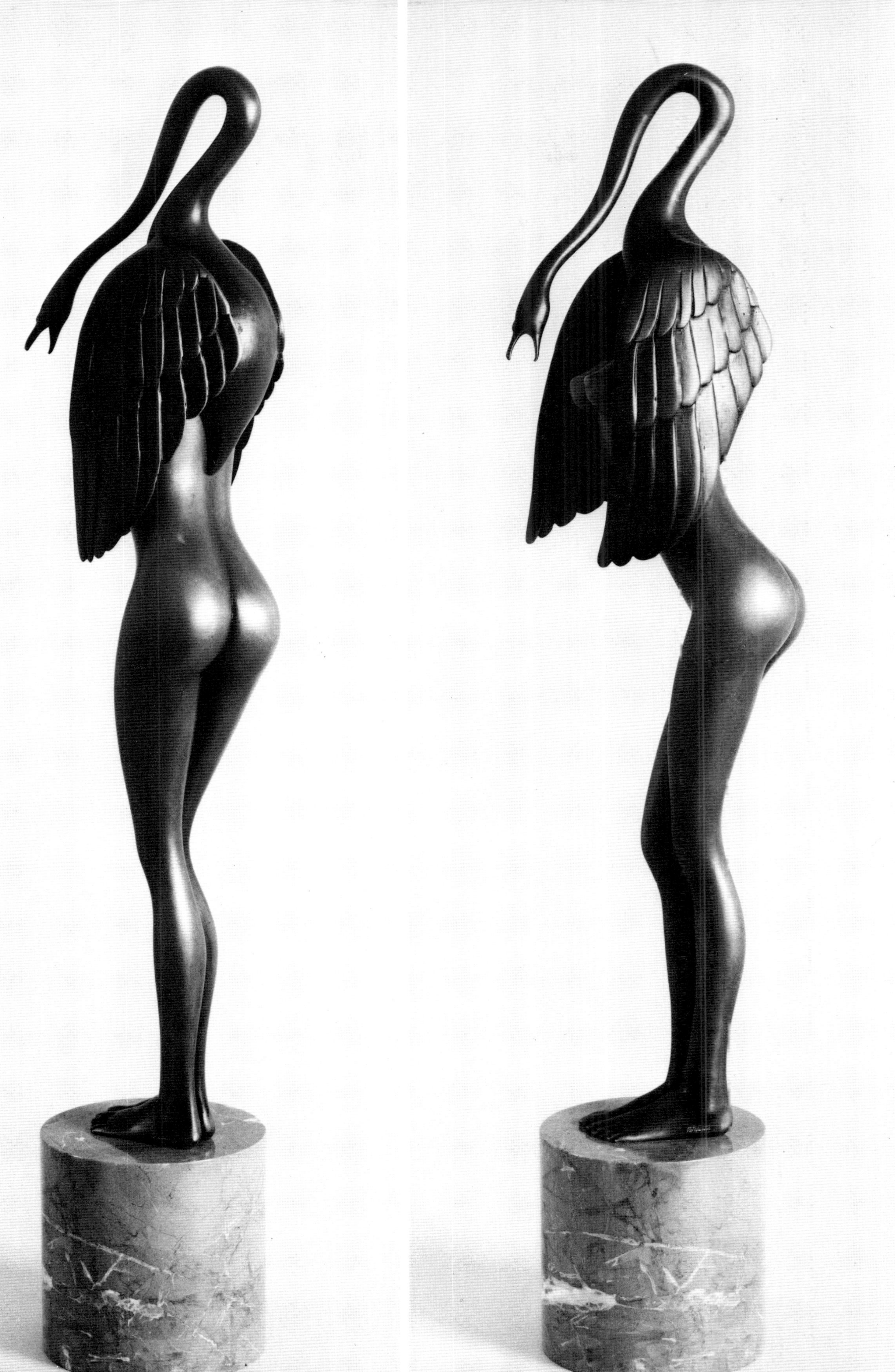

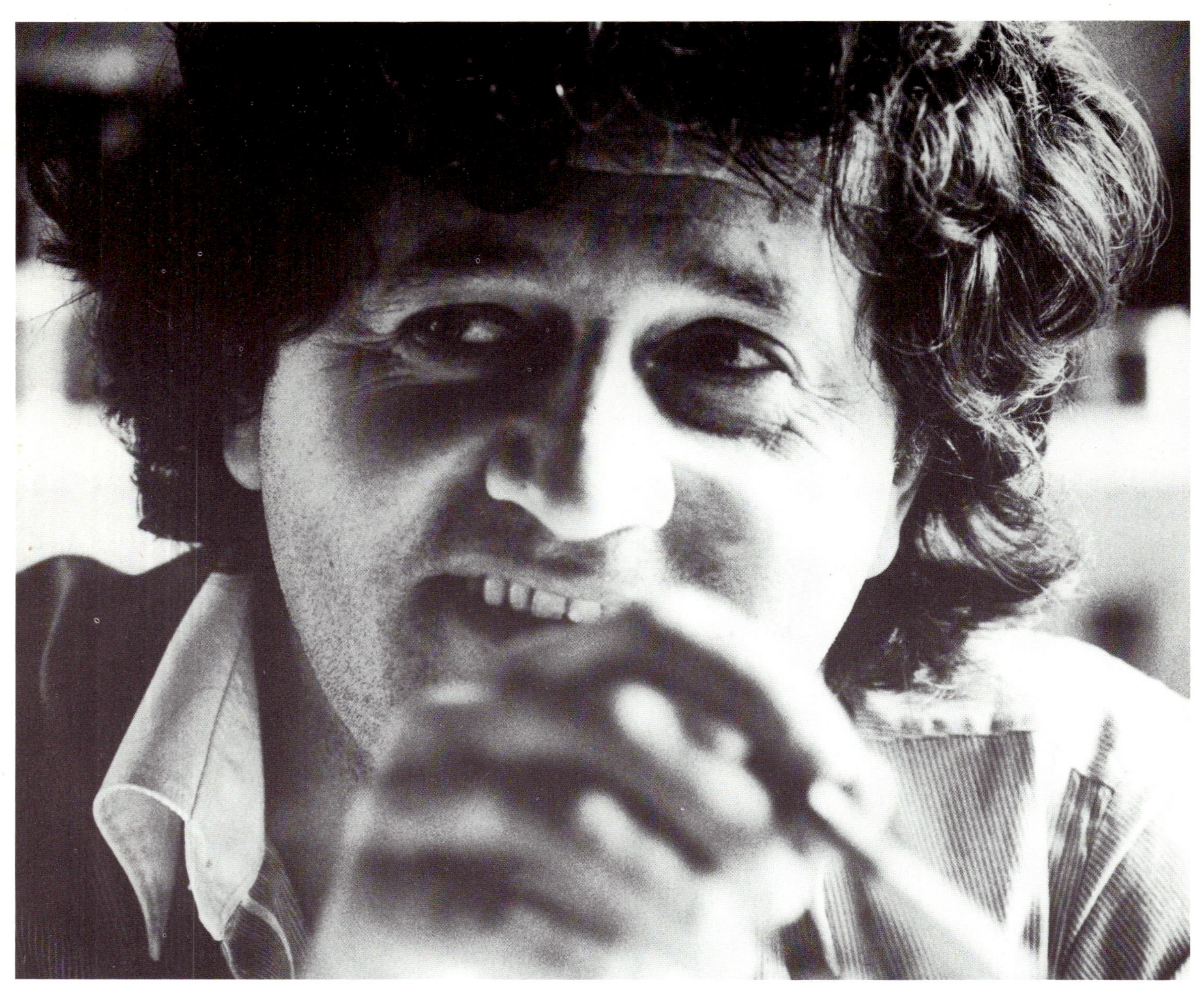

Biography

1935 Born in Gradara (Pesaro)
1953-59 Study at the Istituto d'Arte di Pesaro
1959-60 Stay in London
1960-65 Study at the "Staatliche Hochschule für Bildende Künste" in Hamburg with Gresko and Wunderlich
1967 Lichtwark-Prize Scholarship of the City of Hamburg
Since 1959 Solo exhibitions in:
Pesaro, Florence, London, Rome, Hamburg, Berlin, Milan, Brussels, Amsterdam, Frankfurt, Tokyo, New York, Melbourne, Eremitage Leningrad etc.
1977 International Senefelder-Prize for Lithograph

Bibliography

1960 Charles S. Spencer: "Bruno Bruni" ART NEWS and review No. 4, March 1960 at the occasion of an exhibition in the Whibley Gallery.

1963 Gregor Witt: "Exhibition Bruno Bruni in Pforzheim", Kulturbericht aus Baden und Pfalz of January 13, 1963.

1967 Hanns Theodor Flemming: "Junge Surrealisten in Hamburg – an exhibition in the Gallery Brockstedt", WELTKUNST Nr. 17, page 791, September 1967 with illustrations.

Gallery Assiudia: "Mädchenakte verweben sich mit Blumen und Knospen", Essener Revue No. 7, December 1967 with illustrations.

1968 Detlef Wolff: "Under the Sign of the Rose", Weser-Kurier, No. 204, August 30, 1968 on the occasion of an exhibition in the Gallery Rewolle.

"Gebrochene Eleganz", Frankfurter Allgemeine, No. 223, September 25, 1968.

1972 Exhibition-catalogue "Seconda Triennale dell 'Incisione", Milan, April/May 1972, page 23, with illustrations.

Wilfried Wiegand: "Symbolischer Bildraum", Frankfurter Allgemeine, November 7, 1972, with illustrations.

Hanns Theodor Flemming: "Variationen über Botticelli – Bruno Bruni in the Gallery Brockstedt in Hamburg", WELTKUNST No. 24, page 1894, December 1972, with illustrations.

1973 "Weiden am Untergang", graphic works of Bruno Bruni in the Gallery Gessmann, Offenbach Post, No. 108, May 1973, with illustrations.

1975 Peter Berger: "Afscheid van de wereld in genot", Het Vaderland, Den Haag, May 1, 1975, with illustrations.

Hans Redecker: "Bruno Bruni", Handelsblad, May 9, 1975, with illustrations.

J. C. van der Waals: "Kunstkroniek", Financieel Dagblad, Amsterdam, May 16, 1975, on the occasion of an exhibition in the Gallery Hüsstege.

Hanns Theodor Flemming: "Meister der Graphik" – Die Lithographien von Bruno Bruni" supplement in "Die Kunst und das schöne Heim", 1975.

1976 Bruno Bruni: Das druckgraphische Werk (with texts by Renato Guttuso and Hanns Theodor Flemming) Edition Volker Huber, Offenbach on Main, 116 pages with 111 mostly coloured illustration.

Bruno Bruni: Gouaches, sculptures, lithographs (texts by Henri Alexis Baatsch) Gallery Brockstedt Hamburg, 64 pages with mostly coloured illustrations.

Hanns Theodor Flemming: "Bruno Bruni – Sinnenzauber und Formbewußtsein", WELTKUNST No. 24, December 1976, page 2499, with illustrations.

1977 Guido Mangold: "Zu schön um wahr zu sein" (bronces by Bruno Bruni) photo-series in Playboy No. 8, August 1977, page 74–77, with 4 illustrations.

Dieter Hoffmann: "Bruno Bruni – Leda col cigno" accompanying booklet to Taschen-Graphik No. 5, with illustrations, Edition Volker Huber, Offenbach on Main.

Graphic Design:
Dieter Lincke, Frankfurt am Main

Reproductions:
Repro- und Druckservice Wolfgang Goldbeck
Frankfurt am Main

Paper:
wood free offset 150 g/qm
Koninklijke Nederlandse Papierfabriek N. V.
Maastricht

Set, print and binding:
Beltz Offsetdruck, Hemsbach

Photos

Margrit Bruni, Hamburg: 2, 24, 78, 139, 158 and
inside cover picture
Stephan Jouhoff, Frankfurt: 20, 54, 56, 61, 62, 64
Guido Mangold: 151, 152, 155

Casting of the bronces
under the direction of Günter Stimpfl